The End Has Come !

By: Immanu-el The Alch3mist 555

And the word of the LORD came unto me, saying,

Son of man, prophesy against the prophets of Israel that prophesy, and say thou unto them that prophesy out of their hearts, Hear ye the word of the LORD;

Thus saith the Lord GOD: Woe unto the foolish prophets that follow their spirit, and have seen nothing!

O Israel, thy prophets are like the foxes in the deserts. Ye have not gone up into the gaps, neither made up the hedge for the house of Israel to stand in the battle in the day of the LORD. They have seen vanity and lying divination, saying, The LORD saith: and the LORD hath not sent them: and they have made others to hope that they would confirm the word.

Have ye not seen a vain vision, and have ye not spoken a lying divination, whereas ye say, The LORD saith it; albeit I have not spoken? Therefore, thus saith the Lord GOD: because ye have spoken vanity, and seen lies, therefore, behold, I am against you, saith the Lord GOD. And mine hand shall be upon the prophets that see vanity, and that divine lies:

They shall not be in the assembly of my people; neither shall they be written in the writing of the house of Israel, neither shall they enter into the land of Israel; and ye shall know that I am the Lord GOD. Because, even because they have seduced my people, saying, peace; and there was no peace; and one built up a wall, and, lo, others daubed it with untempered mortar: Therefore ye shall see no more vanity, nor divine divinations: for I will deliver my people out of your hand; and ye shall know that I am the LORD.

Preface

This book is not intended for the general public, nor is it an attempt to persuade anyone to believe that every word recorded in the Scriptures is the infallible Word of the God of truth.

At this point, if you have not realized that this current age has reached its appointed end, you have either been deceived or you are part of the deception. This book is not an attempt to convince you to repent and obey the commandments of God. If you do great! But that is beyond the scope of this book.

Many pastors, ministers, and evangelists have preached repentance and obedience to God's commandments for many years. I am sure you've heard it. That was their calling and the reason God entrusted them with such a ministry. My Job is quite different.

Again, the word of the LORD came unto me, saying,

Son of man, speak to the children of thy people, and say unto them, When I bring the sword upon a land, if the people of the land take a man of their coasts, and set him for their watchman: If when he seeth the sword come upon the land, he blow the trumpet, and warn the people; Then whosoever heareth the sound of the trumpet, and taketh not warning; if the sword come, and take him away, his blood shall be upon his head. He heard the sound of the trumpet, and took no warning; his blood shall be upon him. But he that taketh warning shall deliver his soul. But if the watchman sees the sword come, and blow not the trumpet, and the people be not warned; if the sword come, and take any person from among them, he is taken away in his iniquity; but his blood will I require at the watchman's hand. So thou, O son of man, I have set thee a watchman unto the house of Israel;

therefore thou shalt hear the word at my mouth, and warn them from me.

Here comes the sword!

This book is short, intense, uncut, and straight to the point, intended for the Elect of God. Those wise enough to understand and believe that the Scriptures are the instructions given to mankind by the Creator of all and who keep His Commandments.

The fear of the LORD is the beginning of wisdom: a good understanding have all they that do his commandments (Psalm 111:10)

If thou desirest wisdom, keep the commandments, and the Lord shall give her unto thee. (Sirach 1:26)

If you have been keeping the commandments, you will have a good understanding. If you have not, you simply will not. Nonetheless, I truthfully warn you to start. It is in your best interest, not mine!

This is a Warning and a deep look at Biblical Prophecy as it applies to this very day and time. Diligently searching all Scripture, including the Apocrypha (hidden books), apocalyptical writings, history, and current world events to give you a comprehensive view of what exactly is happening today and what is about to take place. It is the unmasking of the man of sin, the son of perdition, better known as the Antichrist, where Mystery Babylon really is. These revelations will astound you and bring you up to date in prophecy.

Watch ye therefore, and pray always, that ye may be accounted worthy to escape all these things that shall come to pass, and to stand before the Son of man. (Luke 21:36)

I pray that God opens your eyes that you may see and your ears that you may hear, for the time is at hand. Judgment is upon you; sentence is about to be executed. The end has come   .

May God help us all.

Table of Contents

Introduction

The most difficult part of writing this book was trying to compile the incredible and vast amounts of information needed into the simplest, shortest book I could put together. Due to the volume of books and the years of research, it almost seemed as if this goal was contradictory. Nonetheless, large books tend to discourage people from reading them and this was not my intention.

However, please keep in mind that for you to fully understand what the Nation of Islam is, who the Freemasons, Illuminati, and other secret societies are, what symbols they use, the architecture of their buildings, who is known to be part of them, and what their end satanic goal is, you must do your part and research.

You will notice that most books on these subjects are huge and sometimes very complex. Some even dismiss them as some conspiracy theory so big and diabolical that most people cannot begin to conceive in their mind that this is taking place right before their very eyes.

To this, I will put you in remembrance that it has been a conspiracy from the beginning, since the days of Adam and Eve, when the Watchers (Angels) rebelled against God and started mating with the daughters of men. The conspiracy goes back that far .

Besides, the method of this conspiracy is deception, and no one who is being deceived thinks he is being deceived, for had he thought he was being deceived, it would not be called a deception!

And the great dragon was cast out, that old serpent, called the Devil, and Satan, which deceived the whole world: he was cast out into the earth, and his angels were cast out with him. (Revelation 12:9)

To try to add anything to the books written on such subjects would be futile. Nevertheless, although a lot of these books at times refer to Scripture, it always seems as if we are looking in from the outside.

Now, I want to take you inside the very words of God so that you may look from the inside out and see the entire picture the way God intended for His people to see it. For that reason, I challenge anyone to try to refute what is contained in this book. They will not be able to simply because it is the truth. Truth cannot be overthrown, will never fail, and in the end will always triumph.

Howbeit when he, the Spirit of truth, is come, he will guide you into all truth: for he shall not speak of himself; but whatsoever he shall hear, that shall he speak: and he will show you things to come (John 16:13)

About the Author

Jonah was in the belly of the fish three days and three nights. Then Jonah prayed unto the LORD his God out of the fish's belly, and said, I cried because of mine affliction unto the LORD, and he heard me; out of the belly of hell cried I, and thou headrest my voice. For thou hadst cast me into the deep, amid the seas; and the floods compassed me about: all thy billows and thy waves passed over me. Then I said, I am cast out of thy sight; yet I will look again toward thy holy temple.

The waters compassed me about, even to the soul: the depth closed me round about, the weeds were wrapped about my head. I went down to the bottoms of the mountains; the earth with her bars was about me forever: yet hast thou brought up my life from corruption, O LORD my God. When my soul fainted within me, I remembered the LORD: and my prayer came in unto thee, into thine holy temple. Those who observe lying vanities forsake their mercy. But I will sacrifice unto thee with the voice of thanksgiving; I will pay that which I have vowed. Salvation is of the LORD. (Jonah 1:17-2:9)

For the preaching of the cross is to them that perish foolishness; but unto us which are saved it is the power of God. For it is written, I will destroy the wisdom of the wise, and will bring to nothing the understanding of the prudent. Where is the wise? Where is the scribe? Where is the dispute of this world? Hath not God made foolish the wisdom of this world? For after that, in the wisdom of God, the world by wisdom knew not God, it pleased God by the foolishness of preaching to save them that believe. For the Jews require a sign, and the Greeks seek after wisdom: But we preach Christ crucified, unto the Jews a stumbling block, and unto the Greeks foolishness; But unto them which are called, both Jews and Greeks, Christ the power of

God, and the wisdom of God. Because the foolishness of God is wiser than men, and the weakness of God is stronger than men.

 For ye see your calling, brethren, how that not many wise men after the flesh, not many mighty, not many noble, are called: But God hath chosen the foolish things of the world to confound the wise; and God hath chosen the weak things of the world to confound the mighty things; And base things of the world, and things which are despised, hath God chosen, yea, and things which are not, to bring to naught things that are: hat no flesh should glory in his presence. But of him are ye in Christ Jesus, who of God is made unto us wisdom, and righteousness, and sanctification, and redemption: That, according as it is written, He that gloried, let him glory in the Lord. (1Corintians 1:18-31)

Let no man deceive himself. If any man among you seemed to be wise in this world, let him become a fool, that he may be wise. For the wisdom of this world is foolishness with God. For it is written, He taketh the wise in their craftiness. And again, the Lord Koeth the thoughts of the wise, that they are vain. Therefore, let no man glory in men. (1 Corinthians 3:18-20)

Thus, saith the LORD: Let not the wise man glory in his wisdom, neither let the mighty man glory in his might, let not the rich man glory in his riches:

But let him that gloried glory in this, that he understands and Koeth me, that I am the LORD which exercise lovingkindness, judgment, and righteousness, in the earth: for in these things I delight, saith the LORD. (Jeremiah 9:23-24)

Let all glory and honor be given to the all-wise, all-knowing eternal King and Ruler of Heaven and Earth.

As for me, I am just a foolish servant called to be a wise messenger by an extremely merciful and patient King.

Thank you, DAD, I adore you with all my heart, all my soul, and all my might!

Thank you, thank you, thank you!

Chapter 1

The Covenant

A covenant is a consensual agreement made by two or more parties. It is a binding contract. Many people deceive themselves into believing that this Covenant is no longer in effect. This is far from the truth as we shall subsequently see.

Deuteronomy 28

1 And it shall come to pass, if thou shalt hearken diligently unto the voice of the LORD thy God, to observe and to do all his commandments which I command thee this day, that the LORD thy God will set thee on high above all nations of the earth:

2 And all these blessings shall come on thee, and overtake thee, if thou shalt hearken unto the voice of the LORD thy God.

3 Blessed shalt thou be in the city, and blessed shalt thou be in the field.

4 Blessed shall be the fruit of thy body, and the fruit of thy ground, and the fruit of thy cattle, the increase of thy kine, and the flocks of thy sheep.

5 Blessed shall be thy basket and thy store.

6 Blessed shalt thou be when thou comes in, and blessed shalt thou be when thou goest out.

7 The LORD shall cause thine enemies that rise against thee to be smitten before thy face: they shall come out against thee one way, and flee before thee seven ways.

8 The LORD shall command the blessing upon thee in thy store-houses, and in all that thou settest thine hand unto; and he shall bless thee in the land which the LORD thy God giveth thee.

9 The LORD shall establish thee an holy people unto himself, as he hath sworn unto thee, if thou shalt keep the commandments of the LORD thy God, and walk in his ways.

10 And all people of the earth shall see that thou art called by the name of the LORD; and they shall be afraid of thee.

11 And the LORD shall make thee plenteous in goods, in the fruit of thy body, and in the fruit of thy cattle, and the fruit of thy ground, in the land which the LORD swear unto thy fathers to give thee.

12 The LORD shall open unto thee his good treasure, the heaven to give the rain unto thy land in his season, and to bless all the work of thine hand and thou shalt lend unto many nations, and thou shalt not borrow.

13 And the LORD shall make thee the head, and not the tail and thou shalt be above only, and thou shalt not be beneath if that thou hearken unto the commandments of the LORD thy God, which I command thee this day, to observe and to do them

14 And thou shalt not go aside from any of the words which I command thee this day, to the right hand, or to the left, to go after other gods to serve them.

15 But it shall come to pass, if thou wilt not hearken unto the voice of the LORD thy God, to observe to do all his commandments and his statutes which I command thee this day that all these curses shall come upon thee, and overtake thee:

16 Cursed shalt thou be in the city, and cursed shalt thou be in the field.

17 Cursed shall be thy basket and thy store.

18 Cursed shall be the fruit of thy body, and the fruit of thy land, the increase of thy Kine, and the flocks of thy sheep.

19 Cursed shalt thou be when thou comes in, and cursed shalt thou be when thou goes out.

20 The LORD shall send upon thee cursing, vexation, and rebuke, in all that thou set test thine hand unto for to do, until thou be destroyed, and until thou perish quickly; because of the wickedness of thy doings, whereby thou hast forsaken me.

21 The LORD shall make the pestilence cleave unto thee, until he has consumed thee from off the land, whither thou goes to possess it.

22 The LORD shall smite thee with a consumption, and with a fever, and with an inflammation, and with an extreme burning, and with the sword, and with blasting, and with mildew; and they shall pursue thee until thou perish.

23 And thy heaven that is over thy head shall be brass, and the earth that is under thee shall be iron.

24 The LORD shall make the rain of thy land powder and dust: from heaven shall it come down upon thee, until thou be destroyed.

25 The LORD shall cause thee to be smitten before thine enemies: thou shalt go out one way against them, and flee seven ways before them: and shalt be removed into all the kingdoms of the earth.

26 And thy carcase shall be meat unto all fowls of the air, and unto the beasts of the earth, and no man shall fray them away.

27 The LORD will smite thee with the botch of Egypt, and with the emeralds, and with the scab, and with the itch, whereof thou canst not be healed.

28 The LORD shall smite thee with madness, and blindness, and astonishment of heart:

29 And thou shalt grope at noonday, as the blind groped in darkness, and thou shalt not prosper in thy ways: and thou shalt be only oppressed and spoiled evermore, and no man shall save thee.

30 Thou shalt betroth a wife, and another man shall lie with her: thou shalt build a house, and thou shalt not dwell therein: thou shalt plant a vineyard, and shalt not gather the grapes thereof.

31 Thine ox shall be slain before thine eyes, and thou shalt not eat thereof: thine ass shall be violently taken away from before thy face, and shall not be restored to thee: thy sheep shall be given unto thine enemies, and thou shalt have none to rescue them.

32 Thy sons and thy daughters shall be given unto another people, and thine eyes shall look, and fail with longing for them all the day long: and there shall be no might in thine hand.

33 The fruit of thy land, and all thy labours, shall a nation which thou knowest not eat up; and thou shalt be only oppressed and crushed alway:

34 So that thou shalt be mad for the sight of thine eyes which thou shalt see.

35 The LORD shall smite thee in the knees, and in the legs, with a sore botch that cannot be healed, from the sole of thy foot unto the top of thy head.

36 The LORD shall bring thee, and thy king, which thou shalt set over thee, unto a nation which neither thou nor thy fathers have known; and there shalt thou serve other gods, wood and stone.

37 And thou shalt become an astonishment, a proverb, and a byword, among all nations whither the LORD shall lead thee.

38 Thou shalt carry much seed out into the field, and shalt gather but little in; for the locust shall consume it.

39 Thou shalt plant vineyards, and dress them, but shalt neither drink of the wine, nor gather the grapes; for the worms shall eat them.

40 Thou shalt have olive trees throughout all thy coasts, but thou shalt not anoint thyself with the oil; for thine olive shall cast his fruit.

41 Thou shalt beget sons and daughters, but thou shalt not enjoy them; for they shall go into captivity.

42 All thy trees and fruit of thy land shall the locust consume.

43 The stranger that is within thee shall get up above thee very high and thou shalt come down very low.

44 He shall lend to thee, and thou shalt not lend to him: he shall be the head, and thou shalt be the tail.

45 Moreover, all these curses shall come upon thee, and shall pursue thee, and overtake thee, till thou be destroyed; because thou heark-

ened not unto the voice of the LORD thy God, to keep his commandments and his statutes which he commanded thee:

46 And they shall be upon thee for a sign and a wonder, and upon thy seed for ever.

47 Because thou serves not the LORD thy God with joyfulness, and with gladness of heart, for the abundance of all things;

48 Therefore shalt thou serve thine enemies which the LORD shall send against thee, in hunger, and thirst, and nakedness, and want of all things: and he shall put a yoke of iron upon thy neck, until he hath destroyed thee.

49 The LORD shall bring a nation against thee from far, from the end of the earth, as swift as the eagle filet a nation whose tongue thou shalt not understand

50 A nation of fierce countenance, which shall not regard the person of the old, nor shew favor to the young:

51 And he shall eat the fruit of thy cattle, and the fruit of thy land, until thou be destroyed: which also shall not leave thee either corn, wine, or oil, or the increase of thy Kine, or flocks of thy sheep, until he have destroyed thee.

52 And he shall besiege thee in all thy gates, until thy high and fenced walls come down, wherein thou trusted, throughout all thy land: and he shall besiege thee in all thy gates throughout all thy land, which the LORD thy God hath given thee.

53 And thou shalt eat the fruit of thine own body, the flesh of thy sons and of thy daughters, which the LORD thy God hath given thee, in the siege, and the straightness, wherewith thine enemies shall distress thee:

54 So that the man that is tender among you, and very delicate, his eye shall be evil toward his brother, and toward the wife of his bosom, and toward the remnant of his children which he shall leave:

55 So that he will not give to any of them of the flesh of his children whom he shall eat because he hath nothing left him in the siege, and the straightness, wherewith thine enemies shall distress thee in all thy gates.

56 The tender and delicate woman among you, who would not adventure to set the sole of her foot upon the ground for delicateness and tenderness, her eye shall be evil toward the husband of her bosom, and her son, and her daughter.

57 And toward her young one that cometh out from between her feet, and toward her children which she shall bear: for she shall eat them for want of all things secretly in the siege and straightness, wherewith thine enemy shall distress thee in thy gates.

58 If thou wilt not observe to do all the words of this law that are written in this book, that thou mayest fear this glorious and fearful name, THE LORD THY GOD

59 Then the LORD will make thy plagues wonderful, and the plagues of thy seed, even great plagues, and of long continuance, and sore sicknesses, and long continuance.

60 Moreover, he will bring upon thee all the diseases of Egypt, which thou west afraid of; and they shall cleave unto thee.

61 Also, every sickness, and every plague, which is not written in the book of this law, them will the LORD bring upon thee, until thou be destroyed.

62 And ye shall be left few, whereas ye were as the stars of heaven for multitude; because thou wildest not obey the voice of the LORD thy God.

63 And it shall come to pass, that as the LORD rejoiced over you to do you good, and to multiply you; so the LORD will rejoice over you to destroy you, and to bring you to nought; and ye shall be plucked from off the land whither thou goes to possess it.

64 And the LORD shall scatter thee among all people, from the one end of the earth even unto the other and there thou shalt serve other gods, which neither thou nor thy fathers have known, even wood and stone.

65 And among these nations shalt thou find no ease, neither shall the sole of thy foot have rest: but the LORD shall give thee there a trembling heart, and failing of eyes, and sorrow of mind:

66 And thy life shall hang in doubt before thee; and thou shalt fear day and night, and shalt have none assurance of thy life:

67 In the morning thou shalt say, Would God it was even! And at even thou shalt say, would God it was morning! For the fear of thine heart wherewith thou shalt fear, and for the sight of thine eyes which thou shalt see.

68 And the LORD shall bring thee into Egypt again with ships, by the way whereof I Spake unto thee, thou shalt see it no more again: and there ye shall be sold unto your enemies for bondmen and bondwomen, and no man shall buy you.

Leviticus 26

1 Ye shall make you no idols nor graven image, neither rear you up a standing image, neither shall ye set up any image of stone in your land, to bow down unto it: for I am the LORD your God.

2 Ye shall keep my Sabbaths, and reverence my sanctuary: I am the LORD.

3 If ye walk in my statutes, and keep my commandments, and do them;

4 Then I will give you rain in due season, and the land shall yield her increase, and the trees of the field shall yield their fruit.

5 And your threshing shall reach unto the vintage, and the vintage shall reach unto the sowing time: and ye shall eat your bread to the full, and dwell in your land safely.

6 And I will give peace in the land, and ye shall lie down, and none shall make you afraid: and I will rid evil beasts out of the land, neither shall the sword go through your land.

7 And ye shall chase your enemies, and they shall fall before you by the sword.

8 And five of you shall chase an hundred, and an hundred of you shall put ten thousand to flight: and your enemies shall fall before you by the sword.

9 For I will have respect unto you, and make you fruitful, and multiply you, and establish my covenant with you.

10 And ye shall eat old store, and bring forth the old because of the new.

11 And I will set my tabernacle among you: and my soul shall not ab-hor you.

12 And I will walk among you, and will be your God, and ye shall be my people.

13 I am the LORD your God, who brought you forth out of the land of Egypt, that ye should not be their bondmen; and I have broken the bands of your yoke, and made you go upright.

14 But if ye will not hearken unto me, and will not do all these commandments;

15 And if ye shall despise my statutes, or if your soul abhor my judgments, so that ye will not do all my commandments, but that ye break my covenant:

16 I also will do this unto you; I will even appoint over you terror, consumption, and the burning ague, that shall consume the eyes, and cause sorrow of heart and ye shall sow your seed in vain, for your enemies shall eat it.

17 And I will set my face against you, and ye shall be slain before your enemies: they that hate you shall reign over you; and ye shall flee when none pursueth you.

18 And if ye will not yet for all this hearken unto me, then I will punish you seven times more for your sins.

19 And I will break the pride of your power and I will make your heaven as iron, and your earth as brass

20 And your strength shall be spent in vain: for your land shall not yield her increase, neither shall the trees of the land yield their fruit.

21 And if ye walk contrary unto me, and will not hearken unto me I will bring seven times more plagues upon you according to your sins.

22 I will also send wild beasts among you, which shall rob you of your children, and destroy your cattle, and make you few; and your highways shall be desolate.

23 And if ye will not be reformed by me by these things, but will walk contrary unto me;

24 Then will I also walk contrary unto you, and will punish you yet seven times for your sins.

25 And I will bring a sword upon you that shall avenge the quarrel of my covenant: and when ye are gathered together within your cities, I will send the pestilence among you; and ye shall be delivered into the hand of the enemy.

26 And when I have broken the staff of your bread, ten women shall bake your bread in one oven, and they shall deliver you your bread again by weight: and ye shall eat, and not be satisfied.

27 And if ye will not for all this hearken unto me, but walk contrary unto me

28 Then I will walk contrary unto you also in fury; and I, even I, will chastise you seven times for your sins.

29 And ye shall eat the flesh of your sons, and the flesh of your daughters shall ye eat.

30 And I will destroy your high places, and cut down your images, and cast your carcases upon the carcases of your idols, and my soul shall abhor you.

31 And I will make your cities waste, and bring your sanctuaries unto desolation, and I will not smell the savour of your sweet odours.

32 And I will bring the land into desolation and your enemies which dwell therein shall be astonished at it.

33 And I will scatter you among the heathen, and will draw out a sword after you: and your land shall be desolate, and your cities waste.

34 Then shall the land enjoy her sabbaths, as long as it lieth desolate, and ye be in your enemies ' land; even then shall the land rest, and enjoy her sabbaths.

35 As long as it lieth desolate it shall rest; because it did not rest in your sabbaths, when ye dwelt upon it.

36 And upon them that are left alive of you I will send a faintness into their hearts in the lands of their enemies; and the sound of a shaken leaf shall chase them; and they shall flee, as fleeing from a sword; and they shall fall when none pursueth.

37 And they shall fall one upon another, as it were before a sword, when none pursueth and ye shall have no power to stand before your enemies.

38 And ye shall perish among the heathen, and the land of your enemies shall eat you up.

39 And they that are left of you shall pine away in their iniquity in your enemies ' lands; and also in the iniquities of their fathers shall they pine away with them.

40 If they shall confess their iniquity, and the iniquity of their fathers, with their trespass which they trespassed against me, and that also they have walked contrary unto me;

41 And that I also have walked contrary unto them, and have brought them into the land of their enemies; if then their uncircumcised hearts be humbled, and they then accept of the punishment of their iniquity:

42 Then will I remember my covenant with Jacob, and also my covenant with Isaac, and also my covenant with Abraham, will I remember; and I will remember the land.

43 The land also shall be left of them, and shall enjoy her Sabbaths, while she lieth desolate without them: and they shall accept of the punishment of their iniquity: because, even because they despised my judgments, and because their soul abhorred my statutes.

44 And yet for all that, when they are in the land of their enemies, I will not cast them away, neither will I abhor them, to destroy them utterly, and to break my covenant with them: for I am the LORD their God.

45 But I will for their sakes remember the covenant of their ancestors, whom I brought forth out of the land of Egypt in the sight of the heathen, that I might be their God I am the LORD.

46 These are the statutes and judgments and laws, which the LORD made between him and the children of Israel in Mount Sinai by the hand of Moses.

Chapter 2

Did God give us a religion or a form of government?

One of the greatest deceptions perpetrated upon humanity is the belief that God gave Moses commandments, laws, and statutes as part of a religion rather than as a divine form of government. On the contrary, God established a government system in which He is both King and Lawgiver. His law flows from the top down, not like a democracy (the complete opposite), which goes from the bottom up.

A nation being governed cannot tell its governor how it desires to be governed! God created mankind for His good pleasure. Not the opposite! This is His earth, His people, His creation, and since He owns it all, it is only logical to conclude that He and only He sets the rules in His kingdom.

These laws are the same laws that God administers in the heavens. God never gave mankind some form of moral religion for men to later use as a guide to write the U.S. Constitution and create their version of a democratic government. Do not think that this form of government is inspired in any way, shape, or form by God. The only government inspired by God was the one He gave Moses, and God does not change. He is the same yesterday, today, and forever.

God does not allow anyone to add or diminish anything from His laws.

Deuteronomy 4:1-2, 13, 14

1 Now therefore hearken, O Israel, unto the statutes and unto the judgments, which I teach you, for to do them, that ye may live, and go in and possess the land which the LORD God of your fathers giveth you.

2 Ye shall not add unto the word which I command you, neither shall ye diminish ought from it, that ye may keep the commandments of the LORD your God which I command you.

13 And he declared unto you his covenant, which he commanded you to perform, even the Ten Commandments; and he wrote them upon two tables of stone. Something written in stone is perpetual.

14 And the LORD commanded me at that time to teach you statutes and judgments, that ye might do them in the land whither ye go over to possess it.

Deuteronomy 12:32

32 What thing so ever I command you, observe to do it: thou shalt not add thereto, nor diminish from it.

The notion that people have that the U.S. Constitution was founded on godly principles is beyond ridiculous. Common sense alone would tell you that God would not inspire anything contrary to His laws. Do you think God would inspire anyone to worship any god according to the dictates of their own heart? Not to entertain that notion is to not know the will of God. Have you noticed that the name of Jesus Christ (Yahshua Ha'Mosiac) is not mentioned anywhere in the U.S. Constitution? For a nation that claims to be a Christian Nation, it certainly does not have the name of its Lord anywhere! Instead, this Nation's Founders used vague, Illuminist-coded terms like Nature's god (god of forces, Daniel 11:38) or Providence.

Moreover, Benjamin Franklin, one of this Nation's Founding Fathers and a key leader of the delegates, was both a Grand Master Mason Lodge of nine sisters, Paris, France, and a Rosicrucian. Both of these are secret societies that are Luciferians to the core. Thomas Jefferson, who helped draft the Declaration of Independence, wrote favorably of the Order of the Illuminati and its founder, European Jesuit professor Adam Weishaupt. Even the first president of the United States, George Washington, was a well-documented Freemason.

The U.S. Constitution was written in a way that allows United States Supreme Court justices to interpret it based on their personal opinions. The President of the United States appoints these judges. If the President is a liberal, he would appoint liberal judges, or if a conservative, he would appoint conservative judges. The opinion of these judges shaped the way the Constitution would be interpreted, thereby leading the country as a dog on a leash exactly where they wanted it. This Constitution is twisted and perverted from its inception!

Do you think King David, a man after God's own heart, would have allowed such things while he was in charge of all the tribes of Israel? Of course not! I am sure many people's heads would have flown off their shoulders if anyone tried to pull off this nonsense when kings David, Hezekiah, or Josiah were around!

This topic is vast and could fill an entire book. But let us be clear: God gave Moses commandments, not suggestions!

O LORD, I know that the way of man is not in himself it is not in man that walketh to direct his steps. (Jeremiah 10:23)

Stop believing the deception, do your research! Your eternal future depends on it!

Notice what God's law states:

Deuteronomy 4:1 – 10

1 Now therefore hearken, O Israel, unto the statutes and unto the judgments, which I teach you, for to do them, that ye may live, and go in and possess the land which the LORD God of your fathers giveth you.

2 Ye shall not add unto the word which I command you, neither shall ye diminish ought from it, that ye may keep the commandments of the LORD your God which I command you.

3 Your eyes have seen what the LORD did because of Baalpeor: for all the men that followed Baalpeor, the LORD thy God hath destroyed them from among you.

4 But ye that did cleave unto the LORD your God are alive every one of you this day.

5 Behold, I have taught you statutes and judgments, even as the LORD my God commanded me, that ye should do so in the land whither ye go to possess it.

6 Keep therefore and do them; for this is your wisdom and your understanding in the sight of the nations, which shall hear all these statutes, and say, surely this great nation is a wise and understanding people.

7 For what nation is there so great, who hath God so nigh unto them, as the LORD our God is in all things that we call upon him for?

8 And what nation is there so great, that hath statutes and judgments so righteous as all this law, which I set before you this day?

9 Only take heed to thyself, and keep thy soul diligently, lest thou forget the things which thine eyes have seen, and lest they depart from thy heart all the days of thy life: but teach them thy sons, and thy sons' sons;

10 Especially the day that thou stoutest before the LORD thy God in Horeb, when the LORD said unto me, Gather me the people together, and I will make them hear my words, that they may learn to fear me all the days that they shall live upon the earth, and that they may teach their children.

Deuteronomy 6:1 –9

1 Now these are the commandments, the statutes, and the judgments, which the LORD your God commanded to teach you, that ye might do them in the land whither ye go to possess it:

 2 That thou mightiest fear the LORD thy God, to keep all his statutes and his commandments, which I command thee, thou, and thy son, and thy son's son, all the days of thy life; and that thy days may be prolonged.

3 Hear therefore, O Israel, and observe to do it; that it may be well with thee, and that ye may increase mightily, as the LORD God of thy fathers hath promised thee, in the land that flowed with milk and honey.

4 Hear, O Israel: The LORD our God is one LORD.

5 And thou shalt love the LORD thy God with all thine heart, and with all thy soul, and with all thy might.

6 And these words, which I command thee this day, shall be in thine heart.

7 And thou shalt teach them diligently unto thy children, and shalt talk of them when thou sit test in thine house, and when thou walks by the way, and when thou lies down, and when thou rises up.

8 And thou shalt bind them for a sign upon thine hand, and they shall be as frontlets between thine eyes.

9 And thou shalt write them upon the posts of thy house, and on thy gates.

Deuteronomy 12:1, 8, 32

1 These are the statutes and judgments, which ye shall observe to do in the land, which the LORD God of thy fathers giveth thee to possess it, all the days that ye live upon the earth.

8 Ye shall not do after all the things that we do here this day, every man whatsoever is right in his own eyes.

32 What thing so ever I command you, observe to do it: thou shalt not add thereto, nor diminish from it.

Notice that God's Law was written in stone when given to Moses, and He commanded that when they entered the promised land that the law be written on stone at the gates of the city for all to see. When something is written in stone, it is never meant to be abolished. It is permanent, enduring, and binding.

Deuteronomy 27:1 – 3, 8

1 And Moses with the elders of Israel commanded the people, saying, Keep all the commandments which I command you this day.

2 And it shall be on the day when ye shall pass over Jordan unto the land which the LORD thy God giveth thee, that thou shalt set thee up great stones, and plaster them with plaster

3 And thou shalt write upon them all the words of this law, when thou art passed over, that thou mayest go in unto the land which the LORD thy God giveth thee, a land that flowed with milk and honey as the LORD God of thy fathers hath promised thee.

8 And thou shalt write upon the stones all the words of this law very plainly.

Joshua 1:7-8

7 Only be thou strong and very courageous, that thou mayest observe to do according to all the law, which Moses my servant commanded thee: turn not from it to the right hand or the left, that thou mayest prosper whithersoever thou goes.

8 This book of the law shall not depart out of thy mouth; but thou shalt meditate therein day and night, that thou mayest observe to do according to all that is written therein: for then thou shalt make thy way prosperous, and then thou shalt have success.

Jubilees 2:33

33 This law and testimony were given to the children of Israel as a law forever to their generations.

Testament of Naphtali 1:24

24 Sun and Moon and stars change not their order; so do ye also change not the law of God in the disorderliness of your doings.

In the book Jewish Antiquities, written by first-century historian Flavius Josephus, he records the following:

(BK3, CH8:213)

He also set down in writing the form of their government, and those laws, by obedience to which they would lead their lives to please God, and to have no quarrels one with another.

(BK4, CH8:181)

only do you be obedient to those whom God would have you to follow nor do you prefer any other constitution of the government before the laws now given you; neither do you disregard that way of divine worship which you now have, nor change it for any other form and if you do this, you will be the most courageous of all men and undergoing the fatigues of war, and would not be easily conquered by any of your enemies   .

(BK4, CH8:193-198)

And to prevent your ignorance of virtue, and the degeneracy of your nature into vice, I have also ordained your laws by divine suggestion, and a form of government, which are so good that, if you regularly observe them, you will be esteemed of all men the most happy. When he had spoken thus, he gave them the laws and the constitution of government written in a book. Upon which the people fell into tears, and appeared already touched with the sense that they should have a great want of their conductor, because they remembered what several great dangers he had passed through, and what care he had taken for their preservation. They despaired about what would come upon them after his death, and feared they would never have another governor like him. They also feared that God would take less care of them once Moses was gone, who used to intercede for them. They also repented of what they had said to him in the wilderness when they were angry, and were in grief of those accounts, in so much that the whole body of the people fell into tears with such bitterness, that it was past the power of words to comfort them in their affliction. However, Moses gave them some consolation, and by calling them off the thought of how worthy he was of their weeping for him, he exhorted them to keep to that form of government he had given them; and then the congregation was dissolved at that time.

Accordingly, I shall now first describe this form of government, which was agreeable to the dignity and virtue of Moses, and will thereby inform those who read these antiquities what our original settlements were, and shall then proceed to the remaining histories. Now those settlements are all still in writing, as he left them; and we shall add nothing by the way of ornament or anything besides what Moses left us; only we shall so far innovate, to digest the several kinds of laws into a regular system; for they were by him left in writing as they were accidentally scattered in their delivery, and as he upon inquiry had learned them of God. On which account, I have thought it necessary to premise this observation beforehand, lest any of my countrymen should blame me, as having been guilty of an offense herein. Now, part of our Constitution will include the laws that belong to our political state. As for those laws which Moses left concerning our common conversation and intercourse one with another, I have reserved that for a discourse concerning our manner of life, and the occasions of those laws; which I propose to myself, with God's assistance, to write, after I have finished the work I am now upon.

(BK4, CH8:223)

Aristocracy, and the way of living under it, is the best Constitution; and may you never have any inclination to any other form of government and may you always love that form, and have the laws for your governors, and govern all your actions according to them; for you needed no supreme governor but God.

This type of government was changed during the days of the Prophet Samuel when the children of Israel desired a king to govern them.

1 Samuel 8:4-8

4 Then all the elders of Israel gathered themselves together, and came to Samuel unto Ramah,

5 And said unto him, Behold, thou art old, and thy sons walk not in thy ways: now make us a king to judge us like all the nations.

6 But the thing displeased Samuel, when they said, Give us a king to judge us. And Samuel prayed unto the LORD.

7 And the LORD said unto Samuel, Hearken unto the voice of the people in all that they say unto thee: for they have not rejected thee, but they have rejected me, that I should not reign over them.

8 According to all the works which they have done since the day that I brought them up out of Egypt, even unto this day, wherewith they have forsaken me, and served other gods, so do they also unto thee.

(BK6, CH5:83-85)

And when Samuel had told them that he ought to confirm the kingdom to Saul by a second ordination of him, they all came together to the city of Gilgal, for thither He commanded them to come. So the prophet anointed Saul with the holy oil in the sight of the multitude, and declared him to be king the second time   .

And so the government of the Hebrews was changed into a regal government; for in the days of Moses and his disciple Joshua, who was their general, they continued under an aristocracy. But after the death of Joshua, for 18 years in all, the multitude had no settled form of government, but were in anarchy. After that, they returned to their former government and permitted themselves to be judged by him who appeared to be the best warrior and most courageous Hence, they called this interval of their government the Judges.

In the Book of Jubilees, God tells Moses exactly what would occur in the end times. How the forsaking of the law and form of government would become the downfall of His people.

Jubilees 1:5-15

5 He said, Open your heart to every word which I shall speak to you on this mountain, and write them in a book so that their generations may see how I have not forsaken them for all the evil which they have committed when they transgressed the covenant which I established between Me and you for their generations on this day at Mount Sinai.

6 It will come to pass when all these things come upon them, that they will recognize that I am more righteous than they and all their judgments and in all their actions, and they will recognize that I have truly been with them.

7 Write all these words for yourself which I speak to you today, for I know their rebellion and their stubbornness, before I brought them into the land of which I swore to their fathers, to Abraham and Isaac and Jacob, saying, unto your offspring will I give a land flowing with milk and honey.

8 They will eat and be satisfied, and they will turn to strange gods, to gods that cannot deliver them from any of the tribulation, and this witness shall be heard for a witness against them.

9 They will forget all My commandments, even all that I command them, and they will walk in the ways of the Gentiles, and after their uncleanness, and after their shame, and will serve their gods, and these will prove to them an offense, a tribulation, a sickness, and a trap.

10 Many will perish and they will be taken captive, and will fall into the hands of the enemy, because they have forsaken My laws, My commandments, the festivals of My covenant, My Sabbaths, and My holy place which I have made for myself in their presence, and My tabernacle, and My sanctuary, which I have made holy for Myself amid the land, that I should set My name on it, that it should reside there.

11 They will make themselves high places and places of worship and graven images. Each will worship graven images of his own making thus, they will go astray. They will sacrifice children to demons, and all the errors of their hearts can work.

12 I will send witnesses to them that I may testify against them, but they will not hear. They will kill the witnesses. They will persecute those who seek the law, and they will abolish and change everything in the law to work evil before my eyes.

13 I will hide my face from them. I will deliver them into the hands of the Gentiles. They will be captured like prey for their eating. I will remove them from the land, and I will scatter them among the Gentiles.

14 And they will forget my law and all my commandments and all my judgments. They will go astray regarding the observance of new moons, Sabbaths, festivals, and jubilees, and laws.

15 After this, they will turn to Me from among the Gentiles with all their heart and with all their soul and with all their strength, and I will gather them from among all the Gentiles, and they will seek Me. And I shall be found by them when they seek Me with all their heart and with all their soul.

It is important to note that the word gods does not always refer to a pagan god or an idol. For instance, in Exodus 22:28,

Thou shalt not revile the gods, nor curse the ruler of thy people.

The word gods in this application denotes specifically used in the plural sense occasionally applied by way of deference to magistrate (judges), plural in number refers to (1) rulers, judges, either as divine, representatives. (Strong's # 430 & # 2316)

A perfect example of the use of this word in that form is in John 10:34-35, Jesus answered them,

Is it not written in your law, I said, Ye are gods? If he called them gods, unto whom the word of God came, and the scripture cannot be broken

In other words, representatives (prophets, magistrates, judges, rulers) of the Government of God were also called gods. Not because they were divine but because they spoke on behalf of God (The Only Law Giver). The laws, statutes, and judgments did not proceed from themselves but from God.

When an ambassador of a country is sent to another country to conduct governmental business and an agreement is reached, both parties acknowledge that the ones who agreed were the countries, not the ambassadors themselves personally. They were merely the representatives of the country they spoke on behalf of, as was the case when God sent Moses to speak to the Pharaoh.

Exodus 4:12, 15-16

12 Now therefore go, and I will be with thy mouth, and teach thee what thou shalt say.

15 And thou shalt speak unto him (Aaron), and put words in his mouth: and I will be with thy mouth, and with his mouth, and will teach you what ye shall do.

16 And he shall be thy spokesman unto the people: and he shall be, even he shall be to thee instead of a mouth, and thou shalt be to him instead of God.

Exodus 7:1-2

1 And the LORD said unto Moses, See, I have made thee a god to Pharaoh: and Aaron thy brother shall be thy prophet.

2 Thou shalt speak all that I command thee: and Aaron thy brother shall speak unto Pharaoh, that he send the children of Israel out of his land.

With this in mind, there are many verses in which God admonishes His people not to serve other gods. For example, the First Commandment,

Thou shalt have no other gods before Me.

God is not only speaking of pagan gods or idols, He is advising us that He is the Supreme authority and only Law Giver. No other magistrate, judge, ruler, king, president, etc, gives you a law that is contrary to the one God originally gave you to obey. If you do, you are serving other gods (another law giver).

Isaiah 10:1-3

1 Woe unto them that decree unrighteous decrees An order with the power of legislation issued by a ruler or other person or group with authority., and that write grievousness which they have prescribed To recommend a particular course of action or treatment as a remedy for something.

2 To turn aside the needy from judgment, and to take away the right from the poor of my people, that widows may be their prey, and that they may rob the fatherless!

3 and what will they do on the day of visitation, and in the desolation which shall come from afar? To whom will you flee for help? And where would you leave your glory?

The evidence of the fact that God gave mankind a form of government and not a religion is overwhelming. When Jesus Christ returns to earth to establish the Kingdom of God, what laws do you think His government will enforce? That's right, the laws God gave Moses! Not the U.S. Constitution, federal, state, or local laws, which directly contradict the laws of God. No agencies like the FBI, CIA, DEA, or police department enforcing their man-made laws will even exist. God did not inspire any man-made governments to write laws that are contrary to the ones He originally gave Moses. Satan did! God is not the author of confusion Satan is! Man is not the lawgiver; God is!

Every government established by man has and will fail because it is not governed by the laws of God. And if it is not God's law, then it is of the adversary. You are either a friend or a foe, here or there, hot or cold. If you choose to be lukewarm, God is going to get rid of you.

Matthew 12:30

He that is not with me is against me and he that gathereth not with me scattereth abroad.

Revelation 3:15-16

15 I know thy works, that thou art neither cold nor hot: I would thou wert cold or hot.

16 So then, because thou art lukewarm, and neither cold nor hot, I will spew thee out of my mouth.

Who do you think Jesus Christ is going to war with upon his return to Earth?

Psalms 2

1 Why do the heathen rage, and the people imagine a vain thing?

2 The kings of the earth set themselves, and the rulers take counsel together, against the Lord and his anointed, saying,

3 Let us break their bands asunder, and cast away their cords from us.

4 He that sitteth in the heavens shall laugh: the Lord shall have them in derision.

5 Then shall he speak unto them in his wrath, and vex them in his sore displeasure.

6 Yet have I set my king upon my holy hill of Zion.

7 I will declare the decree: the Lord has said unto me, Thou art my Son; this day have I begotten thee.

8 Asked of me, and I shall give the heathen for thine inheritance, and the uttermost parts of the earth for thy possession.

9 Thou shalt break them with a rod of iron; and thou shalt dash them in pieces like a potter's vessel.

10 Be wise now therefore, O ye kings be instructed, ye judges of the earth.

11 Serve the Lord with fear, and rejoice with trembling.

12 Kiss the Son, lest he be angry, and ye perish from the way, when his wrath is kindled but a little. Blessed are all who put their trust in him.

Revelation 16:14

For they are the spirits of devils, working miracles, which go forth onto the kings of the earth and of the whole world, to gather them to the battle of the great day of God Almighty.

Revelation 19:19

And I saw the beast, and the kings of the earth, and their armies, gathered together to make war against him that sat on the horse, and against his army.

Enoch 46:4 -7

4 And this Son of Man who thou hast seen shall raise the kings and the mighty from their seats (Dethrone them, take away their authori-

ty.), and the strong from their thrones and shall loosen the reins of the strong, and break the teeth of the sinners.

5 And he shall put down the kings from their thrones and kingdoms because they do not extol and praise him, nor humbly acknowledge whence the kingdom was bestowed upon them.

6 And he shall put down the countenance of the strong, and shall fill them with shame. And the darkness shall be their dwelling, and worms shall be their bed, and they shall have no hope of rising from their beds, because they do not extol the name of the Lord of spirits.

7 And these are they who judge the stars of heaven, and raise their hands against the Most High, and tread upon the earth and dwell upon it. And all their deeds manifest unrighteousness, and their power rests on the riches, and their faith is in the gods which they have made with their hands, and they deny the name of the Lord of spirits.

Enoch 48:8

In these days, downcast and countenance shall the kings of the earth have become, and the strong who possess the land because of the works of their hands, for on the day of their anguish and affliction, they should not be able to save themselves.

Enoch 53:3-5

3 For I saw all the angels of punishment abiding there and preparing all the instruments of Satan.

4 And I asked the angel of peace who went with me: For are they preparing these instruments?

5 And he said unto me: They prepare these for the kings and the mighty of this Earth, that they may thereby be destroyed.

Enoch 54:1-6

1 And I looked and turned to another part of the earth, and I saw there a deep valley with a burning fire.

2 And they brought the Kings and the mighty, and began to cast them into this deep valley.

3 And there mine eyes saw how they made these their instruments, iron chains of immeasurable weight.

4 And I asked the angel of peace who went with me, saying: For whom are these chains being prepared? And he said to me: these are being prepared for the host of Azazel (Satan), so that they may take them and cast them into the abyss of complete condemnation, and he shall cover their jaws with rough stones as the Lord of spirits commanded.

6 And Michael, and Gabriel, and Raphael, and Phanuel shall take hold of them on that great day, and cast him on that day into the burning furnace, that the Lord of spirits may take vengeance on them for their unrighteousness in becoming subject to Satan and leading astray those who dwell on the earth.

Wisdom of Solomon 6: 1-10

1 Hear therefore, O ye kings, and understand; learn, ye that be judges of the ends of the earth.

2 Give ear, ye that rule the people, and glory in the multitude of nations.

3 For power is given you of the Lord, and sovereignty from the Highest, who shall try your works, and search out your counsels.

4 Because, being ministers of his kingdom, ye have not judged aright, nor kept the law, nor walked after the counsel of God;

5 Horribly and speedily shall he come upon you: for a sharp judgment shall be to them that be in high places.

6 For mercy will soon pardon the meanest, but mighty men shall be mightily tormented.

7 For He who is Lord over all shall fear no man's person, neither shall He stand in awe of any man's greatness: for He has made the small and great, and cares for all alike.

8 But a sore trial shall come upon the mighty.

9 Unto you therefore, O kings, do I speak, that ye may learn wisdom, and not fall away.

10 For they that keep holiness holily shall be judged holy: and they that have learned such things shall find what to answer.

If by the end of this book you still cannot understand that when the Scriptures speak of the beast, kings, and armies, God is referring to the government, rulers, and their military, you have been deceived. For those who are wise enough to understand, it is common sense.

Furthermore, if you work for the government in any way, shape, or form, you are furthering their godless agenda, whether you know it or would like to admit it; you work for the beast! Especially, if you work in some form of law enforcement enforcing laws contrary to God's law. Do not deceive yourself, the tentacles cannot tell the head of the octopus. I am not part of you. I have heard many people say, I don't agree with what the government is doing, I just work here because of the benefits. Is that so? Do you think that if parent company A owns corporations B, C, and D, and you work for corporation D, you are not part of parent company A? Are people really that naïve or simply trying to take God for a fool? You are a servant to whom you serve, whether it is God or the beast.

Know ye not, that to whom ye yield yourselves servants to obey, his servants ye are to whom ye obey. (Romans 6:16)

During the reign of Roman Emperor Caesar, his top government officials came to the same logical conclusion that even though they were following the Emperor's orders, they were the ones furthering his agenda.

Jewish Antiquities BK 19, CH1:35-41

Cherea cruelly tortured this woman; unwillingly indeed, but because he could not help it. He then brought her, without being in the least moved at what she suffered, into the presence of Caius, and that in such a state as was sad to behold. This matter sorely grieved Cherea, as having been the cause as far as he could, or the instrument, of those miseries to men, which seemed worthy of consolation to Caius himself; on which account he said to Clement and to Papinius (of whom Clement was general of the Army, and Papinius was a tribune): to be sure, O Clement, we have no way failed in our guarding the Emperor; for us to those that have made conspiracies against his government, some have been slain by our care and pains, and some have been by us tortured, and this to such a degree, that he (Caius) hath himself pitied them. How great then is our virtue in submitting to conduct his armies! Clement held his peace, but showed the shame he was under in obeying Caius' orders, both by his eyes and his blushing countenance. We may indeed pretend in words that

Caius is the person onto whom the cause of such miseries ought to be imputed; but, in the opinion of such as can judge rightly, it is I, O Clement! And this Papinius, and before us thou thyself, who bring these tortures upon the Romans, and upon all mankind. It is not done by our being subservient to the commands of Caius, but it is done by our consent. We are his guard in mischief and his executioners, instead of his soldiers, and are the instruments of his cruelty.

When Herod ordered the killing of every two-year-old in Bethlehem in the hopes of killing Jesus, who went out and did the killing? Certainly not Herod, but his soldiers! If his soldiers would not have consented, Herod could not have killed the children.

The same principle applies now, in the opinion of such as can judge uprightly!

2 Timothy 2:3-4

3 Thou therefore endure hardness, as a good soldier of Jesus Christ.

4 No man that warmth entangled himself with the affairs of this life; that he may please him who has chosen him to be a soldier.

Do not entangle yourself in the affairs of any government. That includes working for them less; you should suddenly find yourself warring against God.

Isaiah 31:2-3

2 Yet He also is wise, and will bring evil, and will not call back his words: and will arise against the house of the evildoers, and against the help of them that work iniquity.

3 When the Lord shall stretch out his hand, that helped shall fall, and he that is helped shall fall, and they shall all fail together.

Now, do not misinterpret this. You are to obey all the laws put in place by the government. I am in no way telling anyone to fight against the government, take up arms, or join any kind of militia. Doing so would be going against God's will.

God is fully in control of the affairs in Heaven and Earth, and He has allowed the government to function according to His purpose rather than to have people in complete anarchy. God has allowed this government to continue, and when He is good and ready, He will destroy it, and He certainly does not need your help to do it. However, when the laws enforced by the government are in direct contradiction with God's law, God's law must take precedence; you are to obey God rather than men.

1 Corinthians 7:23

Ye are bought with a price; be not ye servants of men.

Especially in this very end time, keep in mind Ecclesiastes 3: there is a time for everything, and this is the time that God is judging the world. Do not compromise any of His laws, for He is taking note.

Chapter 3

What is Prophecy?

The word prophe in Hebrew is NABA, NAW-BAH a prime root: to prophecy, i.e speak or sing by inspiration in prediction or simple discourse (2). Most frequently, NABA is used to describe the function of the true prophet as he speaks God's message to the people, under the influence of the Divine Spirit. (2A) to prophecy was a task that the prophet could not avoid: (2B) While the formula The word of the Lord came [to the prophet] is used hundreds of times in the Old Testament, (2B1) there is no real indication as to how it came whether it came through the thought process, through a vision, or in some other way. Strong's Concordance #5012

In Greek it is: PROPHETEIA, PROF-AY-TIAH (prophecy) prediction (scriptural or other) (1) Prophecy is not necessarily common nor even primarily foretelling. (2) It is the declaration of that which cannot be known by natural means. (3) It emanates from God and is the foretelling of the will of God, whether with references to the past, the present, or the future. (4) It signifies the speaking forth of the mind and counsel of God.

The person chosen by God to proclaim a prophecy is called a prophet, which means: one who speaks forth openly, a proclaimer of a divine message. A prophet is one upon whom the Spirit of God rests; to whom and through whom God speaks.

God has always spoken to His people through prophets. He gives instructions or a message to the prophets, and they deliver the message to the people.

Moses made that very clear to the children of Israel.

Deuteronomy 18:15

The Lord thy God will raise unto thee a Prophet from the midst of the, of thy brethren, like unto me: unto him you shall hearken.

1 Samuel 10:6

And the Spirit of the Lord will come upon thee, and thou shalt prophesy with them, and shalt be turned into another man.

1 Samuel 16:13

Then Samuel took the horn of oil, and anointed him among his brethren and the Spirit of the Lord came upon David from that day forward.

Hebrews 1:1

God, who at sundry times and in diverse manners spake in time past unto the fathers by the prophets,...

God also makes this clear.

2 Chronicles 36:15 – 16

15 And the Lord God of their fathers sent to them by His messengers, rising up early and sending them; because He had compassion on His people, and on His dwelling place:

16 But they mocked the messengers of God, and despised His words, and misused His prophets, and to the wrath of the Lord arose against His people, till there was no remedy.

Jeremiah 7:25 – 26

25 Since the day that your fathers came forth out of the land of Egypt unto this day, I have even sent on to you all My servants the prophets, daily rising early and sending them:

26 Yet they hearkened not unto Me, nor inclined their ear, but hardened their neck: they did worse than their fathers.

Jeremiah 25:4

And the Lord hath sent on to you all His servants the prophets, rising early and sending them; but ye have not hearkened, nor inclined your ear to hear.

Jeremiah 26:4 – 5

4 And thou shalt say unto them, thus saith the Lord; if ye will not hearken to me, to walk in My law, which I have set before you,

5 To hearken to the words of My servants the prophets, whom I sent on to you, but ye have not hearkened;

Jeremiah 29:19

Because they have not hearkened to My words, saith the Lord, which I sent on to them by My servants the prophets, rising early and sending them; but ye would not hear, saith the Lord.

God does not come down from His heavenly throne in the sight of everyone and has some sort of press conference to give His people a message. His message is proclaimed through the prophets.

Chapter 4

The Odds and Accuracy of Prophecy

Since this book is not intended for those who are ignorant of the accuracy of Biblical prophecy, we will not go into the details of hundreds of prophecies already fulfilled. Our focus will be on end-time prophecies currently being fulfilled. However, we need to be thoroughly educated as to the mathematical odds of prophecy. After all, God numbered the stars, planets, times, ages, people, etc. Everything has a number, a beginning, and an end.

2 Esdras 4:36-37

36 And the Archangel Jeremiel gave him this answer As soon as the number of those like yourselves is complete.

37 For the Lord has weighed the world in a balance, He has measured and numbered the ages; He will move nothing, or turn nothing, until the appointed number is achieved.

2 Esdras 9:5-6

5 Just as everything that is done on earth has its beginning and end marked, so it is with the times which the Most High has determined:

6 Their beginning is marked by portents and miracles, and their end by manifestations of power.

Wisdom of Solomon 11:20

But thou hast ordered all things in measure and number and weight.

Testament of Naphtali 1:15

For by weight, and measure, and rule was all the creation made.

Apocalypse of Baruch 42:6 pg.59

And time shall succeed to time and season to season, and one shall receive from another, and then with a view to the consummation shall everything be compared according to the measure of the times and the hours of the seasons.

Apocalypse of Baruch 85:14 pg.96

On this account, there is one law for one, one age, and an end for all who are in it.

Mathematical odds of prophecy:

Dr. Peter Stoner (June 16, 1888 – March 21, 1980) was Chairman of the Departments of Mathematics and Astronomy at Pasadena City College until 1953; Chairman of the science division, Westmont College, 1953–57; Professor Emeritus of Science, Westmont College; Professor Emeritus of Mathematics and Astronomy, Pasadena City College. Dr. Stoner is probably best known for his work Science Speaks, which discusses, among other things, Bible prophecies vis-à-vis probability estimates and calculations.

Dr Stoner stated, For one person to even fulfill eight of the prophecies of the Messiah is one in ten to the 157th power (1 with 157 zeros). That is a big number. There is not much chance that even one person could fulfill eight of the prophecies. Let me give you an illustration that I have used before, but I think it helps us get a picture. The odds of someone fulfilling even 8 of the prophecies would be like the odds of taking the state of Texas and filling it with silver dollars, two feet deep throughout the whole state. We take one of those silver dollars and put a big X on the back of it. Then we stuff it into the state of Texas and get some big, strong guys and mix it all up. Then we will take one person and blindfold them. Drop them in Texas and let them wander around. As he/she is wandering around, they finally bend down and pick up the coin with the X. The first time they pick up a coin, no second or third chances. The odds of that coin having the X on it are less than the odds that one person would fulfill even eight of the three hundred and thirty prophecies.

The current population of humans presently on earth it's approximately 6.9 billion. By using the example given above, we will begin a process of eliminating those that do not fulfill the prophecies of the Antichrist.

At the same time, we will direct our attention to the one who has, is, and will fulfill all the prophecies given by God. This will give us further evidence that points directly to only one person. Keep this in mind as we progress through our study of prophecy.

Prophecy is one of the biggest proofs of the existence and the sovereignty of God. Only God, who controls the ages and times, can declare something hundreds, even thousands of years before they occur and bring them to pass exactly as He said.

It is God's divine prerogative to announce beforehand what is to occur, and then to fulfill that declaration without fail.

Isaiah 42:9

Behold, the former things are come to pass, and new things do I declare: before the spring forth I tell you of them.

Isaiah 44:6 – 8

6 Thus saith the Lord the King of Israel, and his Redeemer the Lord of hosts I am the first, and I am the last and besides me there is no God.

7 And who, as I, shall call, and shall declare it, and set for me, since I appointed the ancient peoples? And the things that are coming, and shall come, let them show unto them.

8 Fear ye not, neither be afraid have not I told thee from that time, and have declared it? Ye are even my witnesses. Is there a God beside me? Yeah, there is no God; I know not any.

Isaiah 46:9-10

9 Remember the former things of old: for I am God, and there is none else; I am God, and there is none like me,

10 Declaring the end from the beginning, and from ancient times the things that are not yet done, saying, My counsel shall stand, and I will do all my pleasure.

2 Peter 1:19

We also have a more sure word of prophecy; whereunto ye do well that ye take heed, as unto a light that shines in a dark place, until the day dawn, and the day star arise in your hearts:

The accuracy of prophecy has not only been recorded through the pages of Scripture for our benefit but also through numerous historians from different parts of the world. In the book Jewish Antiquities, Flavius Josephus makes an interesting observation as to the accuracy of prophecy.

(BK 8, CH15:418)

And as what things were foretold should happen to Ahab by the two prophets came to pass, we ought thence to have high notions of God, and everywhere to honor and worship him, and never suppose that what is pleasant and agreeable is worthy of belief before what is true; and to esteem nothing more advantageous than the gift of prophecy, and that fore knowledge of future events which is derived from it, since God shows men thereby what we ought to avoid.

(BK 10, CH2:35)

And whatsoever is done among us, whether it be good or whether it be bad, comes to pass according to their (prophets) prophecies.

(BK 10, CH3:39)

So God was angry at these proceedings, and sent prophets to the King, and to the multitude, by whom He threatened the very same calamities to them which their brethren the Israelites, upon the likes affronts offered to God, were now under. But these men would not believe their words by which belief they might have reaped the advantage of escaping all those miseries yet did they in earnest learn that what the prophets had told them was true.

(BK10, CH8:142)

We have said thus much because it was sufficient to show the nature of God to such as are ignorant of it that it is various, and acts the many different ways, and that all events happen after a regular manner, in their proper season, and that it foretells what must come to pass (prophecy). It is also sufficient to show the ignorance and incredulity of man, whereby they are not permitted to foresee anything future, and are, without any guard, exposed to calamities, so that they can't avoid the experience of those calamities.

(BK10, CH11: 277-280)

All these things did this man leave in writing, as God had shown them to him, in so much that such as read his prophecies, and see how they have been fulfilled, would wonder at the honor wherewith

God honored Daniel; and may thence discover how the Epicureans are in an error, who cast Providence out of human life, and do not believe that God takes care of the affairs of the world, nor that the universe is governed and continued in being by that blessed and immortal nature, but say that the world is carried along of its own accord, without a ruler and a curator; which, were it destitute of a guide to conduct as they imagine, it would be like ships without pilots, which we see drowned by the winds, or like chariots without drivers, which are overturned; so would the world be dashed to pieces by being carried without a Providence, and so perish, and come to not. So that, by the aforementioned predictions of Daniel, those men seem to me very much to err from the truth, who determined that God exercises no Providence over human affairs; for if that were the case, that the world went on by mechanical necessity, we should not see that all things would come to pass according to his prophecy.

One of the keys to understanding prophecy is the principle of dualism or duality. That is many Bible prophecies are not single events, but have a lesser forerunner, and then a major fulfillment. This principle of duality is explained by Solomon in the book of Ecclesiastes.

Ecclesiastes 1:9-10

9 The thing that hath been, it is that which shall be; and that which is done is that which shall be done: and there is no new thing under the sun.

10 Is there anything whereof it may be said, see, this is new? It hath been already of old time, which was before us.

Ecclesiastes 3:14 15

14 I know that, whatsoever God doeth, it shall be forever: nothing can be put to it, nor anything taken from it: and God doeth it, that men should fear before him.

15 That which hath been is now; and that which is to be hath already been; and God required that which is past.

Testament of Asher 1:3-4

3 Two ways hath God given the sons of men, and two inclinations and two kinds of actions, and two modes of action, and two issues.

4 Therefore, all things are by twos, one over against the other.

Ecclesiasticus 33:15

So, look upon all the works of the Highest; and there are two and two, one against another.

Chapter 5

Why the Different Interpretations of End Time Prophecy?

Throughout the years, there have been many different interpretations of prophecy, and there are several reasons why. First of all, we must be humble enough to realize and accept that not everyone has been blessed with the gift of prophecy. The apostle Paul addresses this issue.

Romans 12:3 – 9

3 For I say, through the grace given unto me, to every man that is among you, not to think of himself more highly than he ought to think; but think soberly, according as God hath dealt to every man the measure of faith.

4 For as we have many members in one body, and all members have not the same office.

5 So we, being many, are one body in Christ, and everyone members of one another.

6 Having then gifts differing according to the grace that is given to us, whether prophecy, let us prophesy according to the portion of faith

7 Or ministry, let us wait on our ministering; or he that teaches, on teaching;

8 Or he that exhorted, on exhortation: he that giveth, let him do it with simplicity; he that ruled, with diligence; he that showed mercy, with cheerfulness.

9 Let love be without dissimulation. Abhor that which is evil; cleave to that which is good.

1 Corinthians 12:4 –31

12 The body is a unit, though it is made up of many parts; and though all its parts are many, they form one body. So it is with Christ.

13 For we were all baptized by one Spirit into one body--whether Jews or Greeks, slave or free and we were all given the one Spirit to drink.

14 Now the body is not made up of one part but of many.

15 If the foot should say, Because I am not a hand, I do not belong to the body, it would not for that reason cease to be part of the body.

16 And if the ear should say, Because I am not an eye, I do not belong to the body, it would not for that reason cease to be part of the body.

17 If the whole body were an eye, where would the sense of hearing be? If the whole body were an ear, where would the sense of smell be?

18 But God has arranged the parts in the body, every one of them, just as He wanted them to be.

19 If they were all one part, where would the body be?

20 As it is, there are many parts, but one body.

21 The eye cannot say to the hand, I don't need you! And the head cannot say to the feet, I don't need you!

22 On the contrary, those parts of the body that seem to be weaker are indispensable,

23, and the parts that we think are less honorable, we treat with special honor. And the unpresentable parts are treated with special modesty,

24, while our presentable parts need no special treatment. But God has combined the members of the body and has given greater honor to the parts that lacked it,

25 so that there should be no division in the body, but that its parts should have equal concern for each other.

26 If one part suffers, every part suffers with it; if one part is honored, every part rejoices with it.

27 Now you are the body of Christ, and each one of you is a part of it.

28 And in the church God has appointed first of all apostles, second prophets, third teachers, then workers of miracles, also those having gifts of healing, those able to help others, those with gifts of administration, and those speaking in different kinds of tongues.

29 Are all apostles? Are all prophets? Are all teachers? Do all work miracles?

30 Do all have gifts of healing? Do all speak in tongues? Do all interpret?

31 But eagerly desire the greater gifts. And now I will show you the most excellent way.

Ephesians: 11-14

11 It was He who gave some to be apostles, some to be prophets, some to be evangelists, and some to be pastors and teachers,

12 to prepare God's people for works of service, so that the body of Christ may be built up

13 until we all reach unity in the faith and the knowledge of the Son of God and become mature, attaining to the whole measure of the fullness of Christ.

14 Then we will no longer be infants, tossed back and forth by the waves, and blown here and there by every wind of teaching and by the cunning and craftiness of men in their deceitful scheming.

We all have different gifts from God, and God bless the pastors and teachers of righteousness who have worked so hard and endured many trials and temptations. Your reward is recorded in heaven, but if we are to abide by every word that proceeds from the mouth of God, we ought to realize that we all have a specific position in this ministry. I, for instance, am not a minister, pastor, or evangelist. I do not have a church to lead, nor do I pastor the precious flock of God. The Lord did not bless me with such a privileged ministry. I like Moses, Gideon, Jeremiah, and others who prayed that God would choose himself a more qualified person for the job. Not one was completely covered in sin from head to toe. After all, if there is someone who deserves to bust the gates of hell wide open, head-first, and at neck-breaking speed, it is I! But I noticed something about those whom God calls.

Epistle of Barnabas 4:12

And when He chose His apostles, who were afterwards to publish His gospel, He took men who had been very great sinners that thereby

He might plainly show that He came not to call the righteous but sinners to repentance.

The great mercy, forgiveness, and patience of God; indescribable!

Secondly, most pastors, ministers, and theologians have all had some form of formal education from a biblical college. There is nothing wrong with attending such colleges or universities as long as they do not veer from the teachings of the Scriptures either to the left or to the right. The problem comes in with the teachings of these institutions as they pertain to Prophetic Scripture.

For example, a Bible college professor teaches 25 would be pastors what he was taught 30 years ago as a student attending the same class. These 25 pastors go out and teach hundreds of thousands of people what they learned from the pastor as it pertains to Prophetic Scripture. This becomes a never-ending cycle of erroneous interpretations of prophecy. I do not think that this is done with malicious intent on behalf of the Bible College, the professor, or the pastors. This is just the way things work in an imperfect world.

During my research, I found something very interesting that occurred between the prophets Ezekiel and Jeremiah, which many have ignorantly perceived as conflicting statements and have consequently disregarded the entire prophecy to their demise.

(Jewish Antiquities, BK10, CH 7:105-107)

Now, as to Zedekiah himself, while he heard the prophets speak, he believed them, and agreed to everything as true, and supposed it was for his advantage; but then his friends perverted him, and dissuaded him from what the Prophet advised, and obliged him to do what would be pleasing. Ezekiel also foretold in Babylon what calamities were coming upon the people, which when he heard, he sent accounts of them onto Jerusalem; but Zedekiah did not believe their prophecies, for the reason following: it happened that the two prophets agreed with one another in what they said as in all other things, that the city should be taken and Zedekiah himself should be taken captive; but Ezekiel disagreed with him (Jeremiah), and said, that Zedekiah should not see Babylon; while Jeremiah said to him, that the king of Babylon should carry him away thither in bonds; and because they did not both say the same thing as to this circumstance, he disbelieved what they both appeared to agree in, and condemned them as not speaking truth therein, although all the things foretold him did come to pass according to their prophecies, as we shall show upon a fitter opportunity.

(BK 10, CH 8:138-141)

So the enemy took Zedekiah alive, when he was deserted by all but a few, with his children and his wives, and brought him to the king. When he came, Nebuchadnezzar began to call him a wicked wretch, and covenant breaker, and one that had forgotten his former words, when he promised to keep the country for him. He also reproached him for his ingratitude, that when he had received the kingdom from him, who had taken it from Jehoiachin, and given it to him, he had used the power granted to him against the one who gave it. But, said he, God is great who hateth that conduct of thine, and has brought thee under us. And when he had said these words to Zedekiah, he commanded his sons and his friends to be slain, while Zedekiah and the rest of the captains looked on; after which he put out the eyes of Zedekiah, bound him, and carried him to Babylon.

And these things happened to him, as Jeremiah and Ezekiel had foretold him that he should be caught, and brought before the king of Babylon, and should speak to him face-to-face, and should see his eyes with his own eyes; and thus far did Jeremiah prophesy. But he was also made blind and brought to Babylon, so that he did not see it, according to the prediction of Ezekiel.

All prophecies are given in parables, and some are purposely hidden by God and are revealed to whomever God chooses and at the appointed time. There may be certain details of a prophecy not fully revealed to the Prophet, and some things he may not fully understand, as was the case with Daniel.

Daniel 12:8

And I heard, but I understood not: then said I, O my Lord, what shall be the end of these things?

We are not to make the same mistake and completely disregard the entire prophecy as if God will not bring it to pass simply because we do not understand some of it, or because He has chosen not to reveal it until the appointed time. Do not throw the baby out with the bathwater!

Furthermore, Scripture must interpret Scripture, and no one is given a private interpretation.

Isaiah 28:10

For precept must be upon precept, precept upon precept; line upon line, line upon line; here a little: and there a little:

2 Peter 1:20-21

20 Knowing this first, that no prophecy of Scripture is of any private interpretation.

21 For the prophecy came not in old time by the will of man but holy men of God sake as they were moved by the Holy Ghost.

In the Ascension of Isaiah, the Testament of Hezekiah, Hezekiah explains the unfortunate attitude of certain pastors and ministers and how some have given their interpretations to prophecies in these times.

Ascension of Isaiah part 2 – the Testament of Hezekiah 3:29 – 31, pg 37

And there will be great hatred in the shepherds and elders toward each other. For there will be great jealousy in the last days, for everyone will say what is pleasing in his own eyes. And they will make of none effect the prophecy of the prophets which were before me, and these my visions also will be made of none effect, to speak after the impulse of their own heart.

Hosea 9:7

The days of visitation are come, the days of recompense are come; Israel shall know it: the prophet is full, the spiritual man is mad, for the multitude of thine iniquity, and the great hatred.

Another reason for the confusion in end-time prophecy is that God has purposely sealed certain prophecies unto the time He chooses to reveal them.

Isaiah 29:10 – 12

10 For the Lord hath poured out upon you the spirit of deep sleep, and hath closed your eyes: the prophets and your rulers, the seers hath he covered.

11 And the vision of all is become on to you as the words of a book that is sealed, which men deliver to one that is learned, saying, Read this, I pray thee: and he saith, I cannot; for it is sealed

12 And the book is delivered to him that is not learned, saying, Read this, I pray thee: and he saith, I am not learned.

Daniel 12:4, 9-10

4 But thou, O Daniel, shut up the words, and seal the book, even to the time of the end: many shall run to and fro, and knowledge shall be increased.

9 And he said, Go Thy Way, Daniel for the words are closed up and sealed till the time of the end.

10 Many shall be purified, and made white, and tried; but the wicked shall do wickedly: and none of the wicked shall understand; but the wise shall understand.

Furthermore, human beings have simply lost track of time, making it impossible to properly determine when certain prophecies will be fulfilled. (More on this subject later)

Now we move on to the more severe problem. Ministers of Satan, false prophets, purposely deceiving the masses. With smooth, convincing words pointing to the destruction that is to hit the North, while purposely not telling you that it hits the South first, then works its way up. What is the point of prophetic Scripture if it is not clear and we do not know the approximate time of its fulfillment to prepare and get out of harm's way? There would be no point in it, and rendered useless!

1 Corinthians 14:7-8

7 And even things without life giving sound, whether pipe or harp, except they give a distinction in the sounds, how shall it be known what is piped or harped?

8 For if the trumpet gives an uncertain sound, who shall prepare himself to the battle?

God does not operate in a vague manner of confusion; Satan does and is the master of it. God is clear and precise in what he says. He does not say right when he means left or up when he means down. Besides, I do not need God to tell me that a nuclear explosion devastated the city I lived in three days ago. By that time, I will be either a pile of ashes or very well aware of the fact! I need to know before, not after!

Now notice what the Scriptures continue to say about false prophets.

Jeremiah 6:13 – 14

13 For from the least of them even unto the greatest of them everyone is given to covetousness; and from the prophet even unto the priest everyone dealeth falsely.

14 They have healed also the hurt of the daughter of my people slightly, saying, Peace, peace; when there is no peace.

Jeremiah 14:13 – 16

13 Then said I, Ah, Lord God! Behold, the prophets say unto them, ye shall not see the sword, neither shall ye have famine; but I will give you assured peace in this place.

14 Then the Lord said unto me, the prophets prophesy lies in my name: I sent them not, neither have I commanded them, neither

spake unto them: they prophesy unto you a false vision and divination, and a thing of nought, and the deceit of their heart.

15 Therefore, thus saith the Lord concerning the prophets that prophesy in my name, and I sent them not, yet they say, Sword and famine shall not be in this land; By sword and famine shall those prophets be consumed.

16 And the people to whom they prophesy shall be cast into the streets of Jerusalem because of the famine and the sword; and shall have none to bury them, their wives, nor their sons, nor their daughters; for I will pour their wickedness upon them.

Jeremiah 27:10, 15

10 For they prophesy a lie unto you, to remove you far from your land; and that I should drive you out, and you should perish.

15 For I have not sent them, saith the Lord, yet they prophesy a lie in my name; that I may drive you out, and that ye might perish, ye, and the prophets that prophesy unto you.

Micah 3:5

Thus, saith the Lord concerning the prophets that make my people err, that bite with their teeth, and cry, Peace; and he that putteth not into their mouths, they even prepare war against him.

Zephaniah 3:4

Her prophets are light and treacherous persons: her priests have polluted the sanctuary, they have done violence to the law.

Zechariah 10:2

For the idols have spoken vanity, and the diviners have seen a lie, and have told false dreams; they comfort in vain therefore they went their way as a flock; they were troubled, because there was no shepherd.

Zechariah 13:2 – 5

2 And it shall come to pass in that day, saith the LORD of hosts, that I will cut off the names of the idols out of the land, and they shall no more be remembered: and also I will cause the prophets and the unclean spirit to pass out of the land.

3 And it shall come to pass, that when any shall yet prophesy, then his father and his mother that begat him shall say unto him, Thou shalt not live for thou speakest lies in the name of the LORD and his father and his mother that begat him shall thrust him through when he prophesieth.

4 And it shall come to pass in that day, that the prophets shall be ashamed every one of his vision, when he hath prophesied; neither shall they wear a rough garment to deceive:

5 But he shall say, I am no prophet, I am a husbandman; for man taught me to keep cattle from my youth.

Listen to our Savior's warning:

Matthew 24:3 – 5, 11

3 And as he sat upon the Mount of Olives, the disciples came unto him privately, saying; Tell us, when shall these things be? And what shall be the sign of thy coming, and of the end of the world?

4 And Jesus answered and said unto them, Take heed that no man deceive you.

5 For many shall come in my name, saying, I am Christ; and shall deceive many.

11 And many false prophets shall rise, and shall deceive many.

Mark 13:6, 22-23

6 For many shall come in my name, saying, I am Christ; and shall deceive many.

22 For false Christs and false prophets shall rise, and shall shew signs and wonders, to seduce, if it were possible, even the elect.

23 But take ye heed: behold, I have foretold you all things.

Luke 21:8

8 And He said, Take heed that ye be not deceived for many shall come in my name, saying, I am Christ; and, The time draweth near go ye not therefore after them.

Look what Paul tells Timothy.

1 Timothy 4:1-2

1 Now the Spirit speaketh expressly, that in the latter times some shall depart from the faith, giving heed to seducing spirits, and doctrines of devils;

2 Speaking lies in hypocrisy; having their conscience seared with a hot iron

Notice the words of Peter.

2 Peter 2:1-3

1 But there were false prophets also among the people, even as there shall be false teachers among you, who privily shall bring in damnable heresies, even denying the Lord that bought them, and bring upon themselves swift destruction.

2 And many shall follow their pernicious ways, because of whom the way of truth shall be evil spoken of.

3 And through covetousness shall they with feigned words make merchandise of you: whose judgment now of a long time lingereth not, and their damnation slumbereth not.

Satan also has apostles and ministers.

2 Corinthians 11:13 – 15

13 For such are false apostles, deceitful workers, transforming themselves into the apostles of Christ.

14 And no marvel; for Satan himself is transformed into an angel of light.

15 Therefore, it is no great thing if his ministers also be transformed as the ministers of righteousness, whose end shall be according to their works.

Ascension of Isaiah 3:21-31

21 And afterwards. On the eve of His approach, His disciples will forsake the teaching of the Twelve Apostles. And their faith, and their love, and their purity.

22 And there will be many lawless elders and shepherds dealing wrongly by their sheep, and they will ravage them owing to their not having holy shepherds.

25 And many will change the honor of the garments of the Saints for the garments of covetous, and there will be much respect of persons in those days, and lovers of the honor of this world

26 And there will be much slander and vain glory at the approach of the Lord, and the Holy Spirit will withdraw from many.

27 And there will not be in those days many prophets, nor those who speak trustworthy words save one here and there in diverse places,

28 On account of the spirit of error and fornication and of vainglory, and of covetousness, which will be in those who will be called servants of that One (Satan), and in those days who will receive that One

29 And there will be great hatred among the shepherds and elders towards each other.

30 For there will be great jealousy in the last days; for everyone will say what is pleasing in his own eyes.

31 And they will make of none effect the prophecy of the prophets which were before me, and these my visions also will they make of none effect, to speak after the impulse of their own heart.

For instance, did you know that famous Evangelist Billy Graham is a high-level Illuminist and consort of the secret society elite? (See book, Billy Graham and friends, by Dr. Kathy Burns; and video documentary Tower of infamy, by Texe Marrs) What about Robert Schuller, a 33rd degree Freemason, and pastor of California's Crystal Cathedral and host of Hour of Power? Or good old Pat Robertson? Illuminati servant, ordained for the ministry at a Norfolk, Virginia church appropriately named The Freemason St., Baptist Church. Robertson is allied with the Vatican's Sovereign Military Order of the Knights of

Malta (SMOM). Religious rights leader of TV's The 700 Club and founder of the Christian Coalition.

Several years ago, Robertson had two books ghostwritten for him The New Millennium and The New World Order. As happens often in elitist circles, the opinions and materials for both books seem to be decidedly anti-elitist; they even expose the global conspiracy and the Illuminati. These books make a Robertson appear as if he is fighting against the global conspiracy and the evils of the Illuminati. The truth is that the books were for the ignorant of the masses. While reading The New Millennium, the reader, ignorant of the uses of symbolism, probably never notices the fact that at the top of every page, a point within a circle (a Masonic symbol, see: Mackie's Masonic Encyclopedia) could be found. Robertson was sending out his hidden code to his elite friends, advising them that he was still on their team and was just taking the ignorant masses for a ride! (Codex Magica, by Texxe Marrs, pg. 462)

How about Prosperity Preacher Kenneth Copeland, who, before the second election of George W. Bush, said that God had told him to keep America safe (avoid another 9/11), and they needed to elect a Republican President.

Since when does God require the help of the public to achieve his goal, or would he have anything to do with the Beast (Government)? And does he think God does not know about the democrat/republican scheme? Come on, Mr. Copeland, God knew the end from the beginning and even wrote it down for us as a witness. I guess Copeland was the one who did not know that the Dragon/beast has 10 horns, and Bush was the 10th. Or did he know perfectly and was just part of the plan? What Copeland did not say was that he and Bush have quite a history together to long to go into details. I guess he conveniently forgot to mention.

I can't wait to see all their faces when all these things foretold come to pass (which they surely will very soon), and all these people have to stand before Christ, who will no longer play the role of the lamb but will now be the Lion, and is very, very, very angry! What will they do on that day? To whom will they flee, Satan? He is the first one who is going to turn their crooked behind over to Christ!

This comes as no surprise, for even Enoch foresaw the magnitude of the deception long before the deception flourished.

Enoch 104:9 – 10

9 Be not godless in your hearts, and lie not and alter not the words of uprightness, nor charge with lying the words of the Holy Great One, nor take account of your idols;

10 for all your lying and all your godlessness, issue not in righteousness but in great sin. And now I know this mystery, that sinners will alter and pervert the words of righteousness in many ways, and will speak wicked words, and lie, and practice great deceits, and write books concerning their words.

Now, notice how knowledge is increased among the wise when the truth is told.

Enoch 104:11 – 13

11 But when they write down truthfully all my words into their languages, and do not change or diminish ought from my words, but write them all down truthfully, all that I first testified concerning them.

12 Then, I know another mystery, that books (What books? Apocrypha?) will be given to the righteous and the

13 wise to become a cause of joy and uprightness and much wisdom. And to them shall the books be given, and they shall believe in them and rejoice over them, and then shall all the righteous who have learnt there from all the paths of uprightness be recompensed.

It is now high time (urgent) for people to take charge of their relationship with God. Study, not just read the Scriptures, seek the knowledge of God as if you were seeking a hidden treasure. Search for yourself! Quit following these good speaking, Bible verse-quoting (Don't you know that Satan knows the Bible better than you and me both?), motivational speakers who establish themselves as leaders and ministers and who are misguided and sinning fools in God's sight! These Men are always learning, but they are never able to come to the knowledge of the truth. Having a form of godliness but denying its power. Blind leaders of the blind, and if the blind lead the blind, both shall fall into the ditch. From such turn away. In other words, stay away from them, ignore them, don't listen to them! Paul warns in (2 Timothy 4:3-4)

For the time will come when they will not endure sound doctrine (the teaching of the truth), but according to their desires, because they have itching ears (that is what people want to hear), they will heap up for themselves teachers; and they will turn their ear away from the truth, and be turned into fables (lies, fairytales) (William F. Dankenbring, Prophecy Flash 2010)

What about you? Are you taking charge of your walk with God, or are you just believing any man or so-called minister without checking, studying, meditating, and praying that God reveals to you if what they are telling you is the truth or not?

Prove all things; hold fast that which is good (1 Thessalonians 5:21). This includes even what I am telling you. Don't just take my word for it, prove all things! (Research, study, pray, meditate) Do not allow men to mislead and deceive you. This battle for the truth is very real your eternal future is what they want to take, and the stakes are very high.

We stand at a spiritual Armageddon, and the physical is about to begin. So are you willing to take the time to study your Bible, look through the Internet, get a concordance, Bible dictionary, make charts, and study the history of Israel? Are you willing to study to show yourself approved to God, a worker who does not need to be ashamed, rightly dividing the word of God? (2 Timothy 2:15)

Remember this if in these times when the worst human suffering the world has ever seen is about to occur, if you do not know the basics: who, how, when, and where? You have either deceived or you are part of the deception! Do not follow cunningly devised fables. Beware of the trickery of men, in their cunning craftiness of deceitful plotting. (Ephesians 4:14) This is an ancient method of warring, it is called divide and conquer. And Jesus knew their thoughts, and said unto them, Every kingdom divided against itself is brought to desolation and every city or house divided against itself shall not stand: (Matthew 12:25)

The deception is so enormous that no words are sufficiently able to describe it. Satan and his hosts have become the unacknowledged Masters who run most Christian establishments behind the scenes. Most big-name clergy and evangelist today merely follow the script laid down for them by their elite controllers.

Jeremiah 5:30 – 31

30 A wonderful and horrible thing is committed in the land;

31 The prophets prophesy falsely, and the priests bear rule by their means; and my people love to have it so: and what will ye do in the end thereof?

Jeremiah 17:5

5 Thus saith the LORD Cursed be the man that trusted in man, and maketh flesh his arm, and whose heart departed from the LORD.

Jeremiah 23:16 – 32

16 Thus saith the LORD of hosts, Hearken not unto the words of the prophets that prophesy unto you: they make you vain: they speak a vision of their own heart, and not out of the mouth of the LORD.

17 They say still unto them that despise me, The LORD hath said, Ye shall have peace; and they say unto every one that walketh after the imagination of his own heart, No evil shall come upon you.

18 For who hath stood in the counsel of the LORD, and hath perceived and heard his word? Who hath marked his word, and heard it?

19 Behold, a whirlwind of the LORD is gone forth in fury, even a grievous whirlwind: it shall fall grievously upon the head of the wicked.

20 The anger of the LORD shall not return, until he has executed, and till he has performed the thoughts of his heart: in the latter days ye shall consider it perfectly.

21 I have not sent these prophets, yet they ran I have not spoken to them, yet they prophesied.

22 But if they had stood in my counsel, and had caused my people to hear my words, then they should have turned them from their evil way, and the evil of their doings.

23 Am I a God at hand, saith the LORD, and not a God afar off?

24 Can any hide himself in secret places that I shall not see him? Saith the LORD. Don't I fill heaven and earth? Saith the LORD.

25 I have heard what the prophets said, that prophesy lies in my name, saying, I have dreamed, I have dreamed.

26 How long shall this be in the heart of the prophets that prophesy lies? Yeah, they are prophets of the deceit of their own heart

27 Which think to cause my people to forget my name by their dreams which they tell every man to his neighbor, as their fathers have forgotten my name for Baal.

28 The prophet that hath a dream, let him tell a dream; and he that hath my word, let him speak my word faithfully. What is the chaff to the wheat? Saith the LORD.

29 Isn't my word like a fire? Saith the LORD and like a hammer that break the rock in pieces?

30 Therefore, behold, I am against the prophets, saith the LORD, that steal my words from his neighbor.

31 Behold, I am against the prophets, saith the LORD, that use their tongues, and say, He saith   .

32 Behold, I am against them that prophesy false dreams, saith the LORD, and do tell them, and cause my people to err by their lies, and

by their lightness; yet I sent them not, nor commanded them: therefore they shall not profit this people at all, saith the LORD.

God gives us a sign to watch for to know if a prophet is truly sent by God or speaking out of his own heart.

Deuteronomy 18:20-22

20 But the prophet, who shall presume to speak a word in my name, which I have not commanded him to speak, or that shall speak in the name of other gods, even that prophet shall die.

21 And if thou say in thine heart, how shall we know the word which the LORD hath not spoken?

22 When a prophet speak in the name of the LORD, if the thing follow not, nor come to pass, that is the thing which the LORD hath not spoken, but the prophet hath spoken it presumptuously: thou shalt not be afraid of him.

Jeremiah 28:8 –9

8 The prophets that have been before me and before thee of old prophesied both against many countries, and against great kingdoms, of war, and of evil, and pestilence.

9 The prophet who prophesieth of peace, when the word of the prophet shall come to pass, then shall the prophet be known, that the LORD hath truly sent him.

Testament of Judah 4:10 – 11

10 And with the flesh of many shall they wrongfully feed the ravens and the cranes; and they shall advance in evil, and covetousness up-

lifted, and there shall be false prophets like tempest, and they shall persecute all righteous men.

11 And the Lord shall bring upon them divisions one against another.

Chapter 6

What are Apocrypha and Apocalyptic Writings?

Apocrypha is derived from the Greek word (Apokryphos) and simply means hidden unknown to hide away. It is a group of books not considered canonical (authorized recognized; accepted). These books are included in the Septuagint and the Latin Vulgate versions of the Old Testament but are usually omitted from Protestant editions of the Bible.

Apocalyptic writings are prophetic revelations concerning a cataclysm in which the forces of good (God) permanently try up over the forces of evil (Satan). It is a prophecy or divine revelation predicting an imminent disaster and total or universal destruction. The books of 2 Esdras, Enoch, the Assumption of Moses, 2 Baruch, the Apocalypse of Abraham, the Ascension of Isaiah, Daniel, and Revelation are considered apocalyptic writings.

Some of these Apocrypha are not considered Scripture or inspired by God by most theologians, pastors, or doctors of the law. However, as we shall see, it was just that these writings were simply not revealed to them. At that time Jesus answered and said, I thank thee, O Father, Lord of heaven and earth, because thou hast hid these things from the wise and prudent, and hast revealed them unto babes. (Matthew 11:25)

Please note that I simply refer to the Apocrypha Books exactly as God intended for us to use them. They are a means for us to get a deeper understanding and, as historical facts, to further enrich our study of Canonized Scripture. They are not intended to replace Scripture because they cannot. They simply complement Scripture in complete harmony. They do exactly what their author intended for them to do.

The reason why some of these books are hidden is that God, who inspired their writing, commanded it to be so. Look at the instructions given to Ezra the priest.

2 Esdras 12:35-39

35 This is the dream that thou sawest, and these are the interpretations.

36 Thou only hast been meet to know this secret of the Highest.

37 Therefore write all these things that thou hast seen in a book, and hide them:

38 And teach them to the wise of the people, whose hearts thou knowest can comprehend and keep these secrets.

39 But wait thou here thyself yet seven days more, that it may be shewn thee, whatsoever it pleaseth the Highest to declare unto thee. And with that, he went his way.

These revelations are intended to be mysteries, not for the general public, but only for a restricted group of wise men who are capable of understanding them. They are secret revelations intended for a very limited circle of readers in the end times.

2 Esdras 14:20-26

20 Behold, Lord, I will go, as thou hast commanded me, and reprove the people which are present: but they that shall be born afterward, who shall admonish them? Thus, the world is set in darkness, and those who dwell therein are without light.

21 For thy law is burnt, therefore no man knoweth the things that are done of thee, or the work that shall begin.

22 But if I have found grace before thee, send the Holy Ghost into me, and I shall write all that hath been done in the world since the beginning, which were written in thy law, that men may find thy path, and that they which will live in the latter days may live.

23 And he answered me, saying, Go thy way, gather the people together, and say unto them, that they seek thee not for forty days.

24 But look thou prepare thee many box trees, and take with thee Sarea, Dabria, Selemia, Ecanus, and Asiel, these five which are ready to write swiftly;

25 And come hither, and I shall light a candle of understanding in thine heart, which shall not be put out, till the things be performed which thou shalt begin to write.

26 And when thou hast done, some things shalt thou publish, and some things shalt thou shew secretly to the wise: tomorrow this hour shalt thou begin to write.

2 Esdras 14: 45-48

45 And it came to pass, when the forty days were filled, that the Highest spake, saying, and the first that thou hast written publish openly, that the worthy and unworthy may read it:

46 But keep the seventy last, that thou mayest deliver them only to such as be wise among the people:

47 For in them is the spring of understanding, the fountain of wisdom, and the stream of knowledge.

48 And I did so.

There are many mysteries the Lord has purposely hidden according to His good pleasure.

Deuteronomy 29:29

The secret things belong to the Lord our God: but those things which are revealed belong to us and our children forever, that we may do all the words of this law.

However, the Lord always chooses someone to reveal his secrets to.

2 Esdras 3:12-14

12 And it happened that when those who dwelt upon the earth began to multiply, and had gotten them many children, and were a great people, they began again to be more ungodly than the first.

13 Now, when they lived so wickedly before thee, thou didst choose thee a man from among them, whose name was Abraham.

14 Him thou lovedst, and unto him only thou shewedst the end of the ages:

2 Esdras 14:1-6

1 And it came to pass upon the third day, I sat under an oak, and, behold, there came a voice out of a bush over against me, and said, Esdras, Esdras.

2 And I said, Here am I, Lord, and I stood up upon my feet.

3 Then said he unto me, in the bush I did manifestly reveal myself unto Moses, and talked with him, when my people served in Egypt:

4 And I sent him and led my people out of Egypt, and brought him up to the mount where I held him by me a long season,

5 And told him many wondrous things, and shewed him the secrets of the times, and the end; and commanded him, saying,

6 These words shalt thou declare, and these shalt thou hide.

Amos 3:7

7 Surely the Lord GOD will do nothing, but he revealeth his secret unto his servants the prophets.

Chapter 7

Humans Lost Track of Time

While many do not consider the Book of Enoch trustworthy, I put you in remembrance that Jude, in the Epistle of Jude (a canonized epistle), found it trustworthy enough to quote from   .

Jude14-15

14 And Enoch also, the seventh from Adam, prophesied of these, saying, Behold, the Lord cometh with ten thousands of his saints,

15 To execute judgment upon all, and to convince all that are ungodly among them of all their ungodly deeds which they have ungodly committed, and of all their hard [speeches] which ungodly sinners have spoken against him.

Jude is quoting Enoch 1:9. Therefore, we ought to take earnest heed to the Book of Enoch.

With this in mind, the question remains Have we lost track of time and, as a result, been unable to properly determine when certain prophecies would be fulfilled? The answer is, positively, yes!

When the law was given to Moses concerning God's feasts, new moons, and how to properly count days and years, everything to be kept at the appointed time, it was for a very specific reason. Violating these heavenly ordinances would cause humans to alter and lose track of the proper timekeeping mechanism instituted by God, thereby erring in many, many things. This includes losing track of the ages and not knowing the appointed time of the fulfillment of prophecy. This is exactly what God said would happen, and of course, it did.

31 And there is no neglecting this commandment for a single year or from year to year.

32 Command the children of Israel that they observe the years according to this counting, 364 days, and these will constitute a complete year, and they will not disturb its time from its days and its feasts; for everything will fall out in them according to their testimony, and they will not leave out any day nor disturb any feasts.

33 But if they neglect and do not observe them according to His commandment, then they will disturb all their seasons and the years will be dislodged from this order, and they will neglect their established rules.

34 And all the children of Israel will forget and will not find the path of the years, and will forget the new moons, and seasons, and sabbaths, and they will wrongly determine all the order of the years.

35 For I know and from now on will I declare it to you and it is not of my devising; for the book lies written in the presence of me, and on the heavenly tablets the division of the days ordained, or they forget the feasts of the covenant and walk according to the feasts of the Gentiles after their error and after their ignorance.

36 For there will be those who will surely make observations of the Moon and how it disturbs the seasons and comes in from year to year, 10 days too soon.

37 For this reason the years will come upon them when they disturbed the order and make an abominable day the day of testimony, and an unclean day a feast day, and they will confound all the days,

the holy with the unclean, and the unclean day with the holy for they will go wrong as to the months and sabbaths and feasts and jubilees.

38 For this reason, I command and testify to you that you may testify to them, for after your death, your children will disturb them, so that they will not make the year 364 days only, and for this reason, they will go wrong as to the new moons and seasons and sabbaths and festivals.

Jubilee 23:18

They shall quarrel with one another, the young with the old, and the old with the young, the poor with the rich, the lowly with the great, and the beggar with the prince, because of the law and the covenant; for they have forgotten the Commandments, and covenant, and feasts, and months, and sabbaths, and jubilees, and all judgments.

This has led to total confusion of times (Ages) in the end times. For this very reason, many have erred in trying to predict the fulfillment of certain prophecies when they simply are not scheduled to be fulfilled at that time. Then, some become discouraged and even begin to doubt the Scriptures, not realizing that there is a timeline and that every prophecy must be fulfilled "at the appointed time" that has been predetermined by the Creator of all.

Before Pentecost, the disciples asked Jesus if he would at this time restore the Kingdom to Israel, and He said,

it is not for you to know the times or the seasons, which the Father hath put in his power. (Acts 1:7)

This in no way implies that we, who are living in the time of the end, were to be in the dark. Times and seasons did not concern the disciples living in that era, but they most certainly apply to those living in the end times. Had it not, Christ Himself would not have given us signs to watch for or repeat the word WATCH for the approaching end.

God is not the author of confusion and does not pride Himself in giving us vague prophecies without a timeline for their fulfillment. Or else, how would we mere humans know when to expect what is written? The problem is that, through the passing of time, humans have lost this vital knowledge.

In the book of Enoch, chapter 93 (The Apocalypse of Weeks), God gives us the precise time as to when all things would be accomplished on earth.

The key to finding these things is this:

Proverbs 25:2

It is the glory of God to conceal a thing: but the honor of Kings is to search out a matter. You must search!!!

Enoch 91:18

And now I tell you, my sons, and show you the paths of righteousness and the paths of violence. Yea, I would show them to you again that ye may know what will come to pass.

Enoch 92:1 –2

1 The book written by Enoch [Enoch indeed wrote this complete doctrine of wisdom, which is praised by all men and a judge of all the earth] for all my children who shall dwell on the earth. And for the future generations who shall observe uprightness and peace.

2 Let not your spirit be troubled on account of the times *(Ages)*; for the Holy and Great One has appointed days for all things.

Enoch 93: The Apocalypse of Weeks

1-2 And after that, Enoch began to recount from the books. And he said:

Concerning the children of righteousness (Referring to the children of Israel) and concerning the elect of the world, (Those called and chosen out of the world) And concerning the plant of uprightness, (Son of man, the Messiah from the seed of Abraham.) I will speak these things, Yeah, I Enoch will declare (them) unto you, my sons:

According to that which appeared (He saw) to me in the heavenly vision, And which I have known through the word of the holy angels, (It was told to him) And have learnt from the heavenly tablets. (he read it; this is complete confirmation of the future events that Enoch is about to describe.)

3 And Enoch began to recount from the books and said: (Enoch confirms to us the accuracy of what he saw, was told, he read, and the timeline of events from the heavenly tablets).

I was born the seventh in the first week, while judgment and righteousness still endured.

(Why Enoch chose to call it weeks, I am not sure. However, it is obvious that in this particular prophecy, a week refers to every 1000 years. Enoch was the seventh born from Adam in the first 1000 years of creation history. Secrets of Enoch 33:1 gives further proof that each week refers to 1000 years. And I appointed the eighth day also, that the eight day should be the first – created after my work, and that the first seven revolve in the form of 7000, and that at the beginning of the 8000 there should be a time of not counting, endless, with neither years nor months nor weeks nor days nor hours.)

4 And after me there shall arise in the second week (In the 2000 years of creation history) great wickedness, and deceit shall have sprung up;

And in it there shall be the first end.

(Fragment of Noah 106:13-19 And I, Enoch, answered and said unto him The Lord will do a new thing on the earth, and this I have already seen in a vision, and make it known to thee that, in the generation of my father Jared some of the angels of heaven transgressed the word of the Lord. And behold, they committed sin and transgressed the law, and have united themselves with women and commit sin with them, and have married some of them, and have begot children by them. And they shall produce on the earth giants not according to the spirit, but according to the flesh, and there shall be a great punishment on the earth, and the earth shall be cleansed from all impurity. Yea, there shall come a great destruction over the whole earth, and there shall be a deluge and 16 a great destruction for one year. And this son who has been born unto you shall be left on the earth, and his three children shall be saved with him: when all mankind that are on the earth shall die [he and his sons shall be saved]. And now make known to thy son Lamech that he who has been born is in truth his son, and call his name Noah; for he shall be left to you, and he and his sons shall be saved from the destruction, which shall come upon the earth on account of all the sin and all the unrighteousness, which shall be consummated on the earth in his days. And after that there shall be still more unrighteousness than that which was first consummated on the earth; for I know the mysteries of the holy ones; for He, the Lord, has showed me and informed me, and I have read (them) in the heavenly tablets.

During the days of Jared, Enoch's father, the Watchers/Angels started going into the daughters of men, and giants were born to them, and all the earth became filled with violence. As a result, God condemned the earth through Noah's flood. This was the first end.

And in it a man shall be saved; (Noah)

And after it is ended after the 2000 years of creation history are ended unrighteousness shall grow up, and a law shall be made for the sinners.

This law made for sinners points to God's covenant with Noah a new beginning after the flood:

Genesis 6:18

But with thee will I establish my covenant; and thou shalt come into the ark, thou, and thy sons, and thy wife, and thy sons' wives with thee.

Genesis 9:1 – 9

1 And God blessed Noah and his sons, and said unto them, be fruitful, and multiply, and replenish the earth.

2 And the fear of you and the dread of you shall be upon every beast of the earth, and every fowl of the air, upon all that moveth upon the earth, and all the fishes of the sea; into your hand are they delivered.

3 Every moving thing that liveth shall be meat for you; even as the green herb have, I given you all things.

4 But flesh with the life thereof, which is the blood thereof, shall ye not eat.

5 And surely your blood of your lives will I require; at the hand of every beast will I require it, and at the hand of man; at the hand of every man's brother will I require the life of man.

6 Whoso sheddeth man's blood, by man shall his blood be shed: for in the image of God made He man.

7 And you, be ye fruitful, and multiply; bring forth abundantly in the earth, and multiply therein.

8 And God spake unto Noah, and to his sons with him, saying,

9 And I, behold, I establish my covenant with you, and with your seed after you;

And after that, in the third week at its close (towards the end of the 3000 years from creation history)

A man shall be elected as the plant of righteous judgment. (Abraham, father of the faithful)

And his posterity shall become the plant of righteousness forevermore. (From Abraham's seed would come the Deliverer, the Messiah, who would redeem the children of Israel.)

6 And after that, in the fourth week, at its close, (towards the end of the 4000 years from creation history) Visions of the holy and righteous shall be seen, And a law for all generations and an enclosure shall be made for them. (During this period, God delivered the children of Israel from Egyptian slavery, and began to manifest Himself unto Moses with many signs and wonders, and later unto the entire

congregation of the children of Israel, in which the Commandments and Covenant were made.)

7 And after that, in the fifth week, at its close, (towards the end of the 5000 years from creation history) The house of glory and dominion shall be built forever. (It was a well-known fact that the Messiah would be born after 5500 years from creation.

In 1 Adam and Eve 3:1-6,

1 God said to Adam, I have ordained on this earth days and years, and you and your descendants shall live and walk in them, until the days and years are fulfilled; when I shall send the Word that created you, and against which you have transgressed, the Word that made you come out of the garden, and that raised you when you were fallen.

 2 Yes, the Word that will again save you when the five and a half days are fulfilled.

3 But when Adam heard these words from God, and of the great five and a half days, he did not understand the meaning of them.

4 For Adam was thinking there would be only five and a half days for him until the end of the world.

5 And Adam cried and prayed to God to explain it to him.

6 Then God, in his mercy, for Adam who was made after His image and likeness, explained to him that these were 5,000 and 500 years; and how One would then come and save him and his descendants.

2 Adam and Eve 12:6,

And God accepted his offering, and sent His blessing upon him and his children. And then God made a promise to Seth, saying, At the end of the great five days and a half, concerning which I have made a promise to thee and thy father, I will send My Word and save thee and thy seed.

Gospel of Nicodemus 22:3 –7, 10- 13,

3 And when the great book, carried by four ministers of the Temple, and adorned with gold and precious stones, was brought, Pilate said to them all, I adjure you by the God of your fathers, who made and commanded this temple to be built, that ye conceal not the truth from me.

4 Ye know all the things which are written in that book tell me therefore now, if ye in the Scriptures have found anything of that Jesus whom ye crucified, and at what time of the world he ought to have come: show it me.

5 Then, having sworn Annas and Caiaphas, they commanded all the rest who were with them to go out of the chapel.

6 They shut the gates of the Temple and of the chapel, and said to Pilate, thou hast made us to swear, O judge, by the building of this temple, to declare to thee that which is true and right.

7 After we had crucified Jesus, not knowing that he was the son of God, but supposing he wrought his miracles by some magical arts, we summoned a large assembly in this temple.

10 is our custom annually to open this holy book before an assembly, and to search there for the counsel of God.

11 And we found in the first of the 70 books, where Michael the Archangel is speaking to the third son of Adam, the first man (Seth),

and account that after 5500 years, Christ, the most beloved son of God, would come to earth.

12 further considered that perhaps he was the very God of Israel who spoke to Moses, thou shalt make the ark of the testimony two cubits and a half shall be the length thereof, and a cubit and a half the breadth thereof, and a cubit and a half the height thereof.

13 By these five cubits and a half for the building of the ark of the Old Testament, we perceived and knew that in 5000 years and a half years, Jesus Christ was to come in the ark or tabernacle of a body

Malachi 3:1,

Behold, I will send my messenger, and he shall prepare the way before Me and the Lord, whom ye seek (God the father), shall suddenly come to his temple (Jesus the Temple of God), even the messenger of the covenant, whom ye delight in: behold, he shall come, saith the LORD of hosts.

John 2:19 – 21,

19 Jesus answered and said unto them, Destroy this temple, and in three days I will raise it.

20 Then said the Jews, Forty and six years was this temple in building, and wilt thou rear it up in three days?

21 But He spake of the temple of his body.

Acts 17:24- 25,

24 God that made the world and all things therein, seeing that He is Lord of heaven and earth, dwelleth not in temples made with hands

25 Neither is worshipped with men's hands, as though He needed anything, seeing He giveth to all life, and breath, and all things;

Furthermore, the Messiah came to announce the good news of the coming Kingdom of God, offer the ultimate sacrifice, and establish the church, a body of believers, as a habitation of God through the Holy Spirit.

1 Corinthians 3:16   -17,

16 Know ye not that ye are the temple of God, and that the Spirit of God dwelleth in you? 17 If any man defile the temple of God, him shall God destroy; for the temple of God is holy, which temple ye are.

1 Corinthians: 6:19,

19 What? Know ye not that your body is the temple of the Holy Ghost which is in you, which ye have of God, and ye are not your own?

Enoch 93:8- The Sixth Week

8 And after that, in the sixth week, all who live in it shall be blinded, (In the beginning of the 6000 years from creation, when the Messiah began his ministry, blindness engrossed his people.) And the hearts of all of them shall godlessly forsake wisdom (They crucified the Son of God.)

 1 Corinthians 1:24,

24 But unto them which are called, both Jews and Greeks, Christ the power of God, and the wisdom of God.

And in it a man shall ascend; (Christ ascended to heaven.) And at its close, the house of dominion shall be burnt with fire (The Temple built by Herod, destroyed by fire by the Romans in 70 AD.),

And the whole race of the chosen root shall be dispersed. (The beginning persecution of the Church and them being scattered through the four corners of the earth)

Enoch 93:9-10 – week seven

9 And after that, in the seventh week (the 7000 years from creation history), shall an apostate generation arise. And many shall be its deeds, And all its deeds shall be apostate. (Now, we know that from the birth of Christ, towards the end of the 5500 years from creation, entering the beginning of the 6000 years from creation, to the current date of 2010, a little over 2000 years have passed. The 1000 years from the crucifixion of Christ, which ended 1000 years ago, a complete apostate generation arose. Humans lost all true knowledge of God this age is also known as The Dark Age.)

10 And at its close (at the end of the 7000 years from creation history, the millennium that just passed as we entered the year 2000), shall be elected The elect righteous of the eternal plant of righteousness (God, according to his predetermined plan, elected those destined for salvation). To receive sevenfold instruction concerning all His creation. (God has restored the knowledge that was lost to His elect, and they have received many more revelations than in the previous 1000 years)

11 For who is there of all the children of men that can hear the voice of the Holy One without being troubled? And who can think His thoughts? And who is there that can behold all the works.

12 of Heaven? And how should there be one who could behold the Heaven, and who is there that could understand the things of Heaven and see a soul or a spirit and could tell thereof, or ascend and see

13 all their ends and think them or do like them? And who is there of all men that could know what is the breadth and the length of the earth, and to whom has the measure of all things been shown?

14 Or is there anyone who could discern the length of the Heaven and how great is its height, and upon what it is founded, and how great is the number of the stars, and where all the luminaries rest ?

(Here, Enoch is once again advising us of the accuracy of this prophecy, which was given to him by the Most High. For who could know the division of the ages without God revealing it to him?)

Enoch 93:12 — The Eighth Week

12 And after that there shall be another, the eighth week, (the 8000 years from creation history, 2000 years after the crucifixion of Christ, which began approximately in the year 2000) that of righteousness, (As we are about to enter the millennium reign of Christ)

And a sword shall be given to it that a righteous judgment may be executed on the oppressors, And sinners shall be delivered into the hands of the righteous. (But, before the millennium reign of Christ begins, the Almighty God will execute judgment on the earth. This is the time we are presently living in, and the reason why end-time prophecies are being fulfilled at such a rapid pace. This prophecy that explains the ages of the world is a major factor in order to properly understanding when these end-time prophecies would be fulfilled. None of the prophecies of the coming judgment would have been fulfilled at any other time in history because Divine Judgment is executed at the beginning of the eighth week, the beginning of the 8000 years from creation history, not before.)

Secrets of Enoch 33:1,

And I appointed the eighth day also, that the eight day should be the first – created after my work, and that the first seven revolve in the form of 7000, and that at the beginning of the 8000 there should be a time of not counting, endless, with neither years nor months nor weeks nor days nor hours.

Epistle of Barnabas 13:16,

For it is written; And it shall be that as soon as the week shall be completed the Temple of the Lord shall be gloriously built in the name of the Lord.

In the Apocalypse of Abraham 29, part 2, pg. 79

God gives Abraham an interesting parable concerning the time of the end. in the last days, in the twelfth hour of the Age of ungodliness. But in the twelfth year of My final age I will set up this man from thy generation, whom thou sawest (issue) from thy people; this one all will follow

Carefully analyzing all past and current world events and using Prophecy as the ultimate guide, an approximate year of 2012 is not far-fetched. Whether in the beginning or the end we don't know but in light of the timeline of events currently being fulfilled and the significance of the number 12 (12 tribes, 12 apostles, Jesus healed the woman that had the issue of blood for 12 years, He raised the 12 year old girl from the dead, 12,000 sealed at the end from each of the 12 tribes, 12 foundations of the Heavenly Jerusalem, etc.) God might very well be giving us an approximate time of His 2nd coming. We will just have to wait and see.

13 And at its close (at the end of the 8000 years from creation history, at the end of the millennium reign of Christ), they shall acquire houses through their righteousness, And a house shall be built for the Great King in glory forevermore,

14d And all mankind shall look to the path of uprightness. (Christ's millennial reign is a time for restoration and perfection for the chosen. A time for God's Spirit to align perfectly with our DNA, once perfection is achieved, the elect will undergo a physical transformation into a glorified body. Once this transformation is completed, each individual becomes a lively stone perfectly joined and fitted together for a habitation of God through the fullness of God's Spirit in each lively stone. Thereby, all of it put together becomes a Temple of God forevermore. This is truly amazing!

Ephesians 2:20-22,

20 "And are built upon the foundation of the apostles and prophets, Jesus Christ himself being the chief cornerstone;

21 In whom all the building fitly framed together groweth unto a holy temple in the Lord:

22 In whom ye also are builded together for an habitation of God through the Spirit.

1 Corinthians 15:21-28,

21 For since by man came death, came also the resurrection of the dead. 22 For as in Adam all die, even so in Christ shall all be made alive.

23 But every man in his order Christ the firstfruits; afterward they that are Christ's at his coming.

24 Then cometh the end, when he shall have delivered up the kingdom to God, even the Father when he shall have put down all rule and all authority and power.

25 For he must reign, till he hath put all enemies under his feet.

26 The last enemy that shall be destroyed is death.

27 For He hath put all things under his feet. But when he saith all things are put under him, it is manifest that he is excepted, which did put all things under him.

28 And when all things shall be subdued unto him, then shall the Son also himself be subject unto him that put all things under him, that God may be all in all.

Revelations 3:12,

Him that overcometh will I make a pillar in the temple of My God, and he shall go no more out: and I will write upon him the name of My God, and the name of the city of My God, which is new Jerusalem, which cometh down out of heaven from My God and I will write upon him my new name.

Enoch 93:14a–c — The Ninth Week

14a And after that, in the ninth week (the 9000 years from creation history, during the millennial reign of Christ), the righteous judgment shall be revealed to the whole world,

b And all the works of the godless shall vanish from all the earth,
c And the world shall be written down for destruction. (Those born

during Christ's millennial reign will be blessed to grow up in God's kingdom without the evil influences of Satan. Physical life will be extended; sickness and disease will no longer be a factor.

Isaiah 65:17 25,

17 For, behold, I create new heavens and a new earth: and the former shall not be remembered, nor come into mind.

18 But be ye glad and rejoice forever in that which I create: for, behold, I create Jerusalem a rejoicing, and her people a joy.

19 And I will rejoice in Jerusalem, and joy in my people: and the voice of weeping shall be no more heard in her, nor the voice of crying.

20 There shall be no more thence an infant of days, nor an old man that hath not filled his days: for the child shall die an hundred years old; but the sinner being an hundred years old shall be accursed.

21 And they shall build houses, and inhabit them and they shall plant vineyards, and eat the fruit of them.

22 They shall not build, and another inhabit; they shall not plant, and another eat: for as the days of a tree are the days of my people, and mine elect shall long enjoy the work of their hands.

23 They shall not labour in vain, nor bring forth for trouble for they are the seed of the blessed of the LORD, and their offspring with them.

24 And it shall come to pass, that before they call, I will answer and while they are yet speaking, I will hear.

25 The wolf and the lamb shall feed together, and the lion shall eat straw like the bullock and dust shall be the serpent's meat. They shall not hurt nor destroy in all My holy mountain, saith the LORD.

Revelations 20:1 – 6,

1 And I saw an angel come down from heaven, having the key of the bottomless pit and a great chain in his hand.

 2 And he laid hold on the dragon, that old serpent, which is the Devil, and Satan, and bound him for a thousand years,

3 And cast him into the bottomless pit, and shut him up, and set a seal upon him, that he should deceive the nations no more, till the thousand years should be fulfilled and after that he must be loosed for a little season.

4 And I saw thrones, and they sat upon them, and judgment was given unto them: and I saw the souls of them that were beheaded for the witness of Jesus, and for the word of God, and which had not worshipped the beast, neither his image, neither had received his mark upon their foreheads, or in their hands; and they lived and reigned with Christ a thousand years.

5 But the rest of the dead lived not again until the thousand years were finished. This is the first resurrection.

6 Blessed and holy is he that hath part in the first resurrection on such the second death hath no power, but they shall be priests of God and Christ, and shall reign with him for a thousand years.

Enoch 10:16 – 22,

and let the plant of righteousness and truth appear and it shall prove a blessing; the works of righteousness and truth shall be planted in truth and joy forevermore.

17 And then shall all the righteous escape, and shall live till they beget thousands of children, and all the days of their youth and their old age shall they complete in peace.

18 And then shall the whole earth be tilled in righteousness, and shall all be planted with trees and

19 be full of blessing. And all desirable trees shall be planted on it, and they shall plant vines on it: and the vine which they plant thereon shall yield wine in abundance, and as for all the seed which is sown thereon, each measure (of it) shall bear a thousand, and each measure of olives shall yield

20 ten presses of oil. And cleanse thou the earth from all oppression, and from all unrighteousness, and all sin, and all godlessness: and all the uncleanness that is wrought upon the earth,

21 destroy from off the earth. And all the children of men shall become righteous, and all nations

22 shall offer adoration and shall praise Me, and all shall worship Me. And the earth shall be cleansed from all defilement, and all sin, and all punishment, and all torment, and I will never again send (them) upon it from generation to generation and forever.

Enoch 45,

1 And this is the second Parable concerning those who deny the name of the dwelling of the holy ones and the Lord of Spirits.

2 And into heaven they shall not ascend, and on the earth they shall not come: Such shall be the lot of the sinners who have denied the name of the Lord of Spirits, who are thus preserved for the day of suffering and tribulation.

3 On that day Mine Elect One shall sit on the throne of glory, and shall try their works, and their places of rest shall be innumerable. And their souls shall grow strong within them when they see Mine Elect Ones, and those who have called upon My glorious name:

4 Then will I cause Mine Elect One to dwell among them. And I will transform the heaven and make it an eternal blessing and light   .

5 And I will transform the earth and make it a blessing: And I will cause Mine elect ones to dwell upon it: But the sinners and evil-doers shall not set foot thereon.

6 For I have provided and satisfied with peace My righteous ones, And have caused them to dwell before Me: But for the sinners there is   judgment impending with Me, so that I shall destroy them from the face of the earth.

15 And after this, in the tenth week in the seventh part, (the seventh part of the 10,000 years from creation history) There shall be the great eternal judgement, In which He will execute vengeance amongst the angels.

(Enoch 18:14-16,

14 and to me, when I inquired regarding them, the angel said: 'This place is the end of heaven and earth: this has become a prison for the stars and the host of heaven. And the stars which roll over the fire are they which have transgressed the commandment of the Lord in the beginning of

16 their rising, because they did not come forth at their appointed times. And He was wroth with them, and bound them till the time when their guilt should be consummated (even) for ten thousand years.

Enoch 21:6,

These are of the number of the stars of heaven, which have transgressed the commandment of the Lord, and are bound here till ten thousand years.

Revelations 20:7-15,

7 And when the thousand years are expired, Satan shall be loosed out of his prison,

8 And shall go out to deceive the nations which are in the four quarters of the earth, Gog and Magog, to gather them together to battle: the number of whom is as the sand of the sea.

9 And they went up on the breadth of the earth, and compassed the camp of the saints about, and the beloved city and fire came down from God out of heaven, and devoured them.

10 And the devil that deceived them was cast into the lake of fire and brimstone, where the beast and the false prophet are, and shall be tormented day and night forever and ever.

11 And I saw a great white throne, and him that sat on it, from whose face the earth and the heaven fled away and there was found no place for them.

12 And I saw the dead, small and great, stand before God; and the books were opened and another book was opened, which is the

book of life: and the dead were judged out of those things which were written in the books, according to their works.

13 And the sea gave up the dead which were in it; and death and hell delivered up the dead which were in them: and they were judged every man according to their works.

14 And death and hell were cast into the lake of fire. This is the second death.

15 And whosoever was not found written in the Book of Life was cast into the lake of fire.

16 And the first heaven shall depart and pass away, And a new heaven shall appear, And all the powers of the heavens shall give sevenfold light.

Revelation 21:1-5,

1 And I saw a new heaven and a new earth: for the first heaven and the first earth were passed away; and there was no more sea.

2 And I, John, saw the holy city, New Jerusalem, coming down from God out of heaven, prepared as a bride adorned for her husband.

3 And I heard a great voice out of heaven saying, Behold, the tabernacle of God is with men, and he will dwell with them, and they shall be his people, and God himself shall be with them, and be their God.

4 And God shall wipe away all tears from their eyes; and there shall be no more death, neither sorrow, nor crying, neither shall there be any more pain: for the former things are passed away.

5 And he that sat upon the throne said, Behold, I make all things new. And he said unto me, Write: for these words are true and faithful.

17 And after that, there will be many weeks without number forever, And all shall be in goodness and righteousness, And sin shall no more be mentioned forever.

Revelation 21:6,

And he said unto me, It is done. I am Alpha and Omega, the beginning and the end.

This is God's prescribed timeline of events for the history of the world, written on the Heavenly Tablets. Everything has been fulfilled according to what is described in this prophecy. There is no indication that future events will not follow suit. The fact remains that humans lost track of time for not following God's prescribed chronological order.

Ecclesiastes 7:29, Lo, this only have I found, that God hath made man upright; but they have sought out many inventions.

We are currently living at the beginning of the 8000 years from Adam, the 8th millennium, the time when judgment is to be executed on earth! Not the 6th millennium (6000 years from Adam) as so many wrongly believe.

Proverbs 16:25, There is a way that seemeth right unto a man, but the end thereof are the ways of death.

Chapter 8

The Origin of Evil

Matthew 12:43-45

43 When the unclean spirit is gone out of a man, he walketh through dry places, seeking rest, and findeth none.

44 Then he saith, I will return into my house from whence I came out; and when he is come, he findeth it empty, swept, and garnished.

45 Then he, and taketh with himself seven other spirits more wicked than himself, and they enter in and dwell there: and the last state of that man is worse than the first. Even so shall it be also unto this wicked generation.

Luke 11:24 – 26

24 When the unclean spirit is gone out of a man, he walketh through dry places, seeking rest and finding none, he saith, I will return unto my house whence I came out   .

25 And when he cometh, he findeth it swept and garnished.

26 Then he, and taketh to him seven other spirits more wicked than himself; and they enter in, and dwell there: and the last state of that man is worse than the first.

Have you ever wondered where exactly these evil spirits come from? Most people automatically assume that these evil spirits are fallen Angels. However, this is not the case. These evil spirits have to do with fallen Angels, but are not the Fallen Angels as we shall soon learn.

Genesis 6:1 – 4

1 And it came to pass, when men began to multiply on the face of the earth, and daughters were born unto them,

2 That the sons of God saw the daughters of men that they were fair; and they took them wives of all which they chose.

3 And the LORD said, My spirit shall not always strive with man, for that he also is flesh: yet his days shall be an hundred and twenty years.

4 There were giants in the earth in those days; and also after that, when the sons of God came in unto the daughters of men, and they bare children to them, the same became mighty men which were of old, men of renown.

These verses, briefly recorded in Genesis, have always puzzled many. Who were these sons of God that began to mate with the daughters of men, and how did they bear giants? What does all this mean? Let's let Scripture interpret Scripture.

Enoch 6: 1-8

1 And it came to pass when the children of men had multiplied that in those days were born unto

2 their beautiful and comely daughters. And the angels, the children of the heaven, saw and lusted after them, and said to one another: 'Come, let us choose us wives from among the children of men

3 and beget us children.' And Semjaza, who was their leader, said unto them: 'I fear ye will not

4 indeed agree to do this deed, and I alone shall have to pay the penalty of a great sin.' And they all answered him and said: 'Let us all swear an oath, and all bind ourselves by mutual imprecations

5 not to abandon this plan but to do this thing.' Then swore they all together and bound themselves

6 by mutual imprecations upon it. And they were in all two hundred , who descended in the days of Jared on the summit of Mount Hermon, and they called it Mount Hermon, because they had sworn

7 and bound themselves by mutual imprecations upon it. And these are the names of their leaders: Samlazaz, their leader, Araklba, Rameel, Kokablel, Tamlel, Ramlel, Danel, Ezeqeel, Baraqijal,

8 Asael, Armaros, Batarel, Ananel, Zaqiel, Samsapeel, Satarel, Turel, Jomjael, Sariel. These are their chiefs of tens.

Enoch 7

1 And all the others together with them took unto themselves wives, and each chose for himself one, and they began to go in unto them and to defile themselves with them, and they taught them charms

2 and enchantments, and the cutting of roots, and made them acquainted with plants. And they

3 became pregnant and bore great giants, whose height was three thousand ells, who consumed

4 all the acquisitions of men. And when men could no longer sustain them, the giants turned against

5 them and devoured mankind. And they began to sin against birds, and beasts, and reptiles, and

6 fish, and to devour one another's flesh, and drink the blood. Then the earth laid accusation against the lawless ones.

These fallen angels were known by men by various names: children of heaven, sons of God, or Watchers. Why watchers? Because they were sent by God to watch over mankind and make sure God's laws were being implemented on earth. Instead, they fell into lust and started mating with the daughters of men.

Jubilees 4:15

In the second week of the 10th Jubilee, Mahalalel took to himself to wife, Dinah, daughter of Barakiel, the daughter of his father's brother, and she gave birth to a son in the third week in the sixth year, and he called his name Jared. For in his days the Angels of the Lord descended on the earth, those who are named the Watchers, that they should instruct the children of men, and that they should do judgment and uprightness on the earth.

Enoch 13:1–10

1 And Enoch went and said: Azazel, thou shalt have no peace: a severe sentence has gone forth

2 against thee to put thee in bonds: And thou shalt not have toleration nor request granted to thee, because of the unrighteousness which thou hast taught, and because of all the works of godlessness

3 and unrighteousness and sin which thou hast shown to men. Then I went and spoke to them all

4 together, and they were all afraid, and fear and trembling seized them. And they besought me to draw up a petition for them that they might find forgiveness, and to read their petition in the presence

5 of the Lord of heaven. From thenceforward, they could not speak (with Him) nor lift their

6 eyes to heaven for shame of their sins for which they had been condemned. Then I wrote out their petition, and the prayer regarding their spirits and their deeds individually, and about their

7 requests that they should have forgiveness and length. And I went off and sat down at the waters of Dan, in the land of Dan, to the south of the west of Hermon: I read their petition till I fell

8 asleep. And behold, a dream came to me, and visions fell upon me, and I saw visions of chastisement, and a voice came bidding me to tell it to the sons of heaven, and reprimand them.

9 And when I awoke, I came unto them, and they were all sitting gathered together, weeping in

10 'Abelsjail, which is between Lebanon and Seneser, with their faces covered. And I recounted before them all the visions which I had seen in sleep, and I began to speak the words of righteousness, and to reprimand the heavenly Watchers.

Enoch 14:4

The Watchers, the children of heaven: I wrote out your petition, and in my vision it appeared thus, that your petition will not be granted unto you throughout all the days of eternity, and that judgment.

Daniel 4:13, 17, 23

13 I saw in the visions of my head upon my bed, and, behold, a Watcher and a holy one came down from heaven;

17 This matter is by the decree of the Watchers, and the demand by the word of the holy ones: to the intent that the living may know that the Most High ruleth in the kingdom of men, and giveth it to whomsoever he will, and setteth up over it the basest of men.

23 And whereas the king saw a Watcher and a holy one coming down from heaven, and saying, Hew the tree down, and destroy it; yet leave the stump of the roots thereof in the earth, even with a band of iron and brass, in the tender grass of the field; and let it be wet with the dew of heaven, and let his portion be with the beasts of the field, till seven times pass over him

Note that there are good Angel/Watchers and there are evil ones. Now that we know that the sons of God referred to in Genesis 6:2 are the Watchers, the Fallen Angels, notice where these evil spirits come from.

Enoch 15

1 And He answered and said to me, and I heard His voice: 'Fear not, Enoch, thou righteous

2 man and scribe of righteousness: approach hither and hear My voice. And go, say to the Watchers of Heaven, who have sent thee to intercede for them: You should intercede for men, and not men

3 for you: Wherefore have ye left the high, holy, and eternal heaven, and lain with women, and defiled yourselves with the daughters of men, and taken to yourselves wives, and done like the children

4 of earth, and begotten giants (as your) sons? And though ye were holy, spiritual, living the eternal life, you have defiled yourselves with the blood of women, and have begotten children with the blood of

flesh, and, as the children of men, have lusted after flesh and blood as those also do who die

5 and perish. Therefore, have I not given them wives also that they might impregnate them, and beget

6 children by them, that thus nothing might be wanting to them on earth. But ye were formerly

7 spiritual, living the eternal life, and immortal for all generations of the world. And therefore I have not appointed wives for you; for, as for the spiritual ones of the heaven, in heaven is their dwelling.

8 And now, the giants who are produced from the spirits and flesh shall be called evil spirits upon

9 the earth, and on the earth shall be their dwelling. Evil spirits have proceeded from their bodies, because they are born from men, and the holy Watchers are their beginning and primal origin   .

10 They shall be evil spirits on earth, and evil spirits shall they be called. [As for the spirits of heaven, in heaven shall be their dwelling, but as for the spirits of the earth which were born upon the earth, on the earth shall be their dwelling.]

11 And the spirits of the giants afflict, oppress, destroy, attack, do battle, and work destruction on the earth, and cause trouble: they take no food, but nevertheless

12 hunger and thirst, and cause offences. And these spirits shall rise against the children of men and the women, because they have proceeded from them.

Enoch 16

1 From the days of the slaughter and destruction and death of the giants, from the souls of whose flesh the spirits, having gone forth, shall destroy without incurring judgement -thus shall they destroy until the day of the consummation, the great judgement in which the age shall be

2 consummated, over the Watchers and the godless; yea, it shall be wholly consummated.

And now as to the watchers who have sent thee to intercede for them, who had been aforetime in heaven,

3 say to them: You have been in heaven, but all the mysteries had not yet been revealed to you, and you knew worthless ones, and these in the hardness of your hearts you have made known to the women, and through these mysteries, women and men work much evil on earth.

4 Say to them therefore: You have no peace.

Dead Sea Scrolls

The outcome of the demonic corruption was violence, perversion, and a brood of monstrous beings. (Compare Genesis 6:4.)

4Q531 Frag. 2

[. . .] They defiled [. . .]

2 [. . .] they begot giants and monsters [. . .]

3 they begot, and, behold, all [the earth was corrupted [. . .]

4 with its blood and by the hand of [. . .]

5[giant's] which did not suffice for them and [. . .]

6   [. . .] and they were seeking to devour many [. . .]

7   [. . .]

8   [. . .] the monsters attacked it.

4Q532 Col. 2 Frags. 1 - 6

2   [. . .] flesh [. . .]

3 all [. . .] monsters   [. . .] will be [. . .]

4   [. . .] they would arise [. . .] lacking in true knowledge [. . .] because   [. . .]

5   [. . .] the earth [grew corrupt . . .] mighty [. . .]

6   [. . .] they were considering [. . .]

7   [. . .] from the angels upon [. . .]

8   [. . .] in the end it will perish and die   [. . .]

9   [. . .] they caused great corruption in the [earth . .   .] [. . . this
did not] suffice to   [. . .] "they will be   [. . .]"

There is a general rule that we must abide by, and that is not to mix
the 'seed' of anything, whether it is harvest, clothing, animals, or
humans. The mixing of 'seeds' has serious and lasting consequences,
especially the intermingling of angelic beings with human DNA. What
results from such a union is something profoundly abnormal and
contrary to God's intended design.

Deuteronomy 22:9-11

9 Thou shalt not sow thy vineyard with divers seeds: lest the fruit of thy seed which thou hast sown, and the fruit of thy vineyard, be defiled.

10 Thou shalt not plow with an ox and an ass together. (The word plow used here as a verb is charash, khaw-rash' to fabricate to cut in, plough, engrave, devise (Qal) to cut in, engrave to plough to devise In layman's terms, do not genetically manipulate or deviate from the prescribed order of anything!)

11 Thou shalt not wear a garment of divers sorts, as of woollen and linen together.

Leviticus 19:19

Ye shall keep my statutes. Thou shalt not let thy cattle gender with a diverse kind: thou shalt not sow thy field with mingled seed neither shall a garment mingled of linen and woollen come upon thee.

Dead Sea Scrolls

The two hundred angels choose animals on which to perform unnatural acts (manipulate), including, presumably, humans.

1Q23 Frag. 1 + 6 [. . . two hundred] 2donkeys, two hundred asses, two hundred . . . rams of the] 3flock, two hundred goats, two hundred [. . . beast of the] 4field from every animal, from every [bird . . .] 5   [. . .] for miscegenation [. . .]

These evil spirits are the spirits of deceased giants, the sons of the Watchers (the fallen angels), who were the product of the unlawful union between the Watchers and the daughters of men. Since they have no access to the heavens or a place of rest once their spirit leaves their body at the time of death, they simply roam the earth seeking a body in which they may dwell. These spiritual mediums, soothsayers, and diviners who claim to be in contact with a spirit guide are channeling a spirit of a deceased son of the Watchers who has been roaming the earth for thousands of years; this is why they are sometimes able to accurately predict future events.

Chapter 9

As In the Days of Noah

Matthew 24:37–39

37 But as the days of Noe were, so shall also the coming of the Son of man be.

38 For as in the days that were before the flood they (The Watchers) were eating and drinking, marrying and giving in marriage (Mating with the daughters of men and humans were oblivious to the whole thing or carrying on in their godlessness as if everything were normal.), until the day that Noe entered into the ark,

39 And knew not until the flood came, and took them all away; so shall also the coming of the Son of man be.

Luke 17:26–27

26 And as it was in the days of Noe, so shall it be also in the days of the Son of man.

27 They (The Watchers) did eat, they drank, they married wives, they were given in marriage, until the day that Noe entered into the ark, and the flood came, and destroyed them all.

These words of Christ were recorded by both Matthew and Luke, and it is evident that something very serious was occurring in those days that would be prevalent today, besides mankind's attitude of carelessness and sinful behavior. It was something much more than just eating and drinking, and being given in marriage. Let us see what brought the wrath of God in the days of Noah.

When these Fallen Angels (Watchers) began to mate with the daughters of men, total rebellion against God's laws ensued, and they began to teach mankind all sorts of sinful acts. Notice it reads in Genesis 6:4, There were giants in the earth in those days; and also after that This implies that after the flood, somehow, the same thing began to occur. Exactly how it is not clear, for the Scriptures do not specify.

However, the fact remains that there were giants during the time of Joshua when he sent spies to scout out the land of Canaan, and the report was brought back that the children of Israel were as grasshoppers compared to the inhabitants of Canaan. Furthermore, throughout the pages of Scripture, there are many references to the children of the giants, one of whom was Goliath, whom David killed. This was one of the reasons why the sword of Israel was needed.

In the book of Jude, verse 6, it reads: And the Angels which kept not their first estate, but left their habitation, he hath reserved in everlasting chains under darkness unto the judgment of the great day.

So we know that the Fallen Angels themselves were bound. Nevertheless, in the book of Enoch 10:12 it reads bind them fast for 70 generations in the valleys of the earth to the day of their judgment and of their consummation,. This means that at some point, some of these Fallen Angels were once again released for their final rebellion against God. This also aligns with Revelation 18:2, And he cried mightily with a strong voice, saying, Babylon the great is fallen, is fallen, and is become the habitation of devils, and the hold of every foul spirit, and a cage of every unclean and hateful bird.

Furthermore, in the Ascension of Isaiah chapter 4:1-2, we read:

1 And now Hezekiah and Josab, my son, these are the days of the completion of the world.

2 after it is completed, Beliar (another name for Satan), the great ruler, the King of this world, will descend, who hath ruled it since it came into being; yea, he will descend from his firmament in the likeness of a man.

We know that throughout Scripture, angels have appeared to mankind in the form of men. In Genesis 3:15, it is established that Satan has a seed And I will put enmity between thee and the woman, and between thy seed (offspring) and her seed (offspring)

In Daniel 2:43 speaking of the end time kingdom, it reads: And whereas thou sawest iron mixed with miry clay, they shall mingle themselves with the seed of men Who are they? Who are these who mingle themselves with the seed of men? It seems rather clear that they must not be of the seed of men since they mix themselves with the seed or offspring of men. Who could they be? The only other seed the Scriptures speak about is the seed of Satan. Obviously, Satan has seed and they mingle with the children of men.

Daniel's words also imply that some of the end-time world leaders, or kings, would be of this mixed genetic heritage. Notice that Daniel connected the intermingling of seed with the days of these kings (Daniel 2:44).

This implies that some of the world leaders today, or Kings who seem so charismatic and devilishly clever, such as androids and congenial liars, are really of their father, the devil in a literal sense.

In Matthew 13:37-39, Jesus Christ declares a parable in which some people are compared to wheat and others to tares. Both are different plants, yet they appear very similar on the outside. In the parable, Jesus said, "He that soweth the good seed is the Son of Man; the field is the world; the good seed are the children of the kingdom but the tares are the children of the wicked one; the enemy that sowed

124

them is the Devil. Could this have a dual meaning? It is a parable; all parables have a hidden meaning! He is not only speaking of those who give themselves over to Satan's evil spiritual influences and follow his ways.

But He is also speaking of certain ones whose actual birth or begettal was influenced or engineered by the Devil or his fallen angels. (William F. Dankenbring, Return of the Nephilim)

Satan's rebellion against God included his experimenting with human genetics in the womb of unsuspecting women, causing them to be impregnated by him or his fallen angels since the beginning of time. It is obvious that we have both the genetic seed and the spiritual seed of Satan alive in the world today under his influence and doing his deeds. Such beings would appear as humans but would be a mixed, mingled seed of an ancient angelic race. Hybrids, half-breeds of a most unusual kind.

All these alien abductions and UFO sightings are none other than the Watchers up to their old tricks again. Notice that all victims of alien abductions give the same account of being on some sort of operating table, with aliens performing strange medical experiments on them. Women even give accounts of being impregnated by these aliens.

A leading UFO Researcher and the scientist who headed Project Blue Book is Dr. J. Allen Hynek. Dr. Hynek commented, An expert has studied UFOs long enough to realize he is utterly ignorant. The UFO phenomenon is the outstanding strange dilemma of our age. We don't know what they are.

Dr. Hynek asserts that he possesses a computerized list of some 63,000 sightings. The Australian computer bank passed the 80,000 mark as of 1977. Many of these sightings were seen by dozens, even hundreds, and thousands of people at the same time. In 1954, there were numerous reports of UFO landings in France, witnessed by multiple witnesses 85% of the time. Dr. Stanton Friedman, a nuclear scientist and UFO Researcher, says, A close encounter of the third kind occurs somewhere on planet Earth every day.

The most common explanation offered to account for UFOs is, of course, the Extraterrestrial Hypothesis. According to this belief, UFOs come from amazingly advanced civilizations out in the cosmos that are seeking to study, contact, and influence mankind on Earth. However, editor Gordon Creighton of the British Journal, Flying Saucer Review, a widely hailed leading UFO publication which has investigated the phenomenon for 40 years, founded in 1955, and which has viewed the subject objectively and thoroughly now says: There seems to be no evidence yet that any of these craft or beings originate from outer space.

Two of the most highly respected and qualified researchers, Jacques Vallee and J. Allen Hynek, have discarded the Extraterrestrial Hypothesis completely. They point out with sense and rational logic:

If UFOs are indeed somebody else's nuts-and-bolts hardware, then we must still explain how such tangible hardware can change shape before our eyes, vanish in a Cheshire Cat manner (not even leaving a grin), seemingly melt away in front of us, materialize mysteriously before us without apparent detection by persons or in neighboring towns. We must wonder too, where UFOs are hiding when not manifesting themselves to human eyes (Hynek, Edge of Reality, pg. 7-8)

Brad Steiger, another UFO researcher, believes that very likely we are dealing with a multi-dimensional paraphysical phenomenon which is largely indigenous to planet Earth. Many researchers now believe that the Extraterrestrial Hypothesis is impossible. They point out that most believable UFOs conform to the following theory They are an intelligent life form. They have been with mankind from the beginning of time, although assuming different forms throughout history. They did not originate from advanced civilizations in outer space, but rather came from another dimension of reality that coexists with mankind in an unseen world invisible to human eyes. They represent a psychic phenomenon with the capacity to operate, at least at times, on a physical level.

UFO Researchers John Ankerberg and John Weldon declare:

Indeed, few unbiased researchers can logically deny that UFO experiences are occultic. If we catalogue the basic characteristics of the occult and compare them to UFO phenomena, we discover an essential similarity.

Consider just a few parallels between classical demonology and ufology. An examination of 19th-century literature on the occult, such as Francis Barrett's authoritative work The Magus, Book 2 (1801), describes Fallen Angels or demons in the following manner

Some that are near to us wander up and down in this obscure air; others inhabit lakes, rivers and seas; others the earth and terrify earthly things and vex not only men but also other creatures; some being content with laughter and derision only, do contrive rather to weary men than to hurt them; some heightening themselves to the length of a giant's body, and again shrinking themselves down to the smallest pygmies, and changing themselves into different forms do disturb men with vain fear. (William F. Dankenbring, Return of the Nephilim)

The Watchers have been trying to manipulate human genetics since the beginning of time. Satan even attempted to have sexual intercourse with Adam by taking on the form of a woman.

2 Adam & Eve 3:4, 9-11

4 Then Satan, the hater of all good, when he saw Adam thus alone, fasting and praying, appeared unto him in the form of a beautiful woman, who came and stood before him in the night of the fortieth day, and said unto him:

9 But I rejoiced over the birth of thy son Seth; yet after a little while I sorrowed greatly over Eve, because she is my sister. For when God sent a deep sleep over thee, and drew her out of thy side, He also brought me out of her. But He raised her by placing her with thee, while He lowered me.

10 I rejoiced over my sister for her being with thee. But God had made me a promise before, and said, Grieve not when Adam has gone up on the roof of the Cave of Treasures, and is separated from Eve his wife, I will send thee to him, thou shalt join thyself to him in marriage, and bear him five children, as Eve did bear him five.

11 And now, lo! God's promise to me is fulfilled; for it is He who has sent me to thee for the wedding, because if thou wed me, I shall bear thee finer and better children than those of Eve.

Why would Satan want to have sexual intercourse with Adam? He wanted Adam's seed/DNA!

Now, notice what Satan tried to do to Seth (the son born to Adam after Cain killed Abel).

2 Adam & Eve 5:1-10

1 As for Seth, when he was seven years old, he knew good and evil, and was consistent in fasting and praying, and spent all his nights in entreating God for mercy and forgiveness.

2 He also fasted when bringing up his offering every day, more than his father did; for he was of a fair countenance, like unto an angel of God. He also had a good heart, preserved the finest qualities of his soul, and for this reason, he brought up his offering every day.

3 And God was pleased with his offering, but He was also pleased with his purity. And he continued thus in doing the will of God, and of his father and mother, until he was seven years old.

4 After that, as he was coming down from the altar, having ended his offering, Satan appeared unto him in the form of a beautiful angel, brilliant with light; with a staff of light in his hand, himself girt about with a girdle of light.

5 He greeted Seth with a beautiful smile and began to beguile him with fair words, saying to him, O Seth, why abidest thou in this mountain? For it is rough, full of stones and sand, and trees with no good fruit on them; a wilderness without habitations and towns; no good place to dwell in. But all is heat, weariness, and trouble.

6 He said further, 'But we dwell in beautiful places, in another world than this earth. Our world is one of light, and our condition is the best. Our women are fairer than any others, and I wish thee, O Seth, to wed one of them, because I see that thou art fair to look upon. In this land, there is not one woman good enough for thee. Besides, all those who live in this world are only five souls.

7 But in our world, there are very many men and many maidens, all more beautiful than the other. I wish, therefore, to remove thee hence, that thou mayest see my relations and be wedded to which-ever thou likest.

8 Thou shalt then abide with me and be at peace; thou shalt be filled with splendour and light, as we are.

9 Thou shalt remain in our world and rest from this world and the misery of it. Thou shalt never again feel faint and weary; thou shalt never bring up an offering, nor sue for mercy; for thou shalt commit no more sin, nor be swayed by passions.

10 And if thou wilt hearken to what I say, thou shalt wed one of my daughters; for with us it is no sin so to do; neither is it reckoned as animal lust.

11 For in our world we have no God; but we all are gods; we all are of the light, heavenly, powerful, strong, and glorious.

Satan was trying to abduct Seth to use his genetic makeup for his devious purposes. What the Watchers are doing is something they have been doing for a very long time: Human Genetic/DNA Manipulation. God never mentions anywhere that we need to be on the lookout for aliens from another planet. Nowhere!!! But He does warn us to guard ourselves from the WATCHERS! These aliens are none other than some of the Watchers/Fallen Angels released for their final rebellion against the Almighty God.

Knowing this information gives us a better understanding of what was going on in the days prior to the flood of Noah. Now, notice what the Watchers began to teach mankind   :

Enoch 7

1 And all the others together with them took unto themselves wives, and each chose for himself one, and they began to go in unto them and to defile themselves with them, and they taught them charms

 2 and enchantments, and the cutting of roots, and made them acquainted with plants. And they

3 became pregnant, and they bore great giants, whose height was three thousand ells. These giants

4 consumed all the acquisitions of men. And when men could no longer sustain them, the giants turned against

5 them and devoured mankind. And they began to sin against birds, and beasts, and reptiles, and

6 fish, (The Watchers began to scientifically manipulate the genetic code of all kinds of animals, i.e., cloning, cross-breeding, and synthetically altering) and to devour one another's flesh, and drink the blood. (The documented strange and very disgusting phenomenon of cattle mutilation seen around the world has puzzled scientists and researchers alike. In all of these occurrences, the animal is mutilated, but there is no blood spilled near the carcass. The dead animal is found completely drained of all its blood. Researchers have concluded that something not of this world is behind this phenomenon. Little do they know that this is the work of the Watchers? This is nothing new. It was happening back in the days of Noah, and once some of the Watchers were released into the world again, it is no surprise that they are doing the same things.) Then the earth laid accusation against the lawless ones.

Enoch 8

1 And Azazel taught men to make swords, and knives, and shields, and breastplates, and made known to them the metals of the earth and the art of working them, and bracelets, and ornaments, and the use of antimony, and the beautifying of the eyelids, and all kinds of costly stones, and all

2 colouring tinctures. And there arose much godlessness, and they committed fornication, and they

131

3 were led astray, and became corrupt in all their ways. Semjaza taught enchantments and root-cuttings, 'Armaros the resolving of enchantments, Baraqijal (taught) astrology, Kokabel the constellations, Ezeqeel the knowledge of the clouds, Araqiel the signs of the earth, Shamsiel the signs of the sun, and Sariel the course of the moon. And as men perished, they cried, and their cry went up to heaven. (It is no wonder that in the past centuries humans have experienced a technological boom previously never seen. Whether humans realize it or not, it is the Watchers that are teaching mankind the same things they taught during the days of Noah.)

Enoch 9:6-10

6 Thou seest what Azazel hath done, who hath taught all unrighteousness on earth and revealed the eternal secrets which were (preserved) in heaven, which

7 men were striving to learn: And Semjaza, to whom Thou hast given authority to bear rule over his associates. And they have gone to the daughters of men upon the earth, and have slept with the

9 women, and have defiled themselves, and revealed to them all kinds of sins. And the women have

10 borne giants, and the whole earth has thereby been filled with blood and unrighteousness. And now, behold, the souls of those who have died are crying and making their suit to the gates of heaven, and their lamentations have ascended, and cannot cease because of the lawless deeds which are wrought on the earth.

Enoch 65

1, 2 And in those days Noah saw that the earth had sunk and its destruction was nigh. And he arose from thence and went to the ends of the earth, and cried aloud to his grandfather Enoch

3 and Noah said three times with an embittered voice: Hear me, hear me, hear me.' And I said unto him ' Tell me what it is that is falling out on the earth that the earth is in such evil plight

4 and shaken, lest perchance I shall perish with it? 'And thereupon there was a great commotion on the earth, and a voice was heard from heaven, and I fell on my face. And Enoch, my grandfather, came and stood by me, and said unto me: ' Why hast thou cried unto me with a bitter cry and weeping

6 And a command has gone forth from the presence of the Lord concerning those who dwell on the earth that their ruin is accomplished because they have learnt all the secrets of the angels, and all the violence of the Satans, and all their powers -the most secret ones- and all the power of those who practice sorcery, and the power of witchcraft, and the power of those who make molten images

7 for the whole earth: And how silver is produced from the dust of the earth, and how soft metal

8 originates in the earth. Lead and tin are not produced from the earth like the first it is the fountain

9 that produces them, and an angel stands therein, and that angel is preeminent.' And after that, my grandfather Enoch took hold of me by my hand and raised me, and said unto me ' Go, for I have

10 asked the Lord of Spirits as touching this commotion on the earth. And He said unto me: "Because of their unrighteousness, their judgment has been determined upon and shall not be withheld by Me

forever. Because of the sorceries which they have searched out and learnt, the earth and those

11 who dwell upon it shall be destroyed. And these they have no place of repentance forever, because they have shown them what was hidden, and they are the damned but as for thee, my son, the Lord of Spirits knows that thou art pure, and guiltless of this reproach concerning the secrets.

Enoch 69:1 – 13

1 And after this judgment, they shall terrify and make them tremble because they have shown this to those who dwell on the earth.

2 And behold the names of those angels [and these are their names: the first of them is Samjaza, the second Artaqifa, and the third Armen, the fourth Kokabel, the fifth Turael, the sixth Rumjal, the seventh Danjal, the eighth Neqael, the ninth Baraqel, the tenth Azazel, the eleventh Armaros, the twelfth Batarjal, the thirteenth Busasejal, the fourteenth Hananel, the fifteenth Turel, and the sixteenth Simapesiel, the seventeenth Jetrel, the eighteenth Tumael, the nineteenth Turel,

3 the twentieth Rumael, the twenty-first Azazel. And these are the chiefs of their angels and their names, and their chief ones over hundreds and fifties and tens   .

4 The name of the first Jeqon: that is, the one who led astray [all] the sons of God, and brought them

5 down to the earth, and led them astray through the daughters of men. And the second was named Asbeel: he imparted to the holy sons of God evil counsel, and led them astray so that they defiled

6 their bodies with the daughters of men. And the third was named Gadreel: he it is who showed the children of men all the blows of death, and he led astray Eve, and showed [the weapons of death to the sons of men] the shield and the coat of mail, and the sword for battle, and all the weapons

7 of death to the children of men. And from his hand they have proceeded against those who dwell

8 on the earth from that day and forevermore. And the fourth was named Penemue: he taught the

9 children of men, the bitter and the sweet, and he taught them all the secrets of their wisdom. And he instructed mankind in writing with ink and paper, and thereby many sinned from eternity to

10 eternity and until this day. For men were not created for such a purpose, to give confirmation

11 to their good faith with pen and ink. For men were created exactly like the angels, to the intent that they should continue pure and righteous, and death, which destroys everything, could not have taken hold of them, but through this their knowledge they are perishing, and through this power

12, it is consuming me. And the fifth was named Kasdeja: this is he who showed the children of men all the wicked smitings of spirits and demons, and the smitings of the embryo in the womb, that it may pass away,(abortion) and [the smitings of the soul] the bites of the serpent, and the smitings

13, which befalls through the noontide heat, the son of the serpent named Taba'et. And this is the task of Kasbeel, the chief of the oath, which he showed to the holy ones when he dwelt high above in glory, and its name is Biqa.

Jubilees 7:20-21

20 In the 28th Jubilee, Noah began to direct his sons in the ordinances and commandments, and all the judgments that he knew, and he exhorted his sons to observe righteousness, and to cover the shame of their flesh, and to bless their Creator, and honor father and mother, and love their neighbor, and guard their souls from fornication and uncleanness and all iniquity.

21 Because of these three things came the flood on the earth, namely, the fornication of the Watchers committed against the law of the ordinances when they went whoring after the daughters of men, and took themselves wives of all they chose, and made the beginning of uncleanness.

Now, notice what the behavior of mankind was during the days of Jared, before the birth of Noah.

2 Adam and Eve 20

After Cain had gone down to the land of dark soil, and his children had multiplied therein, there was one of them, whose name was Genun, son of Lamech the blind, who slew Cain.

2 But as to this Genun, Satan came into him in his childhood and he made sundry trumpets and horns, and string instruments, cymbals and psalteries, and lyres and harps, and flutes; and he played on them at all times and every hour.

3 And when he played on them, Satan came into them, so that from among them was heard a beautiful and sweet sound, that ravished the heart.

4 Then he gathered companies upon companies to play on them; and when they played, it pleased well the children of Cain, who inflamed themselves with sin among themselves, and burnt as with fire; while Satan inflamed their hearts, one with another, and increased lust among them.

5 Satan also taught Genun to bring strong drink out of corn; and this Genun used to bring together companies upon companies in drink-houses; and brought into their hands all manner of fruits and flowers;-and they drank together.

6 Thus did this Genun multiply sin exceedingly; he also acted with pride, and taught the children of Cain to commit all manner of the grossest wickedness, which they knew not, and put them up to manifold doings which they knew not before.

7 Then Satan, when he saw that they yielded to Genun and hearkened to him in everything he told them, rejoiced greatly, increased Genun's understanding, until he took iron and with it made weapons of war.

8 Then, when they were drunk, hatred and murder increased among them; one man used violence against another to teach him evil, taking his children and defiling them before him.

9 And when men saw they were overcome, and saw others that were not overpowered, those who were beaten came to Genun, took refuge with him, and he made them his confederates.

10 Then sin increased among them greatly; until a man married his sister, or daughter, or mother, and others; or the daughter of his father's sister, so that there was no more distinction of relationship, and they no longer knew what is iniquity; but did wickedly, and the

earth was defiled with sin; and they angered God the Judge, who had created them.

11 But Genun gathered together company upon companies, that played on horns and on all the other instruments we have already mentioned, at the foot of the Holy Mountain; and they did so so that the children of Seth who were on the Holy Mountain should hear it.

12 But when the children of Seth heard the noise, they wondered, and came by companies, and stood on the top of the mountain to look at those below and they did thus for a whole year.

13 When, at the end of that year, Genun saw that they were being won over to him little by little, Satan entered into him, and taught him to make dyeing stuffs for garments of divers patterns, and made him understand how to dye crimson and purple and whatnot.

14 And the sons of Cain who wrought all this, and shone in beauty and gorgeous apparel, gathered together at the foot of the mountain in splendour, with horns and gorgeous dresses, and horse races, committing all manner of abominations.

15 Meanwhile, the children of Seth, who were on the Holy Mountain, prayed and praised God, in the place of the hosts of angels who had fallen; wherefore God had called them angels,. Because he rejoiced over them greatly.

16 But after this, they no longer kept His commandment, nor held by the promise He had made to their fathers; but they relaxed from their fasting and praying, and from the counsel of Jared their father. And they kept on gathering together on the top of the mountain, to look upon the children of Cain, from morning until evening, and upon what they did, upon their beautiful dresses and ornaments.

17 Then the children of Cain looked up from below, and saw the children of Seth, standing in troops on the top of the mountain; and they called to them to come down to them.

18 But the children of Seth said to them from above, We don't know the way. Then Genun, the son of Lamech, heard them say they did not know the way, and he bethought himself how he might bring them down.

19 Then Satan appeared to him by night, saying, There is no way for them to come down from the mountain on which they dwell; but when they come to-morrow, say to them, 'Come ye to the western side of the mountain; there you will find the way of a stream of water, that comes down to the foot of the mountain, between two hills; come down that way to us.

20 Then, when it was day, Genun blew the horns and beat drums below the mountain, as he was wont. The children of Seth heard it and came as they used to do.

21 Then Genun said to them from down below, Go to the western side of the mountain, there you will find the way to come down.

22 But when the children of Seth heard these words from him, they went back into the cave to Jared, to tell him all they had heard.

23 Then, when Jared heard it, he was grieved, for he knew that they would transgress his counsel.

24 After this, a hundred men of the children of Seth gathered together, and said among themselves, Come, let us go down to the children of Cain, and see what they do, and enjoy ourselves with them.

25 But when Jared heard this of the hundred men, his very soul was moved, and his heart was grieved. He then arose with great fervor and stood in the midst of them, and adjured them by the blood of Abel the just, Let not one of you go down from this holy and pure mountain, in which our fathers have ordered us to dwell.

26 But when Jared saw that they did not receive his words, he said unto them, O my good and innocent and holy children, know that when once you go down from this holy mountain, God will not allow you to return to it.

 27 He again adjured them, saying, I adjure by the death of our father Adam, and by the blood of Abel, of Seth, of Enos, of Cainan, and Mahalaleel, to hearken to me, and not to go down from this holy mountain; for the moment you leave it, you will be reft of life and mercy and you shall no longer be called 'children of God, 'but' children of the devil.

28 But they would not hearken to his words.

29 Enoch at that time was already grown up, and in his zeal for God, he arose and said, Hear me, O ye sons of Seth, small and great-when ye transgress the commandment of our fathers, and go down from this holy mountain ye shall not come up hither again forever.

30 But they rose against Enoch, and would not hearken to his words, but went down from the Holy Mountain.

31 And when they looked at the daughters of Cain, with beautiful figures, and their hands and feet dyed with colour, and tattooed in ornaments on their faces, the fire of sin was kindled in them

32 Then Satan made them look most beautiful before the sons of Seth, as he also made the sons of Seth appear the fairest in the eyes

of the daughters of Cain, so that the daughters of Cain lusted after the sons of Seth like ravenous beasts, and the sons of Seth after the daughters of Cain, until they committed abomination with them.

33 But after they had thus fallen into this defilement, they returned by the way they had come and tried to ascend the Holy Mountain. But they could not, because the stones of that holy mountain were of fire flashing before them, because of which they could not go up again.

34 And God was angry with them, and repented of them because they had come down from glory, and had thereby lost or forsaken their purity or innocence, and had fallen into the defilement of sin.

35 Then God sent His Word to Jared, saying, These thy children, whom you did call 'My children' - behold, they have transgressed My commandment, and have gone down to the abode of perdition, and of sin. Send a messenger to those that are left, that they may not go down, and be lost.

36 Then Jared wept before the Lord, and asked of Him mercy and forgiveness. But he wished that his soul might depart from his body, rather than hear these words from God about the going down of his children from the Holy Mountain.

37 But he followed God's order, and preached unto them not to go down from that holy mountain, and not to hold intercourse with the children of Cain

38 But they heeded not his message, and would not obey his counsel.

The Watchers taught mankind all sorts of things that God never intended mankind to know. From certain music, strong liquor, houses of music (clubs), knives, tinctures, gangs, abortion, advanced sciences, charms, enchantments, cutting of roots (drugs), astrology, astronomy, witchcraft, voodoo, magic, the use of certain roots for enchantments, etc. They taught them Illuminism, the evil art of magical enchantments to invoke the help of the spirit world. The old mystery religion of Summer and ancient Babylon. Now under the guise of Freemasonry, Jewish Kabbalah, Buddhism, Mormonism, Scientology, New Age, black or white magic, Islam, etc, and whatever other name they wish to call it! Whichever way they put it is a worship of Satan, Satanism! Whatsoever is contrary to God's law is Satanism. You can dress a monkey in a three-piece suit, but the fact remains that it is still a monkey!

There are not many ways or paths to God. There is only one way through Jesus Christ (Yahshua Ha Mosiach).

Luke 17:28-30

28 Likewise also, as it was in the days of Lot; they did eat, they drank, they bought, they sold, they planted, they built

29 But the same day that Lot went out of Sodom, it rained fire and brimstone from heaven, and destroyed them all.

30 Even thus shall it be in the day when the Son of man is revealed.

The main sin running rampant in Sodom and Gomorrah in the days of Lot was homosexuality. What exactly is running rampant in today's world?

Genesis 19:5 −9

5 And they called unto Lot, and said unto him, Where are the men which came in to thee this night? Bring them out unto us, that we may know them. (Sexually)

6 And Lot went out at the door unto them, and shut the door after him,

7 And said, I pray you, brethren, do not so wickedly.

8 Behold now, I have two daughters who have not known man; let me, I pray you, bring them out unto you, and do ye to them as is good in your eyes: only unto these men do nothing; for therefore came they under the shadow of my roof.

9 And they said, Stand back. And they said again, this one fellow came in to sojourn, and he will needs be a judge: now will we deal worse with thee, than with them. And they pressed sore upon the man, even Lot, and came near to break the door.

2 Peter 2:4-8

4 For if God spared not the angels that sinned, but cast them down to hell, and delivered them into chains of darkness, to be reserved unto judgment

5 And spared not the old world, but saved Noah the eighth person, a preacher of righteousness, bringing in the flood upon the world of the ungodly

6 And turning the cities of Sodom and Gomorrah into ashes, con-demned them with an overthrow, making them an ensample unto those that after should live ungodly

7 And delivered just Lot, vexed with the filthy conversation of the wicked

8 (For that righteous man dwelling among them, in seeing and hear-ing, vexed his righteous soul from day to day with their unlawful deeds;

Jude 7-8

7 Even as Sodom and Gomorrah, and the cities about them in like manner, giving themselves over to fornication, and going after strange flesh, are set forth for an example, suffering the vengeance of eternal fire.

8 Likewise also these filthy dreamers defile the flesh and, despising dominion, speak evil of dignities.

Romans 1:27-28, 32

27 And likewise also the men, leaving the natural use of the woman, burned with lust one toward another; men with men working that which is unseemly, and receiving in themselves that recompense of their error which was meet   .

28 And even as they did not like to retain God in their knowledge, God gave them over to a reprobate mind, to do those things which are not convenient;

32 Who, knowing the judgment of God, that they which commit such things are worthy of death, not only do the same, but have pleasure in them that do them.

Chapter 10

Parallels between 2 Esdras, Daniel, and Revelation

It is often said among students of prophecy that to thoroughly understand the book of Revelation, you must thoroughly understand the book of Daniel. What most fail to notice or even realize is that to thoroughly understand the book of Daniel, you must thoroughly understand the book of 2 Esdras, which most people disregard because it is an Apocryphal (hidden book). Some may not even know it exists.

Introduction: The vision of the Eagle and the Lion, 2 Esdras 11-12

In a dream/vision, Ezra sees a monstrous creature rising from the sea, an eagle with 12 wings, 8 rival wings, and 3 heads. The wings and heads rule over the earth in turn (succession, one after the other, not all at once), then disappear. When only 1 head and 2 rival wings are left, the eagle is challenged by a lion, which accuses it of tyrannizing the earth. The lion states that by God's predetermined plan, the time for the eagle to disappear has come, and the vision ends with the body of the eagle bursting into flames. As we subsequently learn, the eagle symbolizes the fourth beast in the vision of Daniel 7, as it is clearly shown in the interpretation of the vision.

This is the most vividly detailed and profound prophecy of the United States of America in all Scripture, down to the number of presidencies. It unveils the Republican/Democrat scheme that the US government is perpetrating to reach its end goal. Furthermore, by this prophecy, we can identify the Lawless One, the Antichrist, and an approximate time of when all hell will break loose on humanity. It is a truly amazing prophecy, and these revelations will shock you!

Before proceeding, I would like to reiterate that in different chapters throughout this book, the reader will be informed as to the basics concerning symbolism, Illuminati, and Freemasonry. However, it is up to the individual to do the research if more in-depth information on these mystery religions (secret societies) and how they affect every facet of governments around the world is wanted. At the end of this book, I will list several excellent sources for further research. You will notice that books on these subjects are lengthy and contain a wealth of information; nonetheless, I highly recommend them. To try to incorporate all that information into this book would probably make it thousands of pages long, which was something I certainly did not want. Please bear this in mind when you notice that my mentioning   of such things is brief and direct to the point.

Before proceeding to this prophecy, let's look at what the eagle symbolizes. "The Herder Dictionary of Symbols notes that the Eagle has long been a symbol of power, endurance, and heavenward flight. It also symbolizes the sun (and the sun god) and spiritual majesty. Coils' Masonic Encyclopedia says that, to the pagans, the eagle was an emblem of Jupiter, and with the Druids (witchcraft) it was a symbol of their supreme god. The Eagle appears in the insignia of many nations, including but not limited to Rome, Nazi and modern-day Germany, Czarist Russia, and the United States of America. It is revered as a holy sign by Sufi Muslims. The Eagle is also represented in the Great Seal of the United States of America (the presidential seal). (Coddex Majica, pg. 247)

To the Illuminati/ Freemasons, the double-headed eagle represents their principal Luciferian Doctrine. Their practice and doctrine are this: a form of witchcraft based on Alchemy and magic, invoking the help spirit world (Demons); while referring to god, the god they worship is Satan, which they call by many names. Fermenting chaos so that order may come out of it using two dynamic and competing

146

forces, i.e, positive and negative, thesis/anti-thesis, left/right (in Latin, Ordo Ab Chaos) Order out of Chaos. Their end goal is to destroy Earth, civilization, and spirituality. Then bring order according to Satan's plan. Earth is to be hell and hell on earth: as above, so below.

The Babylonian and Egyptian pagan god, Mammon Ra, is also a two-headed eagle. Mammon Ra was also known by the ancients as an evil spirit of covetousness that dominated the earth (the god of prosperity). Jesus warned, No man can serve two masters: for either you will hate the one, and love the other; or else he will hold to the one, and despise the other. Ye cannot serve God and Mammon. (Matthew 6:24)

This Satanic symbol (two-headed eagle) is very well hidden from the masses, right in the Oval Office of the President of the United States. In the antique oak desk used by the president, the eagle's head of the Great Seal faces to the right. Directly in front of the desk, the Great Seal is also on the rug, but the eagle's head is facing to the left, a coincidence? Not! We will soon uncover this mystery directly from the words of the Almighty God.

The Vision of the Eagle and the Lion: (Spiritual Judgement Began)

2 Esdras 10:57-59 (The beginning of Ezra's vision)

57 For you are more blessed than many, and you have been called before the Most High, as but few have been.

58 But tomorrow night you shall remain here,

59 and the Most High will show you in those dream visions what the Most High will do to those who dwell on earth in the last days. (Notice that this prophecy was not for Ezra's time but for those living in the end time. This is the main reason why this prophecy has been

disregarded by most. It is to be fulfilled in the time we are currently living in. Remember Enoch's Prophecy of Weeks, judgment is executed at the beginning of the 8th millennium. The millennium we just entered.) So I slept that night and the following one, as he had commanded me.

2 Esdras 11

1 On the second night, I had a dream, and behold, there came up from the sea an eagle that had twelve feathered wings and three heads. (The United States of America, the last remaining superpower, is represented by the bald eagle, which is its national emblem and depicted in the Great Seal (the presidential seal). The first president of the United States, George Washington, was a known Freemason. As were also most of the Founding Fathers, most of the authors of the US Constitution, and most former presidents. The highest degree in Freemasonry is the 33rd degree, whose symbol is an eagle with two heads facing right/left. This symbol can also be found hidden in the Oval Office. In front of the antique oak desk used by the president, the eagle (Great Seal) faces to the right, yet directly in front of the desk, on the rug, is the same seal, but the eagle faces to the left. This symbol is also the one that represents the ancient pagan god/demon Mammon Ra, which was known by the ancients as an evil spirit that controlled the earth with covetousness.)

Right from the mouth of Benjamin Franklin analyze the moral character of the bald eagle: "he is a bird of bad moral character, he does not get his living honestly, you may have seen him perched on some dead tree, where, too lazy to fish for himself, he watches the labor of the fishing-hawk, and when that diligent bird has at length taken a fish, and is bearing it to its nest for the support of his mate and young ones, the bald eagle pursues him and takes it from him. Besides, he is a rank coward; the little kingbird, not bigger than a sparrow, attacks him boldly and drives him out of the district. This is a true description of the moral character of the US Government.

2 And I looked, and behold, he spread his wings over all the earth, and all the winds of heaven blew upon him, and the clouds were gathered about him. (All countries in the world are influenced in some way, shape, or form by the United States.)

3 And I looked, and out of its wings there grew opposing wings (Notice that out of its wings there grew opposing ones, positive/negative, thesis/anti-thesis, Order out of Chaos the Illuminati/Freemason doctrine.) but they became little, puny wings

4 But his heads were at rest (Not yet in office/power); the middle head was larger (Larger could very well refer to its age as we shall see later.) than the other heads (Larger/older than the two heads next to it.), but it also was at rest with them.

5 And I looked, and behold, the eagle flew with his wings, to reign over the earth and over those who dwell in it.

6 And I saw how all things under heaven were subjected to him, and no one spoke against him, not even one creature that was on the earth. (The Eagle became a superpower unable to be stopped.)

7 And I looked, and behold, the eagle rose upon his talons, and uttered a cry to his wings, saying,

8 Do not all watch (Wake up, take office) at the same time; let each sleep in his place, and watch in his turn; (The wings take office in turn, one after the other, not all at once.)

9 but let the heads be reserved for the last. (The heads are kept to the end.)

10 And I looked, and behold, the voice did not come from his head, but from the midst of his body.

11 And I counted his opposing wings, and behold, there were eight of them.

12 And I looked, and behold, on the right side one wing arose, and it reigned over all the earth. (Keep in mind that Republicans are called right wing and Democrats left wing.)

13 And while it was reigning, it came to its end and disappeared, so that its place was not seen. Then the next wing arose and reigned, and it continued to reign a long time.

14 And while it was reigning, its end came also, so that it disappeared like the first.

15 And behold, a voice sounded, saying to it.

16 Hear me, you who have ruled the earth all this time; I announce this to you before you disappear.

17 After you, no one shall rule as long as you, or even half as long.

18 Then the third wing raised itself, and held the rule like the former ones, and it also disappeared.

19 And so it went with all the wings; they wielded power one after another and then were never seen again.

20 And I looked, and behold, in due course the wings that followed also rose on the right side, to rule. Some of them ruled, yet disappeared suddenly;

21 and others of them rose (bid govern), but did not hold the rule (but not according to their plan).

22 And after this, I looked, and behold, the twelve wings and the two little wings disappeared;

23, and nothing remained on the eagle's body except the three heads that were at rest (not yet in office/power) and six little wings.

24 And I looked, and behold, two little wings separated from the six and remained under the head that was on the right side; but four remained in their place. (Two of the left wings, Democrats, positioned themselves under the head of the right Republican, which means that once the head on the right leaves office, these 2 left wings take office.)

25 And I looked, and behold, these little wings (The four that remained in their place) planned to set themselves up and hold the rule.

26 And I looked, and behold, one was set up, but suddenly disappeared;

27 a second, also, and this disappeared more quickly than the first.

28 And I looked, and behold, the two that remained were planning between themselves to reign together

29 and while they were planning, behold, one of the heads that were at rest awoke; for it was greater than the other two heads. (The one which was in the middle, see verse 4.)

30 And I saw how it allied the two heads with itself, (United with the same plan.)

31 and behold, the head turned with those that were with it, and it devoured the two little wings which were planning to reign. (Notice that all heads, whether the middle or on the left Democrats or the right Republicans, were part of the same plan. These two wings never got into power.)

Before we continue with this prophecy, we must notice a very important mathematical equation hidden within this prophecy that tells us the   number of wings/Kings/presidents that reign. This will help us establish an accurate timeline of events and allow us to put names on these wings.

There are 12 wings, 8 rival wings, and 3 heads: 23 in total

Verse 24 tells us that two separate and position themselves to reign. When a president is elected or, better yet, positioned, a vice president is also positioned along with him.

23 in total: X 2 president and vice president = 46 presidencies

Verses 28-31, tells us that the last two wings which remained in the same spot (Not the ones that separated and placed themselves under the head on the right on verse 24, or the ones that had a short reign in verses 26 & 27, were devoured by the three heads in verses 30 & 31, which means that they never took office so we must subtract them.)

46 presidencies, - 2 wings devoured by heads, = 44 presidencies. THIS MARKS THE BEGINNING OF JUDGMENT IN THE SPIRITUAL REALM, FOLLOWED BY THE PHYSICAL. This Trump Presidency is a continuation from his 1st

What presidency are we in? The 47th!!! Now we can go back and start to put names and dates on these wings, and this puzzle will be beautifully assembled together.

Working from the 44th presidency (Obama/Biden) back, let's continue with this amazing prophecy.

32 Moreover this head (Using the formula above now we know that this middle head is referring to George H. Bush, the 41st president, obviously the oldest of the two heads next to him Clinton/Bush.) gained control of the whole earth, and with much oppression dominated its inhabitants; and it had greater power over the world than all the wings that had gone before.

33 And after this, I looked, and behold, the middle head also suddenly disappeared, (Ended his presidential term) just as the wings had done.

34 But the two heads remained, which also ruled over the earth and its inhabitants. (Head on the left, Democrat Bill Clinton, and Head on the right, Republican George W Bush)

35 And I looked, and behold, the head on the right side devoured the one on the left. (Notice it says that. two heads were remaining, I watched the head on the right (Republican, George W. Bush, the 43rd president) devour the head on the left (Democrat, Bill Clinton, the 42nd president).

36 Then I heard a voice saying to me, Look before you and consider what you see.

37 And I looked, and behold, a creature like a lion was aroused out of the forest, roaring (The roaring of an angry lion); and I heard how he uttered a man's voice to the eagle, and spoke, saying,

38 "Listen, and I will speak to you. The Most High says to you

39 Are you not the one that remains of the four beasts which I had made to reign in my world, so that the end of my times might come through them?

40 You, the fourth that has come, have conquered all the beasts that have gone before; and you have held sway over the world with much terror, and over all the earth with grievous oppression; and for so long you have dwelt on the earth with deceit.

41 And you have judged the earth, but not with truth;

42 for you have afflicted the meek and injured the peaceable; you have hated those who tell the truth, and have loved liars; you have destroyed the dwellings of those who brought forth fruit, and have laid low the walls of those who did you no harm.

43 And so your insolence has come up before the Most High, and your pride to the Mighty One.

44 And the Most High has looked upon his times, and behold, they are ended, and his ages are completed! (The beginning of the 8th millennium, the one we entered as of the year 2000.)

45 Therefore, you will surely disappear (Will be no more, cease to exist), you eagle, and your terrifying wings, and your most evil little wings, and your malicious heads, and your most evil talons, and your whole worthless body,

46 so that the whole earth, freed from your violence, may be refreshed and relieved, and may hope for the judgment and mercy of him who made it. In verses 36 – 46, we noticed that the lion which represents Jesus Christ, The Lion of the Tribe of Judah begins to hand

down judgment and upbraids the eagle for its form of governing and harsh oppression, deceit, no regard for truth, loving liars, pride, etc.

Now, if you do not believe or know that the US government has done all this, the answer is right at your fingertips (The Internet). Do your research! I suggest that the reader take a good, hard look at the Conspiratorial View of History and not just accept the Accidental View of History offered by the government-controlled media. Unfortunately, if I were to list all the deceitful practices the US Government has used on its citizens and abroad, this book could not contain them all. This subject would be beyond the scope of this book, and yes, it is one giant conspiracy! It has been a conspiracy from the very beginning when the Watchers fell from heaven. Not because men say so, but because the Eternal God, Ruler of Heaven and Earth, stazes it throughout this and many other prophecies! However, if you do not believe this, then you're calling your Savior Jesus Christ a liar. God does not lie; we were the ones who were ignorant of the entire scheme. Do your research, seek the truth! Most of the so-called conspiracy theories are telling you the truth. The problem is that your human mind cannot fully comprehend the actual magnitude of the conspiracy and the evil that surrounds it. Some may know and simply refuse to acknowledge it, and yet some just don't want to know.

2 Esdras 12

1 While the lion was saying these words to the eagle, I looked,

2 and behold, the remaining head disappeared. (Notice that while the Lion was still addressing the Eagle, Ezra sees the last head, the head on the right (Republican, George W. Bush, the 43rd president) disappear. Towards the end of 2007, the current financial crisis began to take its toll on the economy. Why? Because the Lion began to

hand down judgment during the last year of George W. Bush's 43rd presidency. Approximately towards the end of 2007.)

And the two wings that had gone over to it arose and set themselves up to reign, and their reign was brief and full of trouble. (The last two left-wing Democrats took office (2009 Obama/Biden, the 44th presidency) after a right-wing (Head on the right) Republican (George W. Bush, the 43rd presidency), but their time in office was short and full of trouble.)

3 And I looked, and behold, as they were also about to disappear, (Notice that,. as they were also about to disappear. REMEMBER Spiritual Judgement takes place FIRST; then comes the Physical part.)

The whole body of the eagle burst into flames, and the earth was exceedingly terrified. (Now notice the circumstances surrounding the 44th presidency, Obama/Biden. Their reign was short and full of trouble. From the economy, unemployment, government takeover of banks, General Motors, Fannie Mae, Freddie Mac, Bailouts, Healthcare reform, Wall Street financial reforms, Obama's Marxist agenda, BP oil spill, the list goes on and on. The fact remains that it is a troubled reign. Towards the end of their 1st term, before 4 years are completed (SPIRITUAL JUDGEMENT BEGINS), the Eagle's entire body burst into flames and the earth is struck with terror (NOW COMES THE PHYSICAL MANIFESTATION).

1 Corinthians 15:52

In a moment, in the twinkling of an eye, at the last trump (TRUMP'S last term, GET IT ?): for the trumpet shall sound, and the dead shall be raised incorruptible, and we shall be changed. THIS IS GOD ACTIVATING DIVINE DNA IN HIS CHOSEN ONES.

Then there is some form of nuclear attack before the end of Trump's term in office. This should send chills down your spine as you realize what is about to happen in less than 20 months.)

Now that the goodness of God has revealed this information to us, we can understand this prophecy more clearly. Let's move on to the interpretation of the prophecy so that we can continue piecing it together, Lord willing!

 Then I awoke in great perplexity of mind and great fear, and I said to my spirit,

4 Behold, you have brought this upon me, because you search out the ways of the Most High.

5 Behold, I am still weary in mind and very weak in my spirit, and not even a little strength is left in me, because of the great fear with which I have been terrified this night.

6 Therefore, I will now beseech the Most High that he may strengthen me to the end.

7 And I said, O sovereign Lord, if I have come up before thy face,

8 Strengthen me and show me, thy servant, the interpretation and meaning of this terrifying vision, that thou mayest fully comfort my soul.

9 For thou hast judged me worthy to be shown the end of the times and the last events of the times. (This prophecy is a vision of the events surrounding the very end.)

The Interpretation of this Prophecy:

10 He said to me, This is the interpretation of this vision which you have seen:

11 The eagle which you saw coming up from the sea is the fourth kingdom which appeared in a vision to your brother Daniel.

12 But it was not explained to him as I now explain or have explained it to you. (These two verses are key to comparing this prophecy along with Daniel's vision of the fourth beast and Mystery Babylon in the book of Revelation.)

13 Behold, the days are coming when a kingdom shall arise on earth, and it shall be more terrifying than all the kingdoms that have been before it. (It is a great superpower and much more deceitful than any before it.)

14 And twelve kings shall reign in it, one after another.

15 But the second that is to reign shall hold sway for a longer time than any other of the twelve. (Using the above mathematical equation 12(kings/presidents) X 2(president and vice president) = 24, the 24th president was Grover Cleveland, the 25th president was William McKinley, the 26th president (the 2nd from the 12th—12x2=24) was Theodore Roosevelt, but the 2nd Roosevelt was, Franklin D. Roosevelt the only president in history to serve more than two terms.)

16 This is the interpretation of the twelve wings which you saw.

17 As for your hearing a voice that spoke, coming not from the eagle's heads but from the midst of his body, this is the interpretation:

18 Amid the time of that kingdom, great struggles shall arise, and it shall be in danger of falling; nevertheless, it shall not fall then, but shall regain its former power. (The Syriac and Armenian versions of this prophecy read, in the middle of the time of that kingdom). These

versions most likely preserve more of the original text and correlate with Franklin D. Roosevelt's 32nd presidency, marking the middle time of that kingdom, great struggles shall arise. World War I, World War II, and the Great Depression.)

19 As for your seeing eight little wings clinging to his wings, this is the interpretation:

20 Eight kings shall arise in it, whose times shall be short and their years swift; (Counting backward from Obama the 44th president (excluding George W. Bush, Bill Clinton, and George H. Bush because they are considered the three evil heads of the eagle) you have: Ronald Reagan, Jimmy Carter, Gerald Ford, Richard Nixon, Lyndon Johnson, John F Kennedy, Dwight Eisenhower a total of 8 presidents/kings.)

21 and two of them shall perish when the middle of its time draws near; (Notice in chapter 11 v. 26 And I looked, and behold, one was set up, but suddenly disappeared; Dwight Eisenhower, died March 28, 1969 and v. 27 "a second also, and this disappeared more quickly than the first (The one before it). John F. Kennedy (assassinated, November 22, 1963)

And four shall be kept for the time when its end approaches; (Lyndon Johnson, Richard Nixon, Gerald Ford, Jimmy Carter), but two shall be kept until the end. (Ronald Reagan, Barack Hussein Obama)

22 As for your seeing three heads at rest, this is the interpretation:

23 In its last days, the Most High will raise three kings (George H Bush, Bill Clinton, George W. Bush), and they shall renew many things in it, and shall rule the earth

24 and its inhabitants more oppressively than all who were before them; therefore, they are called the heads of the eagle. (From verses 21 & 22 If we add 2 wings + 4 wings + 2 wings + 3 heads = 11, keep this number in mind as it correlates with the prophecy of Daniel 7:8, the 10 horns then come, another 1 from among them for a total of 11. Also, counting backward from the 44th president, we subtract 11 presidents we reach Dwight Eisenhower. So, from Eisenhower to Obama, we have a total of 11. This also aligns with chapter 11:26 & 27 and chapter 12:21).

25 For it is they who shall sum up his wickedness and perform his last actions. (As you can see for yourself again, the right/Republicans and the left/Democrats were all involved in the same godless scheme, and God has had enough.)

26 As for your seeing that the large head disappeared, one of the kings shall die in his bed, but in agonies. (On June 5, 2004, Ronald Reagan died from pneumonia, a common complication of Alzheimer's disease, in his bed and great agony.)

27 But as for the two who remained, the sword shall devour them (Obama/Biden).

28 For the sword of one (Obama) shall devour him (Bidden) who was with him (Were allied at one point, the problem is that most people don't know who Obama is but they will soon find out the hard way.); but he (Obama) also shall fall by the sword in the last days.

29 As for your seeing two little wings (Obama/Biden) passing over to the head, which was on the right side, (George W. Bush)

30 This is the interpretation: It is these whom the Most High has kept for the eagle's end; (2 Thessalonians 2:7-8, 7 For the mystery of iniquity doth already work: only he who now letteth will let, until he be

taken out of the way. 8 And then shall that Wicked be revealed, whom the Lord shall consume with the spirit of his mouth, and shall destroy with the brightness of his coming:)

This was the reign that was brief and full of tumult, as you have seen. (The 44th and last presidency when Spiritual Judgement takes place. THEN comes the physical. Notice that 44, 4+4=8, the number 8 signifies a new beginning, the 8th day of the week in Secrets of Enoch 33:1, depicting the 8th millennium will be a time of "not counting, endless", Enoch 93:12-14, the beginning of the 8th millennium in where judgment is executed. The year 2008 was also the year when Obama/Biden, the last 2 left wings, began their presidential campaign. Coincidence? Not, God is PERFECTION and He numbers everything, this is purposefully done for our benefit, not His. Take heed!)

31 And as for the lion whom you saw rousing up out of the forest and roaring and speaking to the eagle and reproving him for his unrighteousness, and as for all his words that you have heard,

32 This is the Messiah whom the Most High has kept until the end of days, who will arise from the posterity of David, and will come and speak to them; he will denounce them for their ungodliness and their wickedness, and will cast up before them their contemptuous dealings. (Judgment seat of Christ)

33 First, he will set them living before his judgment seat, and when he has reproved them, then he will destroy them.

34 But he will deliver in mercy the remnant of my people (The few that remain, the Elect.), those who have been saved throughout my borders, and he will make them joyful until the end comes, the day of judgment, of which I spoke to you at the beginning.

35 This is the dream that you saw, and this is its interpretation.

36 And you alone were worthy to learn this secret of the Most High.

37 Therefore, write all these things that you have seen in a book, and put them in a hidden place;

38 and you shall teach them to the wise among your people, whose hearts you know can comprehend and keep these secrets.

39 But wait here seven days more, so that you may be shown whatever it pleases the Most High to show you. Then he left me.

Now that this prophecy is clearly understood, let us proceed to Daniel 7 (The Vision of the Fourth Beast) and dispel the many myths and improper interpretations circulating about this prophecy. Remember that God is not the author of confusion, and no prophecy can contradict another. They must all align perfectly; even if different visions and interpretations are given by God, they must all have the same conclusion. Just as 3+2=5, 4+1=5, 3 ½ + 1 ½=5. No matter which way you put it, the outcome is still 5.

You should be seeing much clearer now and know that the eagle in this prophecy is the US government, down to the precise number of presidencies. That Obama is the 44th and last president, and what has and will occur in detail, marks the Spiritual Judgement FIRST, then comes the physical. Since this prophecy and Daniel's prophecy of the fourth beast share the same conclusion, then obviously means that the fourth beast in Daniel 7 is none other than the US government. And trust me, just like many of God's Elect, I have been the victim of a CIA government watchlist, MK Ultra Mind Control, Gang Stalking, Gas Lighting, Poisoning, witchcraft attacks, attempted Murder MANY TIMES (so many I lost count), and MUCH, MUCH MORE!

Surprised? Don't be! For those of us who have been victims of the US Government's deceitful and illicit practices, this comes as no surprise. But it is comforting to know that although we've been called everything from conspiracy nut case to psycho, the All-Mighty God Himself has redeemed us from the harsh words in which we are constantly subjected to. Very comforting! So what are they going to say now, that God is a conspiracy nut case too? Stop your willful ignorance, my people, WAKE UP!!!

Chapter 11

Daniel 7 (The Vision of the Fourth Beast)

1 In the first year of Belshazzar, king of Babylon, Daniel had a dream and visions in his head upon his bed then he wrote the dream, and told the sum of the matters.

2 Daniel spake and said, I saw in my vision by night, and, behold, the four winds of the heaven strove upon the great sea.

3 And four great beasts came up from the sea, diverse from one another.

4 The first was like a lion, and had eagle's wings: I beheld till the wings thereof were plucked, and it was lifted from the earth, and made stand upon the feet as a man, and a man's heart was given to it.

5 And behold another beast, a second, like to a bear, and it raised itself on one side, and it had three ribs in the mouth of it between the teeth of it: and they said thus unto it, arise, devour much flesh.

6 After this, I beheld, and lo, another, like a leopard, which had upon the back of it four wings of a fowl; the beast had also four heads; and dominion was given to it.

7 After this, I saw in the night visions, and behold a fourth beast, dreadful, and strong exceedingly; and it had great iron teeth: it devoured and brake in pieces, and stamped the residue with the feet of it: (The US armed forces and nuclear capabilities are much superior to any other nation. Its Air Force dominates and makes it dreadful in war. When the US military goes to war, first it strikes its opponent with its superior Air Force, then once the opponent is weakened, the

foot soldiers are sent in, stamped the residue with the feet of it. This is why in 2 Esdras 11 & 12, this beast is referred to as the eagle. Because its superior Air Force dominates the sky. Remember the slogan coined by the Apollo 11 astronauts when they landed on the moon and planted the American flag on it? "The Eagle has landed.)

And it was diverse from all the beasts that were before it; (Compared to all the beasts/governments before it, that not only physically afflicted its victims, this beast/government has made people spiritually captive with its system of confusion, the Babylonian system of government.) And it had ten horns. (10 kings/presidents)

8 I considered the horns (the 10 kings/presidents) and, behold, there came up among them another little horn, (another king/president for a total of 11 kings/presidents. The same number as the prophecy of the Eagle and the Lion in 2 Esdras 12:21-22, 2+4+2+3=11, from Dwight Eisenhower to George W. Bush there are 10 presidents plus 1 Barack Hussein Obama, for a total of 11) Before whom there were three of the first horns plucked up by the roots: (Those running against him in the 2008 – 2009 presidential elections had no chance of defeating him.)

And, behold, in this horn were eyes like the eyes of a man, (In Hebrew, the phrase eyes like the eyes of a man simply means that he looks like a man, but in reality is not a regular man.

In the book the Ascension of Isaiah 4:1-2 it reads, And now Hezekiah and Josab my son, these are the days of the completion of the world. 2 After it is consummated, Beliar (Another name for Satan) the great ruler, the king of this world, will descend, who hath ruled it since it came into being yea, he will descend from his firmament in the likeness of a man

Remember, we are not dealing with a regular man we are dealing with the Arch Fallen Angel. He may look like a regular man, but he's not. It's not the physical that makes him different, but the spirit indwelling him and angelic genes, which are his primal origin.

And a mouth speaking great things. (I don't think I need to elaborate on what a great speaker and a cunning liar Obama is. I believe we are all well aware of the fact.)

9 I beheld till the thrones were cast down, and the Ancient of days did sit, whose garment was white as snow, and the hair of his head like the pure wool: his throne was like the fiery flame, and his wheels as burning fire.

10 A fiery stream issued and came forth from before him: thousand thousands ministered unto him, and ten thousand times ten thousand stood before him the judgment was set, and the books were opened. (Judgment was completed; now God begins the sentencing phase.)

11I beheld then because of the voice of the great words which the horn spake: I beheld even till the beast was slain, and his body destroyed, and given to the burning flame. (Notice that he is still speaking great words/lies when suddenly the beast/eagle is slain and his body destroyed with burning flame (Again, Spiritual first, then the physical). This aligns perfectly with 2 Esdras 12:13, the last reign/presidency, which is a short and troubled one, towards the end of their (Obama/Biden) Spiritual Judgement BEGAN.

12 As concerning the rest of the beasts, they had their dominion taken away yet their lives were prolonged for a season and time. (The rest of the governments around the world had their power taken away from them, but were allowed to continue for a longer time than the fourth beast. Notice that the fourth beast (The eagle is the

first one to be burned. Remember, judgment begins with God's people. Again, Spiritual first, then the physical manifestation.)

13 I saw in the night visions, and, behold, one like the Son of man came with the clouds of heaven, and came to the Ancient of days, and they brought him near before him.

14 And there was given him dominion, and glory, and a kingdom, that all people, nations, and languages, should serve him: his dominion is an everlasting dominion, which shall not pass away, and his kingdom that which shall not be destroyed. (God the Father hands over dominion of the earth to the MESSIAH. The MESSIAH then sets up the Kingdom of God on earth, a kingdom that will remain forever.)

15 I, Daniel, was grieved in my spirit by my body, and the visions of my head troubled me.

16 I came near unto one of them that stood by, and asked him the truth of all this. So he told me, and made me know the interpretation of the things.

17 These great beasts, which are four, are four kings (Kingdoms), which shall arise out of the earth.

18 But the saints of the Most High shall take the kingdom, and possess the kingdom forever, even forever and ever.

19 Then I would know the truth of the fourth beast, which was diverse from all the others, exceeding dreadful, whose teeth were of iron, and his nails of brass; which devoured, broke in pieces, and stamped the residue with his feet; (US government)

20 And of the ten horns (Eisenhower – Bush 10) that were in his head, and of the other (Obama 11) which came up, and before

whom three fell; even of that horn that had eyes (Looked like a man, the likeness of a man),

and a mouth that spake very great things (One of the main characteristics that Daniel describes is his mouth speaking great things meaning lies and blasphemy. Keep in mind that he is a liar and a murderer from the beginning and never abode in the truth.), whose look was more stout (which means: Strong; great. The roaring of the lion, and the voice of the fierce lion,. Your adversary the devil roams around as a roaring lion seeking whom he may devour.) than his fellows.

21 I beheld, and the same horn (the 11th Obama) made war with the saints, and prevailed against them (Bingo! He is the one we must watch out for.. Unfortunately, due to unbelief, a lot of the saints are going to go through a very hard time.)

22 Until the Ancient of days came, and judgment was given to the saints of the most High; and the time came that the saints possessed the kingdom. (Notice that Obama makes war with the saints and prevails until the Lord puts an end to his reign.)

Matthew 24:   21-22,

21 For then shall be great tribulation, such as was not since the beginning of the world to this time, no, nor ever shall be.

22 And except those days should be shortened, there should no flesh be saved but for the elect's sake those days shall be shortened.

2 Thessalonians 2:8-9,

8 And then shall that Wicked be revealed, whom the Lord shall consume with the spirit of his mouth, and shall destroy with the brightness of his coming:

9 Even him, whose coming is after the working (engineered, genetically manipulated by the Watchers) of Satan with all power and signs and lying wonders,

23 Thus he said, the fourth beast shall be the fourth kingdom upon earth, which shall be diverse (Diverse because the main method of operation of this beast is deception.) from all kingdoms, and shall devour the whole earth, and shall tread it down, and break it in pieces   .

24 And the ten horns out of this kingdom are ten kings that shall arise (Eisenhower Bush 10): and another shall rise after them (In turn, succession, one king after the other, not all at once! The popular notion throughout mainstream Christianity is that this is 10 nations emerging out of the European Union, the Holy Roman Empire led by Germany, the Catholic Church, you name it, and I've heard it! The point is that all of those are private interpretations, something 2 Peter 1:20 warns us not to do. Use Scripture to interpret Scripture. It is clear that the 10 horns are 10 kings that shall arise out of this kingdom, and another shall arise AFTER them.

Epistle of Barnabas 3:5-6,

5 For so the prophet speaks; There shall 10 kings reign in the heart, and there shall arise last of all another little one, and he shall humble three kings.

6 And again Daniel speaks in like manner concerning the kingdoms; and I saw the fourth beast dreadful, and strong exceedingly and it had 10 horns. I considered the horns, and behold, there came up among them another little horn, before which were three of the first horns plucked up by the roots.)

And he (The 11ᵗʰ Obama) shall be diverse from the first (Diverse: from the Hebrew word, shena, shen-aw to change or alter i.e., from a Fallen Angel to the likeness of a man, Obama the 11ᵗʰ⋅) and he shall subdue three kings.

25 And he shall speak great words against the Most High (This Obama has already done. For proof of it go to your favorite Internet search engine and look at it for yourself.), and shall wear out (In the Old Testament Hebrew lexicon: wear out is Balah: to wear away, wear out to harass constantly (fig.) wear down, as in a mental state. i.e., Gang stalking, Gas Lighting, MK Ultra Mind Control, Poisoning, BLAH BLAH BLAH. You get the point!) The saints of the Most High, and think to change times and laws (Do you remember the slogan of his presidential campaign? That's right, CHANGE! And YES WE CAN, Which by the way means THANK YOU SATAN when played in reverse. As far as laws, he is changing them daily. Just look at how much damage he has created in a few months   .

And they shall be given into his hand until a time and times and the dividing of time (3 ½ years, this aligns perfectly with 2 Esdras 12:1-3 speaking of the last two left wings/Democrats (Obama/Biden) short reign and full of trouble. Also, Revelation 13:5 says that the beast was allowed to continue for another 42 months. Remember, Spiritual Judgement takes place FIRST; then comes the physical. 26 But the judgment shall sit, and they shall take away his dominion, to consume and to destroy it unto the end.

27 And the kingdom and dominion, and the greatness of the kingdom under the whole heaven, shall be given to the people of the saints of the Most High, whose kingdom is an everlasting kingdom, and all dominions shall serve and obey him.

28 Hitherto is the end of the matter. As for me, Daniel, my cogitations much troubled me, and my countenance changed in me: but I kept the matter in my heart.

We have compared 2 Esdras 11 & 12, The Vision of the Eagle and the Lion, and Daniel 7, The Vision of the Fourth Beast. We know it is the same vision. We know there will only be 44 presidencies; the last 10 presidents (Eisenhower – Bush) mark the end time of this kingdom. We know the 11th (Obama) is a one-term president, and towards the end of his first term, a nuclear disaster will occur in the United States. We know that he is the one we need to watch closely. We also know there is no such thing as right-wing/Republican or left-wing/Democrats; they all have the same agenda and are controlled by their Master.

Remember 3+2=5, 4+1=5, 3 ½ + 1 ½ =5, no matter which way you put it, it is still 5.

Now that we have such vital information, we are able to direct our focus to the 44th president, the 11th horn, Barack Hussein Obama! We need to thoroughly examine what the Almighty God says about him in the Scriptures, then move on to Revelation 17 & 18 to see this amazing prophecy being fulfilled before your very eyes.

Chapter 12

Who is Barack Hussein Obama?

So, who is Barack Hussein Obama? Every name in the Bible has a specific significance. For example: Abraham (father of multitudes), Sarah (mother of many multitudes), Israel (prince that prevails with God), Jeshua (He will be saved), etc.

We name our children just because we like the name. God names people according to their mission. Since Satan is archenemy number one of God and humanity, is it not logical to conclude that, apart from the many prophecies depicting his every move, God would also reveal to us his name when he comes to earth in the likeness of a man? After all, the first way to identify someone is by name. An interesting fact to note is that the Hebrews use a technique called play on words to teach a truth or to get a message across. This is often done with the names of people. Knowing this information, let's start with his name, Barack Hussein Obama.

Luke 10:18, an often overlooked verse in Scripture, Jesus Christ says the following I beheld Satan as lightning fall from heaven. The Old Testament is written in Hebrew, and the New Testament is written in Greek. However, Jesus Christ is a Jew according to the flesh, meaning he did not speak Greek he spoke Aramaic, which is an older form of Hebrew. In the original Hebrew language, the word for lightning is barack. In other words, Luke 10:18 should read, "I beheld Satan as Barack fall from heaven.

In Isaiah 14:12-14, we read, How thou art fallen from heaven, O Lucifer, son of the morning! You are cut down to the ground, you who did weaken the nations. You said in your heart, I will ascend into heaven. I will exalt my throne above the stars of God. I will also sit on the Mount of the Congregation on the farthest sides of the north (North what? North America!). I will ascend above the heights of the clouds and be like the Most High.

The Hebrew word for heights/heavens is bama. The conjunction letter that joins the thoughts of lightning and heights is pronounced U or O, thus read as Barack Obama

Furthermore, in Ezekiel 20, God speaks to the children of Israel and reproves them for a number of violations against God's commandments. One of the things the children of Israel did was make a high place of idolatrous worship. Notice verses 28-29; 28 For when I had brought them into the land, for the which I lifted mine hand to give it to them, then they saw every high hill, and all the thick trees, and they offered there their sacrifices, and there they presented the provocation of their offering: there also they made their sweet savour, and poured out there their drink offerings. 29 Then I said unto them, What is the high place whereunto ye go? And the name thereof is called Bamah unto this day. This means that Bamah is also a proper pronoun (name) of a high place of idolatrous worship, unto this day.

Revelation 13:18 reads: Here is wisdom. Let him that hath understanding count the number of the beast: for it is the number of a man; and his number is Six hundred threescore and six (666). Well, if you calculate 6+6+6 = 18. And there are 18 letters in BARACK HUSSEIN OBAMA. It is interesting to note that this is found in verse 18 (8+1=9), there are 18 letters in his name (8+1=9), and he took office in the year 09. In occult numerology, three 9's indicate finality. Three 9's are also an inverted 666.

On October 9, 2009, in his ninth month in office, Barack Hussein Obama was awarded the Nobel Peace Prize. The world was in shock that a man who had done nothing was given such an honor and a high award. The question heard around the world that day was, What did he do to deserve this award? The answer to that question is a spiritual one. This man, who is worshiped by many of the subjects, is now known as the man of peace.

The Scriptures tell us that a man of peace would rise in the last days and destroy many. In Daniel 8:25 we read as follows: and through his policy also he shall cause craft to prosper in his hand (i.e. Gang stalking, Gas Lighting, MK Ultra Mind Control, Poisoning, BLAH BLAH BLAH. You get the point!); and he shall magnify himself in his heart, and by peace he shall destroy many he should also stand up against the Prince of princes; but he shall be broken without hand. In Jeremiah 6:14, we also read the following They have healed also the hurt of the daughter of my people slightly, saying peace, peace; when there is no peace. We must also take note of 1 Thessalonians 5:3 as follows: For when they shall say, peace and safety; then sudden destruction cometh upon them, as travail upon a woman with child; and they shall not escape.

Let it be noted that the Eternal God gave us a definite sign to watch for regarding the coming of the man of false peace. He described the coming of this man with his destructive peace as a woman in travail and giving birth. The human gestation period is nine months, and Obama received the peace prize during his ninth month in office. It was also stated that Obama received the prize not for what he has done, but for what he is going to do. Obama is now being referred to by the news media as the seed of peace. (Dave Meyer, The Last Trumpet 2010)

Before we continue, let us recap what we have learned so far. From 2 Esdras 11 & 12, The Vision of the Eagle and the Lion, we learn several key things. The eagle is the US Government. There are only 44 presidencies. The Eagle burst into flames towards the end of the 44th presidency, which is only a 1 term presidency.

2 Esdras 12:20-23 gives us a time frame of when the last 11 presidents begin to reign (Eisenhower – Obama). We know these presidents take office in turn, not all at once. This is the same prophecy as the prophecy of the Fourth Beast in Daniel 7.

From Daniel 7, The Vision of the Fourth Beast, we know the fourth beast is the US Government. We know there are 10 horns/presidents (Eisenhower – Bush) and the 11th one (Obama) is the last, most evil, and wages war against the saints.

In the Apocalypse of Abraham 13, part 2, pg. 53 The Angel of the Lord speaking to Satan says: For God, the Eternal, Mighty One hath not permitted that the bodies of the righteous should be in thy hand, so that thereby the life of the righteous and the destruction of the unclean may be assured. Here, friend, begone with shame from me. For it hath not been given to thee to play the tempter regarding all the righteous. Depart from this man (Abraham) thou canst not lead him astray, because he is an enemy to thee, and of those who follow thee and love what thou willest. For, behold, the vesture which in heaven was formerly thine hath been set aside for him (Abraham), and the mortality which was his hath been transferred to thee (Satan).

In the Ascension of Isaiah 4:1-2, it reads: And now Hezekiah and Josab, my son, these are the days of the completion of the world. After it is consummated, Beliar (Another name for Satan) the great ruler, the King of this world, will descend, who hath ruled it since it came into being (Since the beginning of time); yea, he will descend from his firmament in the likeness of a man (eyes like the eyes of man, in human manipulated DNA) a lawless king.

God took on human flesh through the power of the Holy Spirit in the form of Jesus Christ. But Satan has taken on human flesh through human genetic manipulation in the form of Barack Hussein Obama! Remember, Satan has always wanted to be like the Most High. This should not take us by surprise. We know that the Watchers/Fallen Angels have been manipulating Human Genetics/DNA from the very beginning. This is why God made so many references throughout Scripture of the seed, the seed! God was simply referring to DNA, the Genetic Blueprint! Satan knew God's plan from the very beginning, and he tried to thwart it by causing Eve to sin. This is why God commanded the children of Israel to marry within their people and never to marry people of other nations, and would get so angry when they would not listen. God was simply preserving a pure strand of DNA that would serve His purpose reserved for the coming of the Messiah.

In light of these prophecies, using a little common sense and simple math, we know the meaning of his name, the number of his name, that he is the 44th president, and the 11th horn in Daniel. It is extremely clear that Satan has taken on human flesh, and we see him as Barack Hussein Obama. Now we can understand why so many prophecies refer to Satan as a man. It is because, according to the flesh, we simply see a man, eyes like the eyes of man, in the likeness of a man as Barack Hussein Obama. But the spirit indwelling him and the angelic primal/human manipulated genetic makeup (The seed of Satan) is Satan himself! For illustrative purposes, think of this it is the same concept as when the Word of God became flesh in the form of our Lord and Savior Jesus Christ.

Only God did it through His power, and Satan has now done it through his manipulations. After all, Satan has always wanted to imitate God!

Now, let us examine the prophecies that describe this evil and lawless fallen Archangel who became Satan.

This evil tyrant, will do as he pleases; he will magnify himself (he has a terrible case of inflated vanity and supreme egotism!) Above every god, and will speak awful things against the God of gods. You must see the videos of Obama on YouTube mocking and speaking against the Bible. It is truly mind-blowing to see these prophecies being fulfilled in every detail. He will prosper until the wrath is spent, and what has been decreed is accomplished. (Daniel 11:36) This describes why Obama is so wrapped up in himself, cloaked in vanity with a supreme ego.

Daniel goes on to describe Obama as a flattering, insincere, very savvy King, an end time political figure also referred to as a contemptible man (Daniel 11:21), or a vile person (NKJV), a despicable creature" (Moffatt translation), of course, he is a genetic manipulation of Satan, who will come in unawares and seize the kingdom through trickery. intrigue (NKJV). He will gain the position of leadership by cunning wisdom and sleight-of-hand, using deceitful, underhanded, and devious means (Daniel 11:21). Using specious promises, he shall pervert those who bring guilt upon the nation. (Moffatt translation) (Daniel 11:32)

Obama embraces all religions, and while trying to appear to be good, he continually embraces evil. He is the end time King of the North of Daniel 11:21-36, who is a vile person who comes in peaceably (winner of a Nobel Peace Prize) and seizes the kingdom by intrigue (v.21), the little horn of Daniel 7:25 who intends to change times and laws. The end time anti-Messiah, the wicked one who comes in the place of Christ. A false, proud, arrogant, stern-faced dictator having fierce features. (Daniel 8:23-25). The great, lying orator, who is engineered genetically and put in office by Satan, the Devil, who is indwelling him, the god of this world.

Barack Hussein Obama (Satan in the flesh) came out of nowhere, for even his place of birth is in question, and became president of the United States through numerous well orchestrated and preplanned trickeries, deceits, blandishments, smiles, charisma, promises, chants, slogans, songs, spellbinding mass hypnotism, illusion, magic, perversion, and extreme fraud. (William F. Dankenbring, Prophecy Flash 2010)

The world has been deceived! Satan has come in the flesh, and prophecy will show the conclusion of this diabolical hoax portrayed on humanity. How's that Hope and Change working out for you now, America? Since they refused the knowledge of the truth, now they will have to bear the consequences of the lie!

God's people can now understand why almost all the prophecies concerning the Lawless One warned us about him speaking great swelling words and blasphemies. Of course, he is a liar and a murderer from the beginning. He never abode in the truth! I have heard many radio and TV commentators say that they have never seen anyone lie and twist words as well as Barack Hussein Obama. Of course not, they have absolutely no idea who he is, or they are part of his team and just playing right along, according to their diabolical doctrine. Remember that by this point and time in history, you only fall into two categories   either you had formerly been deceived (but now know the truth), or you are part of the deception. He is the father of lies, the originator of trickery, the great evil orator, the master of deceit! There is no truth in him!

Now that we know exactly who Barack Hussein Obama is, let's continue to look at the other prophecies and see what he is doing and will do.

Ascension of Isaiah 4:1-13

1 And now Hezekiah and Josab, my son, these are the days of the completion of the world.

2 After it is consummated, Beliar (another name for Satan), the great ruler, the King of this world, will descend, who hath ruled it since it came into being; (Notice that he has been in charge of the affairs of this world from the beginning. He was the one who created the current form of government, and since he created it, he knows exactly how to dismantle it without being stopped, which is exactly what he is doing.)

Yea, he will descend from his firmament in the likeness of a man (eyes like the eyes of man, taking on genetically manipulated human flesh) a Lawless King (The only law he truly believes in is his law.),

the slayer of his mother (It is reported that Obama's mother Ann Dunham died of ovarian cancer. What a coincidence, ovarian cancer! What caused the ovarian cancer? Scripture tells us that Obama was genetically engineered by Satan. Knowing the genetic manipulation she underwent, it is no surprise that the path through were her 'son' would be born (ovaries) became cancerous, which affected (the King) as well.

3 Will persecute the plant (the people of God) which the 12 apostles of the Beloved (Jesus Christ) have planted. Of the 12 (tribes of Israel), one will be delivered into his hands. (One of the 12 tribes of Israel will be destroyed by him. This is why the tribe of Dan is not mentioned as being sealed in the end time and is missing in Revelation 7.)

4 This ruler in the form (likeness) of that King (president) will come, and there will come with them all the powers of this world, and they will hearken unto him in all that he desireth. (He is very powerful. His Daddy Satan inspired him.)

5 And at his word the sun will rise at night, and he will make the moon appear at the sixth hour (This is an expression that means total confusion among the people.)

6 And all that he hath desired he will do in the world: he will do and speak like the Beloved, and he will say: I am God and before me there hath been none.

7 And all the people in the world will believe him.

8 And they will sacrifice to him and they will serve him, saying, "This is God and beside him there is no other."

9 And the greater number of those who shall have been associated to receive the Beloved, he will turn after him. (Unfortunately, a great number of believers in Christ will be deceived.)

10 And there will be the power of his miracles in every city and region.

11 And he will set up his image before him in every city. (TV ads, newspapers, magazines, posters, etc.) Before his presidential election and during his reign   .

12 And he shall bear sway 3 years and 7 months and 27 days (This timeline aligns perfectly with 2 Esdras 12 short reign and full of trouble, Daniel 7 3 1/2 years, Daniel 12 1290 days, and Revelation 13 42 months) The time when Spiritual Judgment begins.

13 And many believers and Saints having seen him for whom they were hoping who was crucified, Jesus the Lord Christ, [after that I, Isaiah, had seen Him who was crucified and ascended] and those also who were believers in Him, of these few in those days will be left as His servants, while they flee from desert to desert (The physical persecution against God's people was be very intense both physically and spiritually. I along with many of God's Elect are living proof of this.), awaiting the coming of the Beloved.

Revelation 13

1 And I stood upon the sand of the sea, and saw a beast rise out of the sea (A satanic empowered government),

having seven heads (It is necessary to understand that the Federal Reserve is a privately owned bank, and they are not a branch of any federal government. However, these private banks are owned and controlled by some of the richest and most powerful people in the world, who, in turn, control the government, the Illuminati.

The Illuminati, through international banks, in turn, control governmental policies around the world. Their end time goal is to bring all the inhabitants of the world into a complete satanic dictatorship, headed by Satan in the flesh, Barack Hussein Obama. These Federal Reserve banks have a total government-enforced monopoly using dollar bills as their means of controlling the masses. They systematically dictate times of prosperity, depressions, inflation, sudden economic collapses, etc. Knowing that the beast is the US government, and through the Federal Reserve, they use dollar bills to control the country. Notice that there are seven denominations of dollar bills in circulation. The $1, $2, $5, $10, $20, $50, and $100. In front of each bill, there is a head, a beast rises out of the sea, having seven heads.)

And ten horns, and upon his horns ten crowns (Eisenhower – Bush, 10 crowns are a sign of power/kingship/president), and upon his heads the name of blasphemy (In front of each of the seven dollar bills in circulation there is a head with the letters engraved in the back of each bill In God we trust. What god? The god they swore allegiance to was the god of this world, Satan. God considers this blasphemy!)

2 And the beast which I saw was like unto a leopard, and his feet were as the feet of a bear, and his mouth as the mouth of a lion (Characteristics of all previous superpowers rolled up into one.): and the dragon (Satan) gave him (US government) his power, and his seat, and great authority (Government now a superpower).

3 And I saw one of his heads as it were wounded to death (Financial depression of 1939); and his deadly wound was healed (Financial recovery, compare to 2 Esdras 12:17-18 kingdom in danger of falling but recovers): and all the world wondered after the beast. (Democracy/capitalism, the Babylonian system of finance, the Way of Cain)

4 And they worshipped the dragon (Satan, the creator of this system of government), which gave power unto the beast (US government): and they worshipped the beast, saying, Who is like unto the beast? Who can make war with him? (Who can beat the US military's power?)

5 And there was given unto him a mouth speaking great things and blasphemies (the US government has a prideful evil spirit leading it and does not want anything to do with God and rejects His Law);

And power was given unto him to continue forty and two months. (This marks the time of the end of the 10th horn's reign (Bush), same as the last head on the right in 2 Esdras 12:2, the 43rd president. Now, the 11th horn (the little horn) in Daniel 7 is allowed to continue for another 42 months. Same as 2 Esdras 12:2, the last two left wings (Obama/Biden), the 44th presidency's short and troubled reign. Then began Spiritual Judgement)

6 And he (US government) opened his mouth in blasphemy against God, to blaspheme his name, and his tabernacle, and them that dwell in heaven.

7 And it was given unto him to make war with the saints, and to overcome them (The main method of war employed is spiritual through deception. The main weapon used against the people is a Satan induced financial system to enslave the masses. Ephesians 6:12, For we do not wrestle against flesh and blood, but against principalities, against powers, against the rulers of the darkness of this age, against spiritual hosts of wickedness in the heavenly places.)

And power was given him over all kindreds, and tongues, and nations. (This financial system has enslaved the world.)

8 And all that dwells upon the earth shall worship him, whose names are not written in the book of life of the Lamb slain from the foundation of the world. (If anyone desires any other type of government, including this democracy/capitalism with its system of finance, rather than the one God gave Moses, that person will very soon reap the consequences.)

9 If any man has an ear, let him hear. (This is an encoded message able to be deciphered only by the revelation of the Holy Spirit.)

10 He that leadeth into captivity shall go into captivity: he that killeth with the sword must be killed with the sword. Here is the patience and the faith of the saints.

11 And I beheld another beast coming up out of the earth (The 11th one, the little horn in Daniel 7, Obama); and he had two horns like a lamb (He looks innocent), and he spake as a dragon (As Satan in the flesh with great authority).

12 And he exerciseth all the power of the first beast before him, and causeth the earth and them which dwell therein to worship the first beast, whose deadly wound was healed (Obama is now exercising all the power given to him as president of the United States to change existing laws and purposefully and systematically changing the Democratic/Capitalist form of government the United States has been governed under since its founding. By introducing a Marxist/Communist form of government that the American people do not want, he is causing the people to focus all their attention and apply all their effort to restore their former form of government. Thereby, spiritually worshipping the Democratic/Capitalist form of government (the first beast before him, and causeth the earth and them which dwell therein to worship the first beast, whose deadly wound was healed); The Capitalist type of government, which once recovered from a financial depression/deadly wound.

However, in reality, Satan is the one who created all human forms of government, so if you turn to the right (to desire capitalism) or turn to the left (to desire communism), he's got you! You are spiritually worshiping systems of governing that he created. All of which are contrary to God's system of governing. Remember the right/left scheme which is also the Illuminati/Freemason/Mammon Ra's emblem of the eagle with the two heads facing opposite ways and their twisted Luciferian Doctrine (right/left, thesis/anti-thesis, positive/negative, as above, so below, order out of chaos, earth is to be hell and hell on earth). It is the same beast with opposing heads. Nonetheless, it is the same BEAST!!!

This is why we read in Revelation 12:9, And the great dragon was cast out, that old serpent called the Devil, and Satan, which deceiveth the whole world. Unfortunately, a lot of people are being deceived and ignorantly believe that this current system of government (capitalism) is approved by God. Most are unaware that this is exactly what the Scriptures call the Way of Cain and the error of Balaam the son of Peor, as we shall explore later. It is a governmental system of greed and covetousness. Please understand that any form of government, whether it is a democracy, capitalism, communism, etc, is not the form of government that God originally gave Moses; therefore, it is contrary to the Law. This has all to do with GOVERNMENT, not RELIGION!!! I cannot stress this fact enough! Do not let Satan deceive you into believing otherwise! Study the Law and you will learn the will of God.)

13 And he doeth great wonders, so that he maketh fire come down from heaven on the earth in the sight of men, (This term used can mean that because of his doings, God's wrath is falling on the earth. Or this may be that the writer of Revelation, in a vision, actually saw an ordered military air invasion in which bombs are being dropped, he maketh fire come down from heaven.)

14 And deceiveth them that dwell on the earth (Notice that the method of operation is deception. Someone who is being deceived does not know he is being deceived, for had he known it would not be called a deception!)

Using those miracles (The use of the word miracles here is not what we would consider to be a miracle. The word translated as miracles here is the Greek word: semeion, say-mi'-on; (1) semeion is a manifest deed, having in itself an explanation of something hidden and secret. (2) It denotes a sign, mark, indication, token is used (2a) of that which distinguishes a person or thing from others. (Strong's

Concordance #4592) In other words, by the use of something hidden and secret, Satan has deceived the world.

Which he (Obama) had power to do in the sight of the beast (US government); saying to them that dwell on the earth, that they should make an image (A similitude, likeness, to their former form of government.) to the beast, which had the wound by a sword, and did live (This is where Obama will use all the laws to his benefit and dismantle the current system of government and use redistribution of wealth as an excuse to "climb out of the recession" meanwhile systematically impoverishing the United States to bring about a World Caliphate (Muslim World Empire and implement Sharia Law). (More on Islam Later)

15 And he had power to give life unto the image of the beast, that the image of the beast should both speak, and cause that as many as would not worship the image of the beast should be killed (Anyone who does not submit to Sharia Law will be killed.)

16 And he causeth all, both small and great, rich and poor, free and bond, to receive a mark in their right hand, or their foreheads: (And he causeth all This does not mean that this mark is something that Satan does only in the end time. This verse is simply telling us that this is also something else that he does. But keep in mind, he has ruled this earth from the very beginning, so this mark is something that he causeth all to progressively put on.)

17 And that no man might buy or sell, save he that had the mark, or the name of the beast, or the number of his name. (More on the mark of the beast later)

18 Here is wisdom. Let him that hath understanding count the number of the beast: for it is the number of a man; and his number is Six

hundred threescore and six. (6+6+6=18, there are 18 letters in the name Barack Hussein Obama)

Psalm 109

This Psalm, written by King David, inspired by the Holy Spirit, speaks not only of the end-time human enemies of Christ but also of the Watchers who are His principal enemies.

1 To the Chief Musician. A Psalm of David. Do not keep silent, O God of my praise!

2 For the mouth of the wicked and the mouth of the deceitful have opened against me; They have spoken against me with a lying tongue.

3 They have also surrounded me with words of hatred and fought against me without cause.

4 In return for my love, they are my accusers, but I give myself to prayer.

5 Thus, they have rewarded me evil for good, and hatred for my love.

6 Set a wicked man over him (Obama), and let an accuser stand at his right hand (Satan).

7 When he is judged, let him be found guilty, and let his prayer become sin.

8 Let his days be few, And let another take his office (Short reign and full of trouble).

9 Let his children be fatherless (Notice he has children), and his wife a widow (And a wife).

10 Let his children continually be vagabonds, and beg; Let them seek their bread also from their desolate places.

11 Let the creditor seize all that he has, and let strangers plunder his labor.

12 Let there be none to extend mercy to him, Nor let there be any to favor his fatherless children.

13 Let his posterity (seed,offspring) be cut off, and in the generation following let their name be blotted out.

14 Let the iniquity of his fathers (the Watchers) be remembered before the Lord, and let not the sin of his mother be blotted out. (The human genetic manipulation undergone by her.)

15 Let them be continually before the Lord, that He may cut off the memory of them (The Watchers) from the earth;

16 Because he (Satan) did not remember to show mercy, but persecuted the poor and needy man, that he might even slay the broken in heart.

17 As he loved cursing, so let it come to him; As he did not delight in blessing, so let it be far from him.

18 As he clothed himself with cursing as with his garment (Taking on human flesh), so let it enter his body like water, and like oil into his bones.

19 Let it be to him like the garment which covers him, and for a belt with which he girds himself continually (Satan completely indwelling him, a curse).

20 Let this be the Lord's reward to my accusers, and to those who speak evil against my person.

21 But You, O God the Lord, Deal with me for Your name's sake; Because Your mercy is good, deliver me.

22 For I am poor and needy, and my heart is wounded within me.

23 I am gone like a shadow when it lengthens; I am shaken off like a locust.

24 My knees are weak through fasting, and my flesh is feeble from lack of fatness.

25 I also have become a reproach to them; When they look at me, they shake their heads.

26 Help me, O Lord my God! Oh, save me according to Your mercy,

27 That they may know that this is Your hand-- That You, Lord, have done it!

28 Let them curse, but You bless; When they arise (the Watchers), let them be ashamed, But let Your servant rejoice.

29 Let my accusers be clothed with shame, And let them cover themselves with their disgrace as with a mantle (Human Genetic Manipulation, altered DNA).

30 I will greatly praise the Lord with my mouth; Yes, I will praise Him among the multitude.

31 For He shall stand at the right hand of the poor, To save him from those who condemn him.

Isaiah 14:1–24

1 For the Lord will have mercy on Jacob, and will still choose Israel, and settle them in their land. The strangers will be joined with them, and they will cling to the house of Jacob.

2 Then people will take them and bring them to their place, and the house of Israel will possess them for servants and maids in the land of the Lord; they will take them captive, whose captives they were, and rule over their oppressors.

3 It shall come to pass in the day the Lord gives you rest from your sorrow, and from your fear and the hard bondage in which you were made to serve,

4 that you will take up this proverb against the king of Babylon (Obama), and say: "How the oppressor has ceased, the golden city ceased!

5 The Lord has broken the staff of the wicked, The scepter of the rulers;

6 He (Satan, also known in the flesh as Obama), who struck the people in wrath with a continual stroke, He who ruled the nations in anger (Has been in charge since the beginning of time), is persecuted, and no one hinders.

7 The whole earth is at rest and quiet They break forth into singing.

8 Indeed the cypress trees rejoice over you, And the cedars of Lebanon, Saying, 'Since you were cut down, No woodsman has come up against us (What are dollar bills made of? Linen based paper! And paper comes from trees! That is why even the trees rejoice at his fall because no one is going to cut them down anymore.)

9 Hell from beneath is excited about you, to meet you at your coming

(Revelation 20:1-2)

1 "And I saw an angel come down from heaven, having the key of the bottomless pit and a great chain in his hand.

2 And he laid hold on the dragon, that old serpent, which is the Devil, and Satan, and bound him a thousand years,

3 And cast him into the bottomless pit, and shut him up, and set a seal upon him, that he should deceive the nations no more, till the thousand years should be fulfilled)It stirs up the dead for you, all the chief ones of the earth It has raised from their thrones all the kings of the nations.

10 They all shall speak and say to you: 'Have you also become as weak as we? Have you become like us?

11 Your pomp is brought down to Sheol, And the sound of your stringed instruments; The maggot is spread under you, And worms cover you.' (Satan will be bound for 1000 the flesh he used to manifest himself in will be gone.)

12 How you have fallen from heaven, O Lucifer, son of the morning! How you are cut down to the ground, you who weakened the nations!

13 For you have said in your heart: 'I will ascend into heaven, I will exalt my throne above the stars of God; I will also sit on the mount of the congregation on the farthest sides of the north (North America);

14 I will ascend above the heights of the clouds ("o" bama), I will be like the Most High.'

15 Yet you shall be brought down to Sheol, to the lowest depths of the Pit.

16 Those who see you will gaze at you, and consider you, saying: 'Is this the man who made the earth tremble, who shook kingdoms,

17 Who made the world as a wilderness and destroyed its cities, who did not open the house of his prisoners?'

18 "All the kings of the nations, all of them, sleep in glory, everyone in his own house;

19 But you are cast out of your grave like an abominable branch (Genetically Manipulated DNA), like the garment of those who are slain, Thrust through with a sword, who go down to the stones of the pit, like a corpse trodden underfoot.

20 You will not be joined with them in burial, because you have destroyed your land and slain your people. The brood of evildoers (Children of the Watchers) shall never be named.

21 Prepare slaughter for his children, because of the iniquity of their fathers (the Watchers), lest they rise and possess the land, and fill the face of the world with cities (Take over the world).

22 For I will rise against them, says the Lord of hosts, And cut off from Babylon the name and remnant, and offspring and posterity (Of whom? The Watchers), says the Lord.

23 I will also make it a possession for the porcupine, and marshes of muddy water; I will sweep it with the broom of destruction (nuclear device), says the Lord of hosts.

24 The Lord of hosts has sworn, saying, Surely, as I have thought, so it shall come to pass, And as I have purposed, so it shall stand (God will surely bring it to pass.)

Daniel 8:23-26

23 And in the latter time of their kingdom, when the transgressors have reached their fullness (Sin has reached its limit), A king shall arise, having fierce features, who understands sinister schemes (You

think Obama does not know what he is doing? The problem is that he is such a good deceiver that he makes people believe that he is just an incompetent president who just does not know what he is doing. Now everything he did is coming to the light. All the lies and deception are being found out.

24 His power shall be mighty, but not by his power (By the power of Satan); He shall destroy fearfully, and shall prosper and thrive; He shall destroy the mighty, and also the holy people (Notice that the Holy People are in his grasps not Raptured" to a place of safety. More on the Rapture later.).

25 Through his cunning (Clever or artful, in a way that is intended to deceive.) He shall cause deceit (The act or practice of deceiving or misleading somebody) to prosper under his rule, and he shall exalt himself in his heart (He believes he can pull this off). He shall destroy many in their prosperity. He shall even rise against the Prince of princes, but he shall be broken without human means.

26 And the vision of the evenings and mornings which was told is true; Therefore seal up the vision (Vision not to be understood), For it refers to many days in the future (For the end time).

Daniel 9:26-27

26 And the people of the prince (Notice he did not come alone) who is to come shall destroy the city and the sanctuary. The end of it shall be with a flood, and till the end of the war, desolations are determined.

27 Then he shall confirm a covenant with many for one week (7 years), but in the middle of the week (approximately 3 ½ years), He shall bring an end to sacrifice and offering. And on the wing of abominations shall be one who makes desolate (God has left this world under the complete wrath of Satan) until the consummation, which is determined, is poured out on the desolate.

Daniel 11:36-39

36 "Then the king shall do according to his own will: he shall exalt and magnify himself above every god, shall speak blasphemies against the God of gods, and shall prosper till the wrath has been accomplished; for what has been determined shall be done.

37 He shall regard neither the God of his fathers (Jehovah (YHWH) is the Creator and God of the Watchers though they rebelled.) nor the desire of women (Yes Michelle Obama is NOT a woman It is a transgender an ABOMINATION), nor regard any god; for he shall exalt himself above them all (Of course, He is Satan in the flesh.).

38 But in their place, he shall honor a god of fortresses; and a god which his fathers (The Watchers) did not know, he shall honor with gold and silver, with precious stones and pleasant things.

39 Thus he shall act against the strongest fortresses with a foreign god (Allah, the god of Islam, an invention of Satan) (More on Islam Later), which he shall acknowledge, and advance its glory and he shall cause them to rule over many, and divide the land for gain.

Amos 3:11

Therefore, thus says the Lord God: An adversary shall be all around the land (We are currently surrounded.) He shall sap your strength from you, and your palaces shall be plundered.

Nahum 1:11

From you comes forth one who plots evil against the Lord, A wicked counselor.

Nahum 2:1

He who scatters has come up before your face. Man the fort! Watch the road! Strengthen your flanks! Fortify your power mightily (Prepare yourselves.).

Psalms of Solomon 8

They left no sin undone, wherein they surpassed not the heathen. Therefore God mingled for them a spirit of wondering (Amazed, admiration or awe, especially at something very beautiful or new); and gave them to drink a cup of undiluted (Without any attempt to make something less offensive or easier to accept) wine, that they might become drunken (Overly excited by or as if by having consumed too much alcohol). He brought him (Satan) that is from the end of the earth (Sheol, Hell), that smiteth mightily (The destroyer); He decreed war against Jerusalem (God's Holy People), and against her land. The princes of the land (Governors, senators, rulers) went to meet him (Satan/Obama) with joy: they said to him Blessed (Blessed in Arabic means barack once again, God give us his name) be that way! Come ye, enter ye in with peace. They made the rough ways even, before his answering in; they opened the gates to Jerusalem, they crowded its walls.

As a father enters the house of his sons, so he entered Jerusalem in peace; he established his feet there in great safety. He captured her fortresses (Took the White House) and the wall of Jerusalem; for God himself led him in safety (Notice it is the judgment of God), while they wandered (Spiritually lost). He (Obama) destroyed their princes

and everyone wise and counsel he poured out the blood of the inhabitants of Jerusalem, like the water of uncleanness. He led away
their sons and daughters, whom they had begotten in defilement,
they did according to their uncleanness, even as their fathers had
done.

Psalm of Solomon 17:5-19

5 Thou, O Lord, didst choose David (to be) king over Israel, and
swaredst to him touching his seed that never should his kingdom fail
before Thee.

6 But, for our sins, sinners (The Watchers) rose against us; They as-
sailed us and thrust us out; What Thou hadst not promised to them,
they took away (from us) with violence.

7 They in no wise glorified Thy honourable name They set a (worldly)
monarchy (Secular form of government) in place of (that which was)
their excellency (God's form of government)

8 They laid waste to the throne of David in tumultuous arrogance.
But Thou, O God, didst cast them down and remove their seed from
the earth,

9 In that there rose against them a man that was alien to our race (a
Fallen Angele/Watcher).

10 According to their sins didst Thou recompense them, O God; So
that it befell them according to their deeds.

11 God showed them no pity He sought out their seed and let not
one of them go free.

12 Faithful is the Lord in all His judgments, which He doeth upon the
earth.

13 The lawless one (Satan) laid waste our land, leaving it uninhabited. They destroyed both he young and the old, and their children together.

14 In the heat of His anger, He sent them away even unto the west, and He exposed) The rulers of the land are unsparingly subject to derision.

15 Being an alien (a Watcher), the enemy acted proudly, and his heart was alien to our God.

16 And all things whatsoever he did in Jerusalem, as also the nations in the cities to their gods.

17 And the children of the covenant amid the mingled peoples (Genetically Manipulated DNA) surpassed them in evil. There was not among them one that wrought amid Jerusalem mercy and truth.

18 They that loved the synagogues of the pious fled from them, as sparrows that fly from their nest.

19 They wandered in deserts that their lives might be saved from harm, and precious in the eyes of them that lived abroad was any that escaped alive from them.

Now that we know who Barack Hussein Obama let us review this information before we continue:

-We know that the eagle in 2 Esdras 11 & 12 is the US Government

—We know that during the 44th presidency, Spiritual Judgement began

—We know that the 4th Beast in Daniel 7 is the US Government

-We know the 10 horns (Eisenhower – Bush) +1 the 11th is Obama

–We know the meaning of Obama's name

–We know the number associated with his name

-We know that the Watchers have been experimenting with human genetics/DNA

–We know that Satan is indwelling Obama through genetic manipulation

-We know what he has done & what he will soon do

Taking into account Dr. Stone's mathematical odds of prophecy previously discussed in chapter 4, there are not even enough people on earth to satisfy the odds of fulfilling all these prophecies to the most intricate details as he has. At this time, there are approximately 6.9 billion people on Earth! NOT: 1 in 1,000,000,000,000,000,000,000,000,000,000,000,000,000,000,000,000,000,000,000,000,000,000,000,000,000,000,000,000,000,000,000,000,000,000,000,000,000,000,000,000,000,000,000,000. (Whatever this astronomical number means, I can't even count past the third set of zeros.)

The evidence points directly at the face of only one person. The president of the United States is Barack Hussein Obama! I have seen people get convicted of a capital crime with far less evidence and odds than this.

Before we move on to Revelation 17 and 18, it is important to understand exactly what the "abomination of desolation is.

Chapter 13

The Abomination of Desolation Misunderstood

The Hebrew word for abomination is (shiqquwts), shik-koots; detestable thing or idol, abominable thing, abomination, idol, detested thing.

In Greek, the word for abomination is (bdelugma), bdel'-oog-mah; an object of disgust, an abomination; of that which is highly esteemed amongst men, in contrast to its real character in the sight of God.

The Hebrew word for desolation is (shamem), shaw-mame`; to stun or grow numb, i.e., devastate or (fig.) Stupefy, to be desolate. What one sees sometimes is so horrible that it horrifies or appalls [i.e., to be speechless]

In Greek, the word for desolation is (eremosis), er-ay-mo-sis; in the sense of making desolate, the abomination that makes desolate with stress upon the effect of the process.

The abomination of desolation is difficult to understand. However, once you understand the fact that Satan, through Human Genetic Manipulation, has taken on human flesh and is indwelling Barack Hussein Obama, it becomes clear. The fact that Satan has come to earth in the likeness of a man and the fullness of his spirit indwells Obama, we can understand that the abomination of desolation refers to none other than Barack Hussein Obama.

Keep in mind that everything in the Old Testament had more to do with the physical aspect of things. Jesus Christ came to show us the Spiritual Intent of the Law, the Spiritual aspect of things.

King Antiochus Epiphanes was a forerunner of the Antichrist who set up the first abomination of desolation. He did this by forcing the children of Israel to abandon the laws given by God and polluting the Temple and altar with unlawful sacrifices. (1 Maccabees 1:10-64) The 10 horns (Eisenhower-Bush) plus 1 the little horn (Obama) have done the same thing. By slowly and methodically passing laws contrary to God's laws, they have spiritually polluted and enslaved the masses. Most people have spiritually polluted the Temple of the Holy Spirit, which is their body.

Ezekiel 20:1-30 provides a detailed account of how the children of Israel became desolate   .

1 And it came to pass in the seventh year, in the fifth month, the tenth day of the month, that certain of the elders of Israel came to inquire of the LORD, and sat before me. (Notice that even this date (in the current calendar, it is approximately 8/5/07) aligns with the date that the Lion in 2 Esdras 12:1-2 begins to hand down judgment against the Eagle. During the reign of the last head on the right (Bush, the 43rd presidency)

2 Then came the word of the LORD unto me, saying,

3 Son of man, speak unto the elders of Israel, and say unto them, Thus saith the Lord GOD: Are ye come to inquire of me? As I live, saith the Lord GOD, I will not be enquired of by you.

4 Wilt thou judge them, son of man, wilt thou judge them? Cause them to know the abominations of their fathers:

5 And say unto them, Thus saith the Lord GOD In the day when I chose Israel, and lifted mine hand unto the seed of the house of Jacob, and made myself known unto them in the land of Egypt, when I lifted mine hand unto them, saying, I am the LORD your God;

6 In the day that I lifted mine hand unto them, to bring them forth of the land of Egypt into a land that I had espied for them, flowing with milk and honey, which is the glory of all lands:

7 Then said I unto them, Cast ye away every man the abominations of his eyes, and defile not yourselves with the idols of Egypt: I am the LORD your God.

8 But they rebelled against me, and would not hearken unto me they did not every man cast away the abominations of their eyes, neither did they forsake the idols of Egypt: then I said, I will pour out my fury upon them, to accomplish my anger against them in the land of Egypt.

9 But I wrought for my name's sake, that it should not be polluted before the heathen, among whom they were, in whose sight I made myself known unto them, in bringing them forth out of the land of Egypt.

10 Therefore, I caused them to go forth out of the land of Egypt, and brought them into the wilderness (A physical wilderness).

11 And I gave them my statutes, and shewed them my judgments, which if a man do, he shall even live in them.

12 Moreover also I gave them my sabbaths, to be a sign between me and them, that they might know that I am the LORD that sanctifies them.

13 But the house of Israel rebelled against me in the wilderness: they walked not in my statutes, and they despised my judgments, which if a man follow, he shall even live in them; and my sabbaths they greatly polluted then I said, I would pour out my fury upon them in the wilderness, to consume them.

14 But I acted for my name's sake, that it should not be polluted before the heathen, in whose sight I brought them out.

15 Yet also I lifted my hand unto them in the wilderness, that I would not bring them into the land which I had given them, flowing with milk and honey, which is the glory of all lands

16 Because they despised my judgments, and walked not in my statutes, but polluted my Sabbaths: for their heart went after their idols.

17 Nevertheless, my eye spared them from destroying them, nor did I make an end of them in the wilderness.

18 But I said unto their children in the wilderness, Walk ye not in the statutes of your fathers, neither observe their judgments, nor defile yourselves with their idols

19 I am the LORD your God; walk in my statutes, and keep my judgments, and do them;

20 And hallow my Sabbaths; and they shall be a sign between me and you, that ye may know that I am the LORD your God.

21 Notwithstanding, the children rebelled against me: they walked not in my statutes, neither kept my judgments to do them, which if a man do, he shall even live in them; they polluted my Sabbaths: then I said, I would pour out my fury upon them, to accomplish my anger against them in the wilderness.

22 Nevertheless, I withdrew my hand, and wrought for my name's sake, that it should not be polluted in the sight of the heathen, in whose sight I brought them forth.

23 I lifted my hand unto them also in the wilderness, that I would scatter them among the heathen, and disperse them through the countries;

24 Because they had not executed my judgments, but had despised my statutes, and had polluted my Sabbaths, and their eyes were after their fathers' idols.

25 Wherefore I gave them also statutes that were not good, and judgments whereby they should not live; (Notice that because of disobedience, it was God that gave them up, left them desolate.)

26 And I polluted them in their gifts, in that they caused to pass through the fire all that openeth the womb, that I might make them desolate, to the end that they might know that I am the LORD.

27 Therefore, son of man, speak unto the house of Israel, and say unto them, Thus saith the Lord GOD Yet in this your fathers have blasphemed me, in that they have committed a trespass against me.

28 For when I had brought them into the land, for the which I lifted mine hand to give it to them, then they saw every high hill, and all the thick trees, and they offered there their sacrifices, and there they presented the provocation of their offering: there also they made their sweet savour, and poured out there their drink offerings.

29 Then I said unto them, What is the high place whereunto ye go? And the name thereof is called BAMAH unto this day. (They even named the pagan altar BAMAH as it remains, UNTO THIS DAY. And if you connect the human thought process, it is O or U, thus read, O'BAMAH.)

30 Wherefore say unto the house of Israel, Thus saith the Lord GOD; Are ye polluted after the manner of your fathers? And commit ye whoredom after their abominations?

Because of a complete disobedience and contempt for God's laws, God turned away from the children of Israel, polluted them according to their devises. God has done the same thing to America. You see, God does not change. He is the same yesterday, today, and forever. The United States as a nation was left desolate. Once God did this, the abomination of desolation (Obama) came right in and took his position.

In 2 Thessalonians 2:5-10, Paul explains what was holding back the Antichrist from coming.

5 Remember ye not, that, when I was yet with you, I told you these things?

6 And now ye know what withholdeth that he (The Antichrist) might be revealed in his time.

7 For the mystery of iniquity doth already work: only he (God) who now letteth will let, until he (Holy Spirit) be taken out of the way. (Pushed aside)

8 And then shall that Wicked (Obama) be revealed, whom the Lord shall consume with the spirit of his mouth, and shall destroy with the brightness of his coming:

9 Even him, whose coming is after the working of Satan (genetically engineered by Satan) with all power and signs and lying wonders,

10 And with all deceivableness of unrighteousness in those that perish; because they received not the love of the truth, that they might be saved. (did not believe the Scriptures are the very Words of God.)

Notice that Paul's letter to the Romans explains the same concept.

Romans 1:18-32

18 For the wrath of God is revealed from heaven against all ungodliness and unrighteousness of men, who hold the truth in unrighteousness;

19 Because that which may be known of God is manifest in them; for God hath shewed it unto them.

20 For the invisible things of him from the creation of the world are seen, being understood by the things that are made, even his eternal power and Godhead; so that they are without excuse:

21 Because of that, when they knew God, they glorified him not as God, nor were thankful; but became vain in their imaginations, and their foolish heart was darkened.

22 Professing themselves to be wise, they became fools,

23 And changed the glory of the uncorruptible God into an image made like to corruptible man, and to birds, and four-footed beasts, and creeping things.

24 Wherefore God also gave them up to uncleanness through the lusts of their hearts, to dishonor their bodies between themselves:

25 Who changed the truth of God into a lie, and worshipped and served the creature more than the Creator, who is blessed forever. Amen.

26 For this cause God gave them up unto vile affections: for even their women did change the natural use into that which is against nature:

27 And likewise also the men, leaving the natural use of the woman, burned in their lust one toward another; men with men working that which is unseemly, and receiving in themselves that recompense of their error which was meet   .

28 And even as they did not like to retain God in their knowledge, God gave them over to a reprobate mind, to do those things which are not convenient;

29 Being filled with all unrighteousness, fornication, wickedness, covetousness, maliciousness; full of envy, murder, debate, deceit, malignity; whisperers,

30 Backbiters, haters of God, spiteful, proud, boasters, inventors of evil things, disobedient to parents,

31 Without understanding, covenant-breakers, without natural affection, implacable, unmerciful:

32 Who, knowing the judgment of God, that they which commit such things are worthy of death, not only do the same, but have pleasure in them that do them.

And again in Daniel 9:11-18

11 Yea, all Israel have transgressed thy law, even by departing, that they might not obey thy voice; therefore the curse is poured upon us, and the oath that is written in the law of Moses the servant of God, because we have sinned against him.

12 And he hath confirmed his words, which he spake against us, and against our judges that judged us, by bringing upon us a great evil: for under the whole heaven hath not been done as hath been done upon Jerusalem.

13 As it is written in the Law of Moses, all this evil has come upon us: yet made we not our prayer before the LORD our God, that we might turn from our iniquities, and understand thy truth.

14 Therefore hath the LORD watched upon the evil, and brought it upon us: for the LORD our God is righteous in all his works which he doeth: for we obeyed not his voice.

15 And now, O Lord our God, that hast brought thy people forth out of the land of Egypt with a mighty hand, and hast gotten thee renown, as at this day; we have sinned, we have done wickedly .

16 O Lord, according to all thy righteousness, I beseech thee, let thine anger and thy fury be turned away from thy city Jerusalem, thy holy mountain: because for our sins, and the iniquities of our fathers, Jerusalem and thy people are become a reproach to all that are about us.

17 Now therefore, O our God, hear the prayer of thy servant, and his supplications, and cause thy face to shine upon thy desolate sanctuary, for the Lord's sake.

18 O my God, incline thine ear, and hear; open thine eyes, and behold our desolations, and the city which is called by thy name: for we do not present our supplications before thee for our righteousnesses, but for thy great mercies.

Hosea 5:6

They shall go with their flocks and with their herds to seek the LORD , but they shall not find him; he hath withdrawn himself from them.

Hosea 9:12

Though they bring up their children, yet will I bereave them, that there shall not be a man left: yea, woe also to them when I depart from them!

Luke 21:20 is a key verse in knowing when the abomination of desolation was to come.

And when ye shall see Jerusalem compassed with armies, then know that the desolation thereof is nigh. (Currently, the state of Israel is surrounded by hostile Islamic Nations. When this began to occur, this was a sign for us to know that the abomination of desolation was near.)

Mark 13:14

But when ye shall see the abomination of desolation (Barack Hussein Obama), spoken of by Daniel the prophet, standing where it ought not to (In the ultimate positional power, i.e. the White House), (let him that readeth understand,) (This was not something made obvious to the masses but only to a selected few.) then let them that be in Judaea flee to the mountains: (Obama should not be standing in the White House and the fact that he is has dire consequences and marks the beginning of the worst time of human suffering in history.)

Matthew 24:15

When ye therefore shall see the abomination of desolation, spoken of by Daniel the prophet, stand in the holy place (Holy place simply means a place set apart, implying a distinction; in Greek, Hagios; hag'-ee-os, fundamentally it signifies separated.) (whoso readeth, let him understand) In the days of ancient kings the word Temple had a dual application. A Temple was not only what we know as referred to the Temple of God built by King Solomon, but a Temple was also where the King would sit to conduct his duties of governing the people. A place where the laws of a nation would derive from what we would know today as the White House. This is where laws, statutes, and governmental decisions emanate from, yet most of these laws are contrary to God's laws. It is where the abomination of desolation currently lives and operates.

Daniel 9:27

And he (Obama) shall confirm the covenant with many for one week: (7 years) and during the week (3 ½ years) he shall cause the sacrifice and the oblation to cease, (Worship of the God of Israel was greatly hindered) and for the overspreading of abominations he shall make it desolate, (Islam's world caliphate and Sharia law will be accepted as law of the land) even until the consummation, and that determined shall be poured upon the desolate.

More on Islam's plan later.

Daniel 12:11

And from the time that the daily sacrifice shall be taken away, (This marks the time where the Lion in 2 Esdras 12:1 begins to hand down Spiritual Judgment towards the end of the reign of the last head on the right)

And the abomination that maketh desolate set up, (Obama takes office, the abomination of desolation set up in the White House.) there shall be a thousand two hundred and ninety days. (Spiritual Judgement began and lasted approximately 3 1/2 years, of the last two wings on the left, the 44th presidency, Obama/Biden, 2 Esdras 12:2. For the Spiritual side, then comes TRUMP for the physical.)

Revelation 13:5

And there was given unto him (US government) a mouth speaking great things and blasphemies; and power was given unto him to continue forty and two months. (Government allowed to continue for an additional 42 months, headed by Barack Hussein Obama.)

ABOMINATION, OBAMANATION (Obama in control of the nation, get it?)

Now that we understand these prophecies, let us move on to Revelation 17 and 18, The Great Whore, Mystery Babylon.

Chapter 14

Mystery Babylon (The Great Whore)

Revelation 17

1 And there came one of the seven angels which had the seven vials, and talked with me, saying unto me, Come hither; I will shew unto thee the judgment of the great whore (Once a nation formerly blessed by God becomes great and wealthy but then turns against the laws of God she is considered a whore in His sight.)

This is described in detail in Ezekiel 16

1 Again, the word of the LORD came unto me, saying,

2 Son of man, cause Jerusalem to know her abominations,

3 And say, Thus saith the Lord GOD unto Jerusalem; Thy birth and thy nativity is of the land of Canaan; thy father was an Amorite, and thy mother an Hittite.

4 And as for thy nativity, in the day thou waste born thy navel was not cut, neither waste thou washed in water to supple thee; thou waste not salted at all, nor swaddled at all   .

5 None eye pitied thee, to do any of these unto thee, to have compassion upon thee; but thou waste cast out in the open field, to the loathing of thy person, in the day that thou waste born.

6 And when I passed by thee, and saw thee polluted in thine own blood, I said unto thee when thou wast in thy blood, Live; yea, I said unto thee when thou wast in thy blood, Live.

7 I have caused thee to multiply as the bud of the field, and thou hast increased and waxen great, and thou art come to excellent ornaments: thy breasts are fashioned, and thine hair is grown, whereas thou waste naked and bare.

8 Now when I passed by thee, and looked upon thee, behold, thy time was the time of love and I spread my skirt over thee, and covered thy nakedness: yea, I swear unto thee, and entered into a covenant with thee, saith the Lord GOD, and thou becomes mine.

9 Then washed I thee with water yea, I thoroughly washed away thy blood from thee, and I anointed thee with oil.

10 I clothed thee also with embroidered work, and shod thee with badgers' skin, and I girded thee about with fine linen, and I covered thee with silk.

11 I decked thee also with ornaments, and I put bracelets upon thy hands, and a chain on thy neck.

12 And I put a jewel on thy forehead, and earrings in thine ears, and a beautiful crown upon thine head.

13 Thus waste thou decked with gold and silver and thy raiment was of fine linen, and silk, and embroidered work thou didst eat fine flour, and honey, and oil: and thou waste exceeding beautiful, and thou didst prosper into a kingdom.

14 And thy renown went forth among the heathen for thy beauty: for it was perfect through my comeliness, which I had put upon thee, saith the Lord GOD. (God made the nation a great one.)

15 But thou didst trust in thine own beauty, and players the harlot because of thy renown, and poorest out thy fornications on every one that passed by; his it was.

16 And of thy garments thou didst take, and deckedst thy high places with divers colours, and players the harlot thereupon the like things shall not come, neither shall it be so.

17 Thou hast also taken thy fair jewels of my gold and of my silver, which I had given thee, and madest to thyself images of men, and didst commit whoredom with them,

18 And thou hast taken thy embroidered garments, and coveredst them: and thou hast set mine oil and mine incense before them.

19 My meat also, which I gave thee, fine flour, and oil, and honey, wherewith I fed thee, thou hast even set it before them for a sweet savour: and thus it was, saith the Lord GOD.

20 Moreover thou hast taken thy sons and thy daughters, whom thou hast borne unto me, and these hast thou sacrificed unto them to be devoured. Is this of thy whoredoms a small matter,

21 That thou hast slain my children, and delivered them to cause them to pass through the fire for them?

22 And in all thine abominations and thy whoredoms thou hast not remembered the days of thy youth, when thou wast naked and bare, and wast polluted in thy blood (The nation as a whole did not remember when they were nothing and God was the One who made them great.).

23 And it came to pass after all thy wickedness, (woe, woe unto thee! saith the Lord GOD;)

24 That thou hast also built unto thee an eminent place, and hast made thee a high place in every street.

25 Thou hast built thy high place at every head of the way, and hast made thy beauty to be abhorred, and hast opened thy feet to everyone that passed by, and multiplied thy whoredoms.

26 Thou hast also committed fornication with the Egyptians thy neighbours, great of flesh; and hast increased thy whoredoms, to provoke me to anger   .

27 Behold, therefore, I have stretched out my hand over thee, and have diminished thine ordinary food, and delivered thee unto the will of them that hate thee, the daughters of the Philistines, which are ashamed of thy lewd way.

28 Thou hast played the whore also with the Assyrians, because thou wast unsatiable; yea, thou hast played the harlot with them, and yet couldest not be satisfied.

29 Thou hast moreover multiplied thy fornication in the land of Canaan unto Chaldea (Another name for Babylon, notice that there are 7 letters in the name CHALDEA, and 9 letters in the name CHALDEANS; just as there are 7 letters in the name AMERICA, and 9 letters in the name AMERICANS.); and yet thou wast not satisfied herewith.

30 How weak is thine heart, saith the Lord GOD, seeing thou does all these things, the work of an imperious whorish woman;

31 In that thou builds thine eminent place in the head of every way, and makes thine high place in every street; and hast not been as a harlot, in that thou scorns hire;

32 But as a wife that committeth adultery, which taketh strangers instead of her husband! (According to the law, a woman who commits adultery is punishable by death.)

33 They give gifts to all whores: but thou givest thy gifts to all thy lovers, and hirest them, that they may come unto thee on every side for thy whoredom.

34 And the contrary is in thee from other women in thy whoredoms, whereas none followeth thee to commit whoredoms: and in that thou givest a reward, and no reward is given unto thee, therefore thou art contrary.

35 Wherefore, O harlot, hear the word of the LORD

36 Thus saith the Lord GOD; Because thy filthiness was poured out, and thy nakedness discovered through thy whoredoms with thy lovers, and with all the idols of thy abominations, and by the blood of thy children, which thou didst give unto them;

37 Behold, therefore, I will gather all thy lovers, with whom thou hast taken pleasure, and all them that thou hast loved, with all them that thou hast hated; I will even gather them round about against thee, and will discover thy nakedness unto them, that they may see all thy nakedness. (God gathered all the other nations that Israel turned on God for, and He turned them against His people.)

38 And I will judge thee, as women that break wedlock and shed blood are judged; and I will give thee blood in fury and jealousy. (The death penalty)

39 And I will also give thee into their hand, and they shall throw down thine eminent place, and shall break down thy high places: they shall strip thee also of thy clothes, and shall take thy fair jewels, and leave thee naked and bare. (Financial ruin)

40 They shall also bring up a company against thee, and they shall stone thee with stones, and thrust thee through with their swords. (War)

41 And they shall burn thine houses with fire, and execute judgments upon thee in the sight of many women (other nations): and I will cause thee to cease from playing the harlot, and thou also shalt give no hire any more.

42 So will I make my fury toward thee to rest, and my jealousy shall depart from thee, and I will be quiet, and will be no more angry.

43 Because thou hast not remembered the days of thy youth, but hast fretted me in all these things; behold, therefore I also will recompense thy way upon thine head, saith the Lord GOD: and thou shalt not commit this lewdness above all thine abominations.

44 Behold, every one that useth proverbs shall use this proverb against thee, saying, As is the mother, so is her daughter. (Mother & daughter, Babylon?)

45 Thou art thy mother's daughter, that loatheth her husband and her children; and thou art the sister of thy sisters, which loathed their husbands and their children: your mother was a Hittite, and your father an Amorite.

46 And thine elder sister is Samaria, she and her daughters that dwell at thy left hand: and thy younger sister, that dwelleth at thy right hand, is Sodom and her daughters. (Notice that God always refers to nations as women.)

47 Yet hast thou not walked after their ways, nor done after their abominations: but, as if that were a very little thing, thou wast corrupted more than they in all thy ways.

48 As I live, saith the Lord GOD, Sodom thy sister hath not done, she nor her daughters, as thou hast done, thou and thy daughters.

49 Behold, this was the iniquity of thy sister Sodom, pride, fullness of bread, and abundance of idleness was in her and her daughters, neither did she strengthen the hand of the poor and needy.

50 And they were haughty, and committed abomination before me: therefore I took them away as I saw good.

51 Neither hath Samaria committed half of thy sins; but thou hast multiplied thine abominations more than they, and hast justified thy sisters in all thine abominations which thou hast done.

52 Thou also, which hast judged thy sisters, bear thine own shame for thy sins that thou hast committed more abominable than theirs: they are more righteous than thou: yea, be thou confounded also, and bear thy shame, in that thou hast justified thy sisters.

53 When I shall bring again their captivity, the captivity of Sodom and her daughters, and the captivity of Samaria and her daughters, then will I bring again the captivity of thy captives in the midst of them:

54 That thou mayest bear thine own shame, and mayest be confounded in all that thou hast done, in that thou art a comfort unto them.

55 When thy sisters, Sodom and her daughters, shall return to their former estate, and Samaria and her daughters shall return to their former estate, then thou and thy daughters shall return to your former estate.

56 For thy sister Sodom was not mentioned by thy mouth in the day of thy pride,

57 Before thy wickedness was discovered, as at the time of thy re-proach of the daughters of Syria, and all that are round about her, the daughters of the Philistines, which despise thee round about (All Islamic/Arab Nations currently surrounding the State of Israel).

58 Thou hast borne thy lewdness and thine abominations, saith the LORD.

59 For thus saith the Lord GOD; I will even deal with thee as thou hast done, which hast despised the oath in breaking the covenant.

60 Nevertheless, I will remember my covenant with thee in the days of thy youth, and I will establish unto thee an everlasting covenant.

61 Then thou shalt remember thy ways, and be ashamed, when thou shalt receive thy sisters, thine elder and thy younger: and I will give them unto thee for daughters, but not by thy covenant.

62 And I will establish my covenant with thee; and thou shalt know that I am the LORD:

63 That thou mayest remember, and be confounded, and never open thy mouth anymore because of thy shame, when I am pacified toward thee for all that thou hast done, saith the Lord GOD.

And again in Jeremiah 3:1–10, 20

1 They say, If a man puts away his wife, and she goes from him, and becomes another man's, shall he return unto her again? Shall that land not be greatly polluted? But thou hast played the harlot with many lovers; yet return to me, saith the LORD.

2 Lift thine eyes unto the high places, and see where thou hast not been lain with. In the ways hast thou sat for them, as the Arabian in the wilderness; and thou hast polluted the land with thy whoredoms and with thy wickedness.

3 Therefore, the showers have been withheld, and there hath been no latter rain; and thou hadst a whore's forehead, thou refusedst to be ashamed.

4 Wilt thou not from this time cry unto me, my father, thou art the guide of my youth?

5 Will he reserve his anger forever? Will he keep it to the end? Behold, thou hast spoken and done evil things as thou couldest.

6 The LORD said also unto me in the days of Josiah the king, Hast thou seen that which backsliding Israel hath done? She is gone up upon every high mountain and under every green tree, and there hath played the harlot.

7 And I said after she had done all these things, Turn thou unto me. But she returned not. And her treacherous sister Judah saw it.

8 And I saw, when for all the causes whereby backsliding Israel committed adultery, I had put her away, and given her a bill of divorce; yet her treacherous sister Judah feared not, but went and played the harlot also.

9 And it came to pass through the lightness of her whoredom, that she defiled the land, and committed adultery with stones and with stocks.

10 And yet for all this her treacherous sister Judah hath not turned unto me with her whole heart, but feignedly, saith the LORD.

20 Surely as a wife treacherously departeth from her husband, so have ye dealt treacherously with me, O house of Israel, saith the LORD.

Hosea 1:2

The beginning of the word of the LORD by Hosea. And the LORD said to Hosea, Go, take unto thee a wife of whoredoms and children of whoredoms: for the land hath committed great whoredom, departing from the LORD.

Hosea 4:12

My people ask counsel at their stocks, and their staff declareth unto them: for the spirit of whoredoms hath caused them to err, and they have gone a whoring from under their God.

This is precisely what Moses warned about.

Deuteronomy 8:11-20

11 Beware that thou forget not the LORD thy God, in not keeping his commandments, and his judgments, and his statutes, which I command thee this day:

12 Lest when thou hast eaten and art full, and hast built goodly houses, and dwelt therein;

13 And when thy herds and thy flocks multiply, and thy silver and thy gold are multiplied, and all that thou hast is multiplied;

14 Then thine heart be lifted, and thou forget the LORD thy God, which brought thee forth out of the land of Egypt, from the house of bondage;

15 Who led thee through that great and terrible wilderness, wherein were fiery serpents, and scorpions, and drought, where there was no water; who brought thee forth water out of the rock of flint;

16 Who fed thee in the wilderness with manna, which thy fathers knew not, that he might humble thee, and that he might prove thee, to do thee good at thy latter end;

17 And thou say in thine heart, My power and the might of mine hand hath gotten me this wealth.

18 But thou shalt remember the LORD thy God: for it is he that giveth thee power to get wealth, that he may establish his covenant which he sware unto thy fathers, as it is this day.

19 And it shall be, if thou do at all forget the LORD thy God, and walk after other gods, and serve them, and worship them, I testify against you this day that ye shall surely perish.

20 As the nations which the LORD destroyeth before your face, so shall ye perish; because ye would not be obedient unto the voice of the LORD your God.

Revelation 17:1 (cont.)

that sitteth upon many waters: (In the book, Our Great Seal: The Symbols of Our Heritage and Destiny, author Raymond Capt. discovers an incredible fact: An examination of all nations of the world, shows only one, the United States, that is quartered by rivers. The Mississippi takes its rise near the Canadian border and cuts right down to the Gulf of Mexico, dividing our land into two halves. On the Pacific Coast side is the Columbia River. Follow it upward to its junction with the Snake River, follow that upward into proximity with the source of the Missouri River, which starts in Montana and meanders eastward into the Mississippi, dividing the West into halves.

In the Atlantic Coast side begin with the Ohio River and follow it eastward to Pittsburgh and its junction with the Monongahela River that runs by McKeesport, then follow eastward the Youghiogheny River where, at Glencoe, Pennsylvania, it becomes the Castleman River, go upstream unto Wills Creek branches off and takes its source where the Potomac begins and runs to the Bay and the Atlantic and you have the eastern half of the nation divided in two. Thus, the whole land is quartered by rivers. One cannot find any other land on earth divided this way, into four sections: Northeast, Northwest, Southeast, and Southwest, by rivers. pg.76)

The United States of America has turned against the laws of God and has given herself over to Satan for money and prosperity, which makes her a harlot, and the land sits upon many waters.

Furthermore, the Statue of Liberty was made by French sculptor Frederic Auguste Bartholdi, who was a member of Paris, France's Grand Orient Lodge (a branch of Freemasons), and sculpted this Illuminati monumental statue, which sits on the New York Harbor. This statue is replete with secret society encoded messages and symbols of a blasphemous nature. It is said that Bartholdi used the image of his mother's face and his mistress's body to create the statue. Not to mention that the statue stand on an 11 pointed star a hendecagram also known as a Queliphot: a peel, shell or husk in Jewish Kabalah which signifies a host body that houses the essence of light but the host body is evil in nature because it traps the light The whore that sits upon many waters

In Zechariah 5:6-11, there is a prophecy that depicts the images of two women that have significant meaning of two statues in the United States.

6 And I said, What is it? And he said, This is an ephah (a measure of weight, the scale held up by the statue of Blind Justice) that goeth forth. He said, moreover, this is their resemblance throughout all the earth.

7 And, behold, there was lifted a talent of lead: (platform where the statues sit), and this is a woman that sits amid the ephah. (A woman holding the scale)

8 And he said, This is wickedness. And he cast it into the midst of the ephah; and he cast the weight of lead upon the mouth thereof. And the wind was in their wings; for they had wings like the wings of a stork: (They had wings just as an eagle, which made it possible to travel across the sea.) and they lifted the ephah between the earth and the heaven.

10 Then said I to the angel who talked with me, Whither do these bear the ephah go? (Statute of Blind Justice and Statute of Liberty)

11 And he said unto me, To build it a house in the land of Shinar (another name for Babylon), and it shall be established, and set there upon her base. (They establish their system of government and laws)

Revelation 17:2 (cont.)

2 With whom the kings of the earth have committed fornication, and the inhabitants of the earth have been made drunk with the wine of her fornication. (Many leaders of the world have made backroom deals with the US government in the name of their so-called democracy. Nations from around the world have wanted to imitate every

aspect of the American way of life. It's a form of government that includes freedom of religion, homosexual marriages, gay rights, and liberty to do as you please. Whatsoever seems right in your own eyes! This is contrary to the ways of God. This type of government leads to spiritual and physical lawlessness and sin, which leads to death.

2 Peter 2:19, While they promise them liberty, they are the servants of corruption Furthermore, technological advancements in radio and television have brought American culture into people's homes all over the world. America's movies are universal; wherever you go in the world, they are available. The message they send is not a good one. Immorality and violence are often depicted as something to be proud of and the norm. The pervasiveness of American culture has now worsened with satellite television and the Internet. This is why the Bible describes Satan as the prince of the power of the air these are the methods he employs to influence his victims. In addition to the attack on one's spiritual life through the media, covetousness is running rampant in America. Through radio, TV, newspapers, and magazines, their goal is to get you to buy something, whether it is a stick of bubble gum or a house. Advertisement is just another word for subliminal seduction. This vicious merchant system is known in the Bible as the way of Cain, but fed to the American people as Capitalism.

In the book Jewish Antiquities, BK1, CH 2:60-61, this vicious way of Cain is fully described. Josephus goes on to tell us that after Cain traveled through many countries, he, with his wife, built a city named Nod, which is a place so-called, and there he settled his abode, where he also had children. However, he did not accept his punishment to amend his ways, but to increase his wickedness; for he only came to procure everything that was for his bodily pleasure, though it obliged him to be injurious to his neighbors. He augmented his household substance with much wealth, by rapine and violence; he excited his acquaintance to procure pleasures and spoils by robbery, and became a great leader of men into wicked courses. He also introduced a change in that way of simplicity wherein men lived before, and was the author of measures and weights (a merchant). And whereas the lived innocently and generously while they knew nothing of such arts, he changed the world into cunning craftiness.

Thus, when we combine the biblical account with the account of Josephus, we find that Cain was the first man to build cities and to place people inside them, most likely so he could more easily control them. He changed the simplicity in which they lived to a capitalist society. He became the world's first tyrant. He was the first political dictator and founded a society and distinct rebellion against the laws of God. Those laws meant nothing whatsoever to Cain and his followers and his children. The laws of God were considered to be for the weak and foolish, not intended for the "intellectual elite" of Cain and his leadership. No doubt, also, that Cain began the world system of taxation, to compel those in his cities to pay for their city services, protection, and government, and he and his cronies and aides lived very well off the spoils of the conquests, and the taxes they extorted from their followers and slaves. Thus, this whole worldly Babylonian System of government   began with none other than Cain, Satan's firstborn. (William F. Dankenbring, Prophecy Flash 2010)

Jude 11, Woe unto them! For they have gone in the way of Cain, and run greedily after the error of Balaam for reward, and perished in the gainsaying of Core.

Do not be deceived, this current system of covetousness (Capitalism) is contrary to God's way and leads you astray from the laws of God.

Ephesians 5:5, For this ye know, that no whoremonger, nor unclean person, nor covetous man, who is an idolater, hath any inheritance in the kingdom of Christ and God. Covetousness and idolatry are considered the same!

Wisdom of Solomon 14:12, For the devising of idols was the beginning of spiritual fornication, and the invention of them the corruption of life.

Many would try to argue this without researching the Scriptures and history. The fact remains that whosoever prefers (worships) any other type of government system than the one God gave Moses cannot possibly want to partake in the Kingdom of God and will not be around very much longer. God's government is not a socialist dictatorship, a democracy, a capitalist, or any other form of Satan inspired man-made government. In God's government, He is the supreme Ruler and Lawgiver, and His laws are not twisted or compromised in any way, shape, or form. Desiring any other form of government puts you at risk of (spiritually) worshiping the image of something Satan created. The image of the beast!

Revelation 17:3 (cont.)

3 So he carried me away in the spirit into the wilderness: (spiritual wilderness where most are spiritually lost), and I saw a woman (a nation) sit upon a scarlet coloured beast, (A government headed by the last president, Barack Hussein Obama. The word scarlet means, crimson worm - the female 'coccus ilicis' scarlet stuff, crimson, scarlet the dye made from the dried body of the female of the worm coccus ilicis worm, maggot worm, grub the worm coccus ilicis ++ When the female of the scarlet worm species was ready to give birth to her young, she would attach her body to the trunk of a tree, fixing herself so firmly and permanently that she would never leave again.

The eggs deposited beneath her body were thus protected until the larvae were hatched and able to enter their life cycle. As the mother died (Remember, Obama's mother died of ovarian cancer, but what caused it?), the crimson fluid stained her body and the surrounding wood. From the dead bodies of such female scarlet worms, the commercial scarlet dyes of antiquity were extracted.)

Full of names of blasphemy, having seven heads (A monetary/financial system in which the nation operates, established by the Illuminati and run by the Federal Reserve, with seven denominations of dollar bills in circulation, with a head in front of each one.)

And ten horns. The last 10 presidents (Eisenhower – Bush) have passed numerous laws and executive orders that have gone from president to president and will now be at the disposal of the last one (Obama). Sort of like a relay race where the baton is passed from runner to runner till it is finally given to the last to cross the finish line. Now, Obama has all the laws he needs in place to reach his end goal. Now he changes some of the existing laws using the laws already in place (interpreting the U.S. Constitution in any way he wishes), and whether the American people like it or not, he will do as he pleases till the Scriptures are fulfilled.)

4 And the woman (nation) was arrayed in purple and scarlet colour, and decked with gold and precious stones and pearls, (very wealthy) having a golden cup in her hand full of abominations and filthiness of her fornication: (full of sins, her cup is full and her end has come)

5 And upon her forehead was a name written, MYSTERY, (Notice it was a mystery only revealed in the last days), BABYLON THE GREAT, THE MOTHER OF HARLOTS AND ABOMINATIONS OF THE EARTH. (The word Babylon is derived from the word Babel, which means confusion. In politics, one party does this while the other does that. Some

227

argue they are right, others that they are wrong. Yet, most people are so confused and become so discouraged that they refuse to stay up-to-date with what the government is doing; this is part of the plan. This is precisely the Illuminati's method of operation. They contrive opposites of everything, a thesis and an anti-thesis, a positive and negative of everything, to accomplish their end goal, "order out of chaos". This is why the symbol for the 33rd degree Freemasons is an eagle with two heads looking in the opposite direction. This Democrat/Republican scheme is precisely what Jesus Christ warned about.

Matthew 12:25, Every kingdom divided against itself is brought to desolation; and every city or house divided against itself shall not stand:" This is an ancient method of war, divide and conquer. Freedom of religion leads to more confusion and chaos, and in the end, a complete disbelief in the very existence of the Creator.

Proverbs 16:25, There is a way that seemeth right unto a man, but the end thereof are the ways of death.

Jeremiah 10:23, O LORD, I know that the way of man is not in himself: it is not in man that walketh to direct his steps.

Jeremiah 17:9, The heart is deceitful above all things, and desperately wicked: who can know it?

It is interesting to note that if you take the word America and place the numeric value of each letter next to it, i.e., A=1, M=13, E=5, R=18, I=9, C=3, A=1, all the numbers total 50. There are 50 states in America. Furthermore, in Daniel 9:2, Daniel is searching in the book of Jeremiah, looking for clues as to when the end of the punishment of ancient Jerusalem. If you look in the book of Jeremiah 50, you will notice that it reads, Prophecy against Babylon.

Further study reveals that striking parallels exist between ancient Babylon in the United States of America. Both are the hubs of financial enterprise. Both are major banking centers; in fact, ancient Babylon was where the modern-day "banking system originated. Both have major seaports (the port of New York is one of the largest ports in the world ancient Babylon ports lay on the banks of the Euphrates River, a vital trade conduit in ancient times). Both have a cosmopolitan flair where people of many races and nationalities blend as a great melting pot of humanity. Ancient Babylon is located in modern-day Iraq, precisely where the United States military currently has the largest military base in the world. But could modern-day Babylon be the US? The evidence is overwhelming!

For many years, you were probably under the delusion that modern-day Babylon was somewhere in Europe, thus looking for the rise of the antichrist over there. Many have pegged it as modern Rome, where the seat of the Vatican and the headquarters of the Roman Catholic Church are located. But the description of Babylon in Revelation 17 and 18 in No Way fits Rome today. Although it is a major world city in its own right, it is neither a seaport nor a major world center of banking and commerce. It knows where it begins to compare to any major city in the United States of America. For too long, certain ministers and preachers have had blinders on and have passed on the blinders to the masses, mistakenly saying that Mystery Babylon is in Europe. Now, some say it is Germany in control of the European Union. I am not implying that these countries do not play an end-time role in prophecy   they do. However, it is not Mystery Babylon! No city in the world can compare to a city in America like New York City in terms of trade, mercantile power, financial power, and immensity. Today, Wall Street and the New York stock market shake the world.

The World Book Encyclopedia states: New York City is one of the world's most important centers of business, culture, and trade. It is also the home of the United Nations. Such agencies as the World Bank, the International Monetary Fund, and the leading banks of the world are centered in New York City. Much of what happens in New York City affects what happens throughout the United States and around the world. The business, financial, and trading organizations in New York City play a major role in the economy of the nation and the world (New York City, vol.14, pg. 260) (William F. Dankenbring, Prophecy Flash 2010)

These facts, coupled with the prophecies of the Eagle and the Lion (2 Esdras 11 & 12), give us the precise number of presidencies, marking the 11 last presidents and identifying the left/right scheme. The Vision of the Fourth Beast (Daniel 7), which is the same prophecy against the marking of the last 10 presidents +1, the last and very evil one (The rise of Barack Hussein Obama), it becomes clear that Mystery Babylon is no longer a mystery. Mystery Babylon is none other than the apostate nation of the United States of America! These are all different prophecies, but all have the same conclusion and align perfectly with each other. Just as 3+2=5, 4+1=5, and 3.5+1.5=5, there is uniformity and consistency throughout.

Revelation 17:6 (cont.)

6 And I saw the woman drunken with the blood of the saints, and with the blood of the martyrs of Jesus: and when I saw her, I wondered with great admiration.

(Many of God's people have shed their blood and died horrific deaths for the people of America to have the Scriptures. Almost everyone in America has a Bible at home, yet never even reads it. Do not even entertain the thought that God will not require their shed blood and sacrifice at the hands of America. He will! Especially when there are so many ministers preaching the gospel in America and free Bibles available to everyone, yet most completely disregard it.)

7 And the angel said unto me, Wherefore didst thou marvel? I will tell thee the mystery of the woman, and of the beast that carrieth her, which hath the seven heads and ten horns. (The nation that is governed by a very evil government, whose last president was really in charge of the government from the beginning, the first would be last and the last will be first, and used a financial system and the last 10 presidents to bring her under his complete control.)

8 The beast that thou sawest was,(At some point in early history, Satan was here.) And is not; (Remember Paul in 2 Thessalonians 2:7 explains that God was holding back Satan from coming to earth till the appointed time.) And shall descend out of the bottomless pit, and go into perdition: (Remember the prophecy in the Ascension of Isaiah 4:1-2, that Satan has come to earth in the "likeness of a man" (Obama), he is the beast that was, and is not, and yet is. And they that dwell on the earth shall wonder, whose names were not written in the book of life from the foundation of the world, when they behold the beast that was, and is not, and yet is.

9 And here is the mind which hath wisdom. The seven heads are seven mountains, on which the woman sitteth. (The nation operates upon a Satanic-inspired and controlled financial system with seven denominations of dollar bills currently in circulation, with a head engraved in front of each bill.)

10 And there are seven kings: (This also marks the end-time reign of this kingdom.)Five are fallen, (Ford – Clinton) and one is (Bush, the 43rd president, the time when the Lion began handing down judgment, 2 Esdras 12:1.), and the other is not yet come; (But now he

has, Obama, the 44th and when Spiritual Judgement began) when he cometh, he must continue a short space.

11 And the beast that was, and is not, even he is the eighth, and is of the seven, and goeth into perdition. (This verse once again shows us that Satan is indwelling Obama. Satan being the 8[th,] is inside the 7[th,])

12 And the ten horns which thou sawest are ten kings, (Eisenhower – Bush) which have received no kingdom as yet; (At the time John received this revelation, the United States did not exist.) But receive power as kings (presidents) one hour (The phrase one hour in Greek signifies at the appointed time.) with the beast. (Obama)

13 These have one mind, and shall give their power and strength unto the beast. (These presidents have been passing laws with the end objective to hand the beast (Obama) all the power necessary to make war with Jesus Christ upon His return and try to overcome Him. Sort of like the relay race example, where one runner hands the baton to the other till the last one gets it and runs across the finish line.)

14 These shall make war with the Lamb, and the Lamb shall overcome them: for he is Lord of lords, and King of kings: and they that are with him are called, and chosen, and faithful. (The plan will not succeed. In the end, we know who is King of Kings and Lord of Lords.)

15 And he saith unto me, The waters which thou sawest, where the whore sitteth, are peoples, and multitudes, and nations, and tongues. (The U.S. is a melting pot of humanity.)

16 And the ten horns (Eisenhower Bush) which thou sawest upon the beast, (US government headed by Satan from the beginning.) these shall hate the whore, (nation) and shall make her desolate (Caused God to withdraw from the people due to disobedience) and naked,

(In financial ruin) and shall eat her flesh, and burn her with fire. (Nuclear bomb or super volcano erruption) (This is a rude awakening for many to know that the last 10 presidents despise the American people and their nation. It is the ultimate betrayal by any government to systematically dismantle the country it governs and, in the end, hand it over to Satan so that he can destroy it with some form of explosion.)

17 For God hath put in their hearts to fulfill his will, and to agree, and give their kingdom unto the beast, until the words of God shall be fulfilled. (This was God's plan to achieve his overall purpose.)

Hosea 2:8-9, 8 for she did not know that I gave her corn, and wine, and oil, and multiplied her silver and gold, which they prepared for Baal. 9 Therefore will I return, and take away my corn in the time thereof, and my wine in the season thereof, and will recover my wool and my flax given to cover her nakedness.

18 And the woman whom thou sawest is that great city, which reigneth over the kings of the earth.

Chapter 15

The fall of Babylon

Revelation 18

1 And after these things I saw another angel come down from heaven, having great power; and the earth was lightened with his glory.

2 And he cried mightily with a strong voice, saying, Babylon the great is fallen, is fallen, and is become the habitation of devils, and the hold of every foul spirit, and a cage of every unclean and hateful bird. (These Fallen Angels have been released from their prison for judgment, and they have made the U.S. their habitation. This is why you see the rampant lawlessness and contempt for God's laws all around.)

3 For all nations have drunk of the wine of the wrath of her fornication, (All nations have now been influenced by the U.S. system of government. The lawlessness, corruption, greed, covetousness, the way of Cain, and the Babylonian system has now taken hold of all nations.) The kings of the earth have committed fornication with her. (Many world leaders have made backroom deals with the U.S. government.) And the merchants of the earth have waxed rich through the abundance of her its covetousness. (The United States is the number one consumer nation in the world today; 25% of all produced goods are sold to the United States, and the sellers of such things have become rich through the abundance of its covetousness.)

4 And I heard another voice from heaven, saying, Come out of her, my people, that ye be not partakers of her sins, and that ye receive not of her plagues. (This verse is of extreme importance because God

is giving specific instructions to His people. Come out of her, my people, that ye be not partakers of her sins, and that ye receive not of her plagues. God's people are to leave the U.S .The United States of America was spiritually judged at the hands of Barack Hussein Obama before the end of his first term.)

Micah 2:10

Arise ye, and depart; for this is not your rest: because it is polluted, it shall destroy you, even with a sore destruction.

Zechariah 2:6-9

6 Ho, ho, come forth, and flee from the land of the north, saith the LORD: for I have spread you abroad as the four winds of the heaven, saith the LORD.

7 Deliver thyself, O Zion, that dwellest with the daughter of Babylon.

8 For thus saith the LORD of hosts; after the glory hath He sent me unto the nations which spoiled you: for he that toucheth you toucheth the apple of His eye.

9 For, behold, I will shake mine hand upon them, and they shall be a spoil to their servants: and ye shall know that the LORD of hosts hath sent me.

Jeremiah 4:6-10

6 Set up the standard toward Zion: retire, stay not: for I will bring evil from the north, and a great destruction.

7 The lion is come up from his thicket, and the destroyer of the Gentiles is on his way; he is gone forth from his place to make thy land desolate; and thy cities shall be laid waste, without an inhabitant.

8 For this gird you with sackcloth, lament and howl: for the fierce anger of the LORD is not turned back from us.

9 And it shall come to pass at that day, saith the LORD, that the heart of the king shall perish, and the heart of the princes; and the priests shall be astonished, and the prophets shall wonder.

10 Then said I, Ah, Lord GOD! Surely thou hast greatly deceived this people and Jerusalem, saying, ye shall have peace; whereas the sword reacheth unto the soul.

Jeremiah 50:8-9, 16

8 Remove out of the midst of Babylon, and go forth out of the land of the Chaldeans, and be as the he goats before the flocks.

9 For, lo, I will raise and cause to come up against Babylon an assembly of great nations from the north country: and they shall set themselves in array against her;

from thence she shall be taken: their arrows shall be as of a mighty expert man; none shall return in vain.

16 Cut off the sower from Babylon, and him that handleth the sickle in the time of harvest: for fear of the oppressing sword they shall turn everyone to his people, and they shall flee everyone to his land.

Jeremiah 51:6, 9, 45, 50

6 Flee out of the midst of Babylon, and deliver every man his soul: be not cut off in her iniquity; for this is the time of the LORD'S vengeance; he will render unto her a recompense.

9 We would have healed Babylon, but she is not healed: forsake her, and let us go every one into his own country for her judgment reacheth unto heaven, and is lifted even to the skies.

45 My people, go ye out of the midst of her, and deliver ye every man his soul from the fierce anger of the LORD.

50 Ye that have escaped the sword, go away, stand not still: remember the LORD afar off, and let Jerusalem come into your mind.

Isaiah 48:20

Go ye forth of Babylon, flee ye from the Chaldeans, with a voice of singing declare ye, tell this, utter it even to the end of the earth; say ye, The LORD hath redeemed his servant Jacob.

Isaiah 13:14

And it shall be as the chased roe, and as a sheep that no man taketh up: they shall every man turn to his people, and flee every one into his land.

Those who refused to leave the U.S. because of their houses, cars, and businesses listened to the admonition.

2 Esdras 15:1-8

1 Behold, speak thou in the ears of my people the words of prophecy, which I will put in thy mouth, saith the Lord:

2 And cause them to be written in paper: for they are faithful and true.

3 Fear not the imaginations against thee, let not the incredulity of them trouble thee, that speak against thee.

4 For all the unfaithful shall die in their unfaithfulness.

5 Behold, saith the Lord, I will bring plagues upon the world; the sword, famine, death, and destruction.

6 For wickedness hath exceedingly polluted the whole earth, and their hurtful works are fulfilled.

7 Therefore saith the Lord,

8 I will hold my tongue no more as touching their wickedness, which they profanely commit, neither will I suffer them in those things, in which they wickedly exercise themselves: behold, the innocent and righteous blood crieth unto me, and the souls of the just complain continually.

2 Esdras 16:35-52

35 Hear now these things and understand them, ye servants of the Lord.

36 Behold, the word of the Lord, receive it: believe not the gods of whom the Lord spake.

37 Behold, the plagues draw nigh, and are not slack.

38 As when a woman with child in the ninth month bringeth forth her son, with two or three hours of her birth, great pains compass her womb, which pains, when the child cometh forth, they slack not a moment:

39 Even so shall not the plagues be slack to come upon the earth, and the world shall mourn, and sorrows shall come upon it on every side.

40 O my people, hear my word: make you ready to thy battle, and in those evils be even as pilgrims upon the earth.

41 He that selleth, let him be as he that fleeth away: and he that buyeth, as one that will lose:

42 He that occupieth merchandise, as he that hath no profit by it: and he that buildeth, as he that shall not dwell therein:

43 He that soweth, as if he should not reap; so also he that planteth the vineyard, as he that shall not gather the grapes:

44 They that marry, as they that shall get no children; and they that marry not, as the widowers.

45 And therefore they that labour labour in vain:

46 For strangers shall reap their fruits, and spoil their goods, overthrow their houses, and take their children captives, for in captivity and famine shall they get children.

47 And they that occupy their merchandise with robbery, the more they deck their cities, their houses, their possessions, and their persons:

48 The more I will be angry with them for their sin, saith the Lord.

49 Like as a whore envieth a right honest and virtuous woman:

50 So shall righteousness hate iniquity, when she decketh herself, and shall accuse her to her face, when he cometh that shall defend him that diligently searcheth out every sin upon earth.

51 And therefore be ye not like thereunto, nor to the works thereof.

52 For yet a little, and iniquity shall be taken away out of the earth, and righteousness shall reign among you

Jeremiah 51:58

Thus saith the LORD of hosts: The broad walls of Babylon shall be utterly broken, and her high gates shall be burned with fire; and the people shall labour in vain, and the folk in the fire, and they shall be weary .

Similitude 1:1-3

1 And he said unto me, Ye know that ye who are the servants of the Lord, live here as in a pilgrimage; for your city is far off from the city.

2 If, therefore, ye know your city in which ye are to dwell, why do ye here buy states, and provide yourselves with delicacies, and stately buildings, and superfluous houses? For he that provides himself these things in this city, does not think of returning into his city.

3 O foolish, and doubtful, and wretched man; who understandest not that all these things belong to other men, and are under the power of another.

Remember, prophecy is of no useful purpose if you do not know the approximate time of its fulfillment. But once you know and simply refuse to follow the commands of God, you're putting God to the test and not being obedient. In the end, you will be the one to lose. Do not say no one warned you of the soon approaching disaster, or that God should have sent someone to warn you. He just did! This is not the first time God has commanded His people to flee from the evil to come. Notice!

Jeremiah 6:1

O ye children of Benjamin, gather yourselves to flee out of the midst of Jerusalem, and blow the trumpet in Tekoa, and set up a sign of fire in Bethhaccerem: for evil appeareth out of the north, and great destruction.

Jeremiah 48:28

O ye that dwell in Moab, leave the cities, and dwell in the rock, and be like the dove that maketh her nest in the sides of the hole's mouth.

Jeremiah 49:8, 30

8 Flee ye, turn back, dwell deep, O inhabitants of Dedan; for I will bring the calamity of Esau upon him, the time that I will visit him.

30 Flee, get you far off, dwell deep, O ye inhabitants of Hazor, saith the LORD; for Nebuchadrezzar king of Babylon hath taken counsel against you, and hath conceived a purpose against you.

Tobit 14:3-4, 8, 12-15

3 And when he was very aged, he called his son, and the sons of his son, and said to him, My son, take thy children; for, behold, I am aged, and am ready to depart out of this life.

4 Go into Media my son, for I surely believe those things which Jonas the prophet spake of Nineve, that it shall be overthrown; and that for a time peace shall rather be in Media; and that our brethren shall lie scattered in the earth from that good land: and Jerusalem shall be desolate, and the house of God in it shall be burned, and shall be desolate for a time;

2 And when Anna, his mother, was dead, he buried her with his father. But Tobias departed with his wife and children to Ecbatane to Raguel, his father-in-law,

13 Where he became old with honour, and he buried his father and mother-in-law honourably, and he inherited their substance, and his father Tobit's.

14 And he died at Ecbatane in Media, being an hundred and seven and twenty years old.

15 But before he died, he heard of the destruction of Nineveh, which was taken by Nabuchodonosor and Assuerus, and before his death, he rejoiced over Nineveh.

Apocalypse of Baruch 2:1-2, pg. 35

1 For I had said these things to thee that thou mayest tell Jeremiah, and all those who are like you, to retire from this city.

2 For your works are to this city as a firm pillar, and your prayers as a strong wall.

Once again, I will make this as clear as I possibly can. Let us once again review the information the Great God has revealed to us:

From 2 Esdras 11 & 12 (The Vision of the Eagle and the Lion), we learned:

-The eagle is theU.S. government

-Satan has been using the Republican/Democrat scheme to achieve his end goal

-The last 10 presidents mark the end of its dominion (Eisenhower-Bush)

-The last president where Spiritual Judgement begins, the 11th is (Obama), and his reign is full of trouble

-There will be 44 presidencies, and spiritual judgement begins

-This is the same prophecy as Daniel's vision of the fourth beast

From Daniel 7 (The Vision of the Fourth Beast), we learned:

-The 4th beast is the U.S. government

-The 10 horns are the last 10 presidents (Eisenhower-Bush) and mark the end time of this kingdom's dominion

-The little horn, the 11^{th,} is Obama

-Obama wages war on the saints, which he did

From our research, we learned:

-Satan has come to earth in "the likeness of a man"

-Satan is indwelling Barack Hussein Obama

-We know what his name means

-We know the mystery of 666

-We know he is the abomination of desolation.

-His mission is to kill and destroy

From Revelation 17 (Mystery Babylon), we learned:

-Babylon is the U.S.

-The people have been enslaved in a Satan-induced financial system that has entrapped the masses.

-The 10 horns (Eisenhower-Bush)

-The 10 horns (Eisenhower-Bush) have given all their authority to the beast (Obama).

-God began spiritual judgment of the U.S. when Obama was in office.

Furthermore, throughout all these prophecies, God gives us the same time frame:

- Short reign and full of trouble, 3 ½ years, or 42 months, or 1260 days.

Obama took office in 2009, and God began his spiritual judgment cycle approximately 3.5 years later and has brought to pass everything exactly as He said He would, right on to this very day. Do not even entertain the idea that He will not bring to pass what is soon to be fulfilled. He already has! Read it right in the Scriptures.

Romans 3:3-4

3 For what if some did not believe? Shall their unbelief make the faith of God without effect?

4 God forbid: yea, let God be true, but every man a liar; as it is written, That thou mightest be justified in thy sayings, and mightest overcome when thou art judged.

Numbers 23:19

God is not a man, that he should lie; neither the son of man, that he should repent: hath he said, and shall he not do it? Or hath he spoken, and shall he not make it good?

2 Esdras 15:1-4

1 Behold, speak thou in the ears of my people the words of prophecy, which I will put in thy mouth, saith the Lord:

2 And cause them to be written in paper: for they are faithful and true.

3 Fear not the imaginations against thee, let not the incredulity of them trouble thee, that speak against thee.

4 For all the unfaithful shall die in their unfaithfulness.

I cannot understand the logic of certain people. Knowing that the U.S. is Babylon, that Obama is the antichrist, and that some form of nuclear or maybe even volcanic explosion (like Yellowstone, FIRE !) is going to destroy the United States, they continue their daily lives as if everything that is written will not come to pass; Instead of making arrangements and leaving as soon as possible. For those who refused to heed the warning, even with the overwhelming evidence staring directly at them, I have this to say: Do you honestly think that when a volcanic explosion or volcanic eruption (like Yellowstone) goes off that your house, cars, or businesses will remain standing? Everything will be turned to ashes! If by the grace of God you survive, the Bible says your tribulation has just begun. Besides, do you think that God inspired so many verses that specifically command His people to get out of Babylon for the people to just sit around? Of course not! God means exactly what He says!

The life of a servant of God is a life of spiritual struggle. But in this very end time, it also becomes a struggle for survival. Both the spiritual and physical go hand-in-hand.

Matthew 24:15-16, 20–22

15 When ye therefore shall see the abomination of desolation, spoken of by Daniel the prophet, stand in the holy place, (whoso breadth, let him understand:)

16 Then let them which are in Judaea flee into the mountains:

20 But pray ye that your flight be not in the winter, neither on the sabbath day:

21 For then shall be great tribulation, such as was not since the beginning of the world to this time, nor ever shall be.

22 And except those days should be shortened, there should no flesh be saved: but for the elect's sake those days shall be shortened.

Mark 13:18-20

18 And pray ye that your flight be not in the winter.

19 For in those days shall be affliction, such as was not from the beginning of the creation which God created unto this time, neither shall be.

20 And except that the Lord had shortened those days, no flesh should be saved: but for the elect's sake, whom he hath chosen, he hath shortened the days.

Luke 21:20-22, 35-36

20 And when ye shall see Jerusalem compassed with armies, then know that the desolation thereof is nigh.

21 Then let them who are in Judaea flee to the mountains; and let them who are in the midst of it depart out; and let not them that are in the countries enter thereinto.

22 For these be the days of vengeance, that all things which are written may be fulfilled.

35 For as a snare shall it come on all them that dwell on the face of the whole earth.

36 Watch ye therefore, and pray always, that ye may be accounted worthy to escape all these things that shall come to pass, and to stand before the Son of man.

Ascension of Isaiah 4:13

those also who were believers in Him, of these few in those days will be left as His servants, while they flee from desert to desert, awaiting the coming of the Beloved.

In 1 Corinthians 9:24-27, Paul compares the Christian life to a race to win a prize. "Do you not know that in a race all the runners compete, but only one receives the prize? So run [your race] so that you may lay hold of the prize and make it yours Therefore, I do not run uncertainly (without a definite end) (Amplified Parallel Bible)

So, what is your definite end? Is it not to be spiritually and physically prepared for the very soon coming judgment? Or, are you just going through the motions and playing church on Sundays? Do you believe in all the words in the Bible, or do you pick and choose which verses you are or are not going to obey? Examine yourself, for after proclaiming the gospel to others and things about it (faith, sin, judgment), you should become unfit and not stand the test through unbelief. Examine yourselves, whether ye be in the faith; prove yourselves. (2 Corinthians 13:5)

Genesis 19 tells of Lot's family, who lived in the populous but depraved cities of Sodom and Gomorrah, which God was getting ready to destroy. Lot was found to be righteous by God, so he sent two Angels to warn Lot to make haste (flee, get out)! As Lot, his wife, and two daughters lingered, the Angels laid hold upon all their hands and brought them out of the depraved city and told them, Escape to the mountain for your life. Do not look behind you (don't look back) or stay in any part of the plain, or you will be consumed (destroyed).

God granted Lot's plea to stay in a small city. The Lord destroyed Sodom and Gomorrah, the plain, and the inhabitants with fire and brimstone from heaven. But Lot's wife looked back; she could not let go of her life in Sodom (some of her family remained in Sodom, Jasher 19:51-53) and was turned into a pillar of salt in the fiery destruction. She lacked faith, disobeyed, and died. (William F. Dankenbring, Prophecy Flash 2010)

All of God's servants serve Him in faith, even though they did not know everything from the beginning.

Romans 1:17

17 For therein is the righteousness of God revealed from faith to faith: as it is written, The just shall live by faith.

Hebrews 11:1-2, 13-16, 37-40

1 Now faith is the substance of things hoped for, the evidence of things not seen.

2 For by it the elders obtained a good report.

13 These all died in faith, not having received the promises, but having seen them afar off, and were persuaded of them, and embraced them, and confessed that they were strangers and pilgrims on the earth.

14 For they that say such things declare plainly that they seek a country.

15 And truly, if they had been mindful of that country from whence they came out, they might have had the opportunity to have returned.

16 But now they desire a better country, that is, a heavenly: wherefore God is not ashamed to be called their God: for he hath prepared for them a city.

37 They were stoned, they were sawn asunder, were tempted, were slain with the sword: they wandered about in sheepskins and goatskin; being destitute, afflicted, tormented;

38 (Of whom the world was not worthy) they wandered in deserts, and in mountains, and dens and caves of the earth.

39 And these all, having obtained a good report through faith, received not the promise:

40 God, having provided some better thing for us, that they without us should not be made perfect.

Do not get any irrational ideas and think of arming yourself to fight the Antichrist and his army. DO NOT DO THAT!!! I cannot stress this point enough. God's command is to simply get out! Peaceably, orderly, without making any waves or commotions. Not to try to fight your way out of this. You will not win! This is God's will, God's judgment! Trying to fight this is fighting against the will of God and will land you in prison or dead! DO NOT DO IT!!! You are to be subjected (Law Bidding) to the authorities.

Romans 13:1-2

1 Let every soul be subject unto the higher powers. For there is no power but of God: the powers that be are ordained of God.

2 Whosoever therefore resisted the power, resisted the ordinance of God: and they that resist shall receive to themselves damnation.

Ephesians 6:12-13

12 For we wrestle not against flesh and blood, but against principalities, against powers, against the rulers of the darkness of this world, against spiritual wickedness in high places.

13 Wherefore take unto you the whole armor of God, that ye may be able to withstand in the evil day, and having done all, to stand.

2 Corinthians 10:3-6

3 For though we walk in the flesh, we do not war after the flesh:

4 (For the weapons of our warfare are not carnal, but mighty through God to the pulling down of strongholds ;)

5 Casting down imaginations, and every high thing that exalted itself against the knowledge of God, and bringing into captivity every thought to the obedience of Christ;

6 And having in readiness to avenge all disobedience, when your obedience is fulfilled.

Revelation 17:17

For God hath put in their hearts to fulfil his will, and to agree, and give their kingdom unto the beast, until the words of God shall be fulfilled.

Revelation 18:8, 20

8 Therefore shall her plagues come in one day, death, and mourning, and famine and she shall be utterly burned with fire: for strong is the Lord God who judged her.

20 Rejoice over her, thou heaven, and ye holy apostles and prophets; for God hath avenged you on her.

Revelation 19:2

2 For true and righteous are his judgments: for he hath judged the great whore, which did corrupt the earth with her fornication, and hath avenged the blood of his servants at her hand.

This is the avenging of God's covenant! God is the one who brought judgment upon the United States. It is God's doing, please DO NOT TRY TO PHYSICALLY FIGHT THIS!

I think I have made the point very clear and will not extend on this subject any longer. God's people must leave the U.S., or they will receive the plagues coming upon it and be consumed by them. Unfortunately, many will not heed the warning.

WARNING

Do not fall for this Rapture teaching of poorly misconstrued Bible verses circulating in mainstream Christianity. God did not come and pick up the children of Israel in a cloud out of Egyptian slavery. He told them to prepare themselves and, at the appointed time, to leave. Think about that! (MORE ON THIS "RAPTURE" LATER)

5 For her sins have reached unto heaven, and God hath remembered her iniquities. (The amount of sin running rampant in America has now reached its limit. God has had enough.)

6 Reward her even as she rewarded you, and double unto her double according to her works: in the cup which she hath filled fill to her double. (For all the lies, corruption, trickery, abuse of power, covetousness, the government has weaponized agencies like the CIA, FBI, DHS, etc to target those with certain DNA traits (Children of God) and have subjected them to MK-Ultra, voice to skull manipulation, gang stalking, gas lighting, energy ciphering and so much more, America will now be repaid according to what she deserves.)

7 How much she hath glorified herself, and lived deliciously, so much torment and sorrow give her: for she saith in her heart, I sit a queen, and am no widow, and shall see no sorrow. America has lived in an abundance of prosperity and has grown proud. Pride goth before destruction and a haughty spirit before a fall. (Proverbs 16:18). Now torment and sorrow will overtake her   .

8 Therefore shall her plagues come in one day, death, and mourning, and famine; and she shall be utterly (extremely or completely) burned with fire: for strong is the Lord God who judged her. (Notice it is God who has judged her. Satan cannot do anything without God allowing it.)

9 And the kings of the earth, who have committed fornication and lived deliciously with her, shall bewail her, and lament for her, when they shall see the smoke of her burning, (America is the #1 consuming nation in the world. 25% of the world's products are consumed by the US. The nations that sold their goods to her and acquired

massive amounts of wealth through the abundance of her covetousness will lament her destruction.)

10 Standing afar off for the fear of her torment, saying, Alas, alas, that great city Babylon, that mighty city! for in one hour is thy judgment come. (This verse shows that the destruction of Babylon will be seen from a great distance, and no one wants to approach for fear. This is a mushroom cloud made by some form of nuclear device or volcanic eruption that no one wants to approach for fear of radiation fallout.)

11 And the merchants of the earth shall weep and mourn over her; for no man berth their merchandise any more: (More evidence that Mystery Babylon is a great consuming nation, not an exporting nation like Germany.)

12 The merchandise of gold, and silver, and precious stones, and of pearls, and fine linen, and purple, and silk, and scarlet, and all thyine wood, and all manner vessels of ivory, and all manner vessels of most precious wood, and of brass, and iron, and marble,

13 And cinnamon, and odors, and ointments, and frankincense, and wine, and oil, and fine flour, and wheat, and beasts, and sheep, and horses, and chariots, and slaves, and souls of men. (Everything is imported.)

14 And the fruits that thy soul lusted after are departed from thee, and all things which were dainty and goodly are departed from thee, and thou shalt find them no more at all. (All that the American people have ever cared about was their financial prosperity without taking heed to God's laws. Now all these things will be gone. Cars, houses, businesses, retirement, etc., all gone! They have labored in vain! Labor not to be rich: cease from your own wisdom. (Proverbs 23:4)

15 The merchants of these things, which were made rich by her, shall stand afar off for the fear of her torment, weeping and wailing,

16 And saying, Alas, alas, that great city, that was clothed in fine linen, and purple, and scarlet, and decked with gold, and precious stones, and pearls! (Very wealthy, given to luxury.)

17 For in one hour so great riches are come to nought. And every shipmaster, and all the company in ships, and sailors, and as many as trade by sea, stood afar off,

18 And cried when they saw the smoke of her burning, saying, what city is like unto this great city! (Mushroom cloud)

19 And they cast dust on their heads, and cried, weeping and wailing, saying, Alas, alas, that great city, wherein were made rich all that had ships in the sea because of her costliness! For in one hour is she made desolate.

20 Rejoice over her, thou heaven, and ye holy apostles and prophets; for God hath avenged you on her. (God has judged America the great whore and has avenged all the holy prophets and apostles upon her. God's people are to rejoice at His judgment because now the kingdom of God has been established on earth. Those who do not want judgment to fall on Babylon obviously do not want God to establish His Kingdom. Be very careful that your heart is firmly established in the Kingdom of God, not in America or any other nation. Many pray the words Thy Kingdom come, thy will be done without realizing that for God to establish His Kingdom on earth, He must first judge the world and uproot this Satan-inspired government.)

21 And a mighty angel took up a stone like a great millstone, and cast it into the sea, saying, Thus with violence shall that great city Babylon

be thrown down, and shall be found no more at all. (The overthrow of America will be very violent.)

22 And the voice of harpers, and musicians, and of pipers, and trumpeters, shall be heard no more at all in thee; and no craftsman, of whatsoever craft he be, shall be found any more in thee; and the sound of a millstone shall be heard no more at all in thee;

23 And the light of a candle shall shine no more at all in thee; and the voice of the bridegroom and the bride shall be heard no more at all in thee for thy merchants were the great men of the earth; for by thy sorceries were all nations deceived. (By trickery, lies, and deceit, all nations were deceived.)

24 And in her was found the blood of prophets, and of saints, and of all that were slain upon the earth.

America had the choice to follow God's laws and chose not to. Instead, she went the way of Cain and after the error of Balaam for self-gratification and luxuries. Played the role of a whore who sells herself and of Judas who betrayed Jesus Christ, both for money. Changed the glory of an incorruptible God for the image of corruptible things. I am not being anti-Semitic, I am simply relaying a message. Don't be angry with the messenger who is telling you the truth. Would you prefer for me to lie and tell you everything is just fine and that God is not angry with the US and will never judge it? I cannot do that! I am not here to please men, for if I were to please men, I could not please God. Am I, therefore, becoming your enemy because I've told you the truth? Now, it is time for America to be repaid according to her works!

Other prophecies of Babylon:

Isaiah 13 & 47

Jeremiah 50 & 51

Chapter 16

The Role of Islam in the End

Mohammed (the founder and prophet of Islam) was born in Mecca, Saudi Arabia. Mohammed's call to be a prophet took place at about his age 40. He had a custom of going alone to a nearby mountain cave called Ghar Hira to meditate. He claims that on one of these occasions, he was called to be a prophet. Islamic tradition relates that while he was there, the angel Gabriel commanded him to recite in the name of Allah. When he failed to respond, the angel caught him by force and pressed him so hard that he could not bear it anymore. Then the angel repeated the command. Again, Mohammed failed to react, so the angel choked him. This happened 3 times until Mohammed started to recite in the name of Allah (the god Of Islam) what came to be viewed as a series of revelations that constitute the Quran. It is believed that Mohammed committed these revelations to memory during a period of 22 to 23 years from about 610 CE to his death in 632 CE (600 years after the crucifixion of Christ). These revelations were committed to memory by all until after Mohammed's death, and then this collection of revelations was compiled into what is known as the Quran today.

After Mohammed's death, a crisis arose as to who would be his successor. Never was there more bloodshed between Muslims than this one. The question of the true successor of Mohammed became the cause of division in the ranks of Islam. The Sunni Muslims accept the principle of elected office rather than Mohammed's blood descendants. This claim is refuted by the Shiite Muslims, who say that true leadership comes through Mohammed's bloodline. His cousin and son-in-law (Ali ibn Abi Talib) was the first Imam (leader and successor). He married Mohammed's favorite daughter, Fatimah. Their marriage produced sons Hasan & Husayn. The Shiites claim that from the beginning, Allah and Mohammed had appointed Ali as the legitimate successor. Of course, the Sunni Muslims view it differently.

Ali became the first Imam (was murdered), Hasan the second Imam (murdered), Husayn the third Imam (murdered). The majority of Shiites believe that there have only been 12 true Imams, the last of these, Muhammad Al-Muntazar, disappeared (878 CE) in the cave of the great Mosque at Samarra without leaving offspring. Thus, he became the hidden Imam. The Shiites believe that in the end time, he will reappear as the Mahdi (Divinely guided one, the Muslim messiah) to restore Islam, conquer the whole world, and usher in a short millennium where Islam will be the only religion and Sharia (Islamic law) the only law, before the end of all things.

By the time Mohammed founded Islam, as far as he was concerned, Judaism and Christianity had wandered from the path of truth. In fact, according to some Islamic commentators, the Quran implies rejection of Jews and Christians in stating: Not (the path) of those who earn thine anger nor of those who go astray. (Surah 1:7, mmp) Why is that? A Quranic commentary states: The people of the book went wrong: The Jews in breaking their covenant and slandering Mary and Jesus.. And the Christians in raising Jesus the apostle to equality with God.

You might be asking yourself, What does this all have to do with Babylon (America) and the antichrist (Obama)? Well, it has all to do with Islam as we shall see!!!

First of all, let's analyze the founding of Islam. Mohammed claims to have received these revelations from the angel Gabriel. But was this the Archangel Gabriel, or was it Satan pretending to be Gabriel? After all, we are very well aware that Satan transforms himself into an angel of light. (2 Corinthians 11:14)

Let me take you into a compilation of books you probably never even knew existed. They are called The Lost Books of the Bible. Here you will see Satan's method of operation and see for yourself that what he did with Mohammed, he tried to do before with others through many deceitful apparitions.

1 Adam & Eve 27:1-15

1 When Satan, the hater of all good, saw how they continued in prayer, and how God communed with them, and comforted them, and how He had accepted their offering, Satan made an apparition.

2 He began by transforming his hosts; in his hands was a flashing fire, and they were in a great light.

3 He then placed his throne near the mouth of the cave because he could not enter it because of their prayers. And he shed light into the cave, until the cave glistened over Adam and Eve; while his hosts began to sing praises.

4 And Satan did this, so that when Adam saw the light, he should think within himself that it was a heavenly light, and that Satan's hosts were angels; and that God had sent them to watch at the cave, and to give him light in the darkness.

5 So that when Adam came out of the cave and saw them, and Adam and Eve bowed to Satan, then he would overcome Adam thereby, and a second time humble him before God.

6 When, therefore, Adam and Eve saw the light, fancying it was real, they strengthened their hearts; yet, as they were trembling, Adam said to Eve:

7 Look at that great light, and at those many songs of praise, and at that host standing outside who won't come into our cave. Why don't they tell us what they want, where they are from, what the meaning of this light is, what those praises are, why they have been sent to this place, and why they won't come in?

8 If they were from God, they would come into the cave with us, and would tell us why they were sent.

9 Then Adam stood up and prayed to God with a burning heart, and said:

10 "O Lord, is there in the world another god besides You, who created angels and filled them with light, and sent them to keep us, who would come with them?

11 But, look, we see these hosts that stand at the mouth of the cave; they are in a great light; they sing loud praises. If they are of some other god than You, tell me; and if they are sent by you, inform me of the reason for which You have sent them.

12 No sooner had Adam said this than an angel from God appeared to him in the cave, who said to him, O Adam, fear not. This is Satan and his hosts; he wishes to deceive you as he deceived you at first. For the first time, he was hidden in the serpent; but this time he has come to you in the likeness of an angel of light; so that, when you worship him, he might enslave you, in the very presence of God.

13 Then the angel went from Adam and seized Satan at the opening of the cave, and stripped him of the pretense he had assumed, and brought him in his hideous form to Adam and Eve, who were afraid of him when they saw him.

14 And the angel said to Adam, This hideous form has been his ever since God made him fall from heaven. He could not have come near you in it; he therefore transformed himself into an angel of light.

15 Then the angel drove away Satan and his hosts from Adam and Eve, and said to them, Fear not; God who created you, will strengthen you.

1 Adam & Eve 33:1-5

1 But Satan, the hater of all good, sought them in the cave, but found them not, although he searched diligently for them.

2 But he found them standing in the water praying and thought within himself, Adam and Eve are standing like that in that water praying to God to forgive them their transgression, and to restore them to their former state, and to take them from under my hand.

3 But I will deceive them so that they shall come out of the water, and not fulfil their vow.

4 Then the hater of all good went not to Adam, but he went to Eve, and took the form of an angel of God, praising and rejoicing, and said to her:

5 Peace be to you! Be glad and rejoice! God is favorable to you, and He sent me to Adam. I have brought him the glad tidings of salvation and of his being filled with bright light as he was at first.

1 Adam & Eve 59:1-3

1 They were not very far from the cave when Satan came towards them and hid himself between them and the cave, under the form of two ravenous lions, three days without food, that came towards Adam and Eve, as if to break them in pieces and devour them.

2 Then Adam and Eve cried and prayed to God to deliver them from their paws.

3 Then the Word of God came to them and drove away the lions from them.

1 Adam & Eve 60:1-29

1 Then on the eighty-ninth day, Satan came to the cave, clad in a garment of light, and girt about with a bright girdle.

2 In his hands was a staff of light, and he looked most awful, but his face was pleasant, and his speech was sweet.

3 He thus transformed himself to deceive Adam and Eve, and to make them come out of the cave, before they had fulfilled the forty days.

4 For he said within himself, Now that when they had fulfilled the forty days' fasting and praying, God would restore them to their former state; but if He did not do so, He would still be favorable to them; and even if He had not mercy on them, would He yet give them something from the garden to comfort them; as already twice before.

5 Then Satan drew near the cave in this fair appearance, and said:

6 "O Adam, get up, stand up, you and Eve, and come along with me, to a good land; and don't be afraid. I am flesh and bones like you, and at first, I was a creature that God created.

7 And it was so that when He had created me, He placed me in a garden in the north, on the border of the world.

8 And He said to me, 'Stay here!' And I remained there according to His Word, neither did I transgress His commandment.

9 Then He made a slumber to come over me, and He brought you, O Adam, out of my side, but did not make you stay with me.

10 But God took you in His divine hand and placed you in a garden to the east.

11 Then I worried about you, for that while God had taken you out of my side, He had not let you stay with me.

12 But God said to me: 'Do not worry about Adam, whom I brought out of your side; no harm will come to him.

13 For now I have brought out of his side a help-meet for him; and I have given him joy by so doing.'

14 Then Satan said again, "I did not know how it is you are in this cave, nor anything about this trial that has come over you until God said to me, 'Behold, Adam has transgressed, he whom I had taken out of your side, and Eve also, whom I took out of his side; and I have driven them out of the garden; I have made them live in a land of sorrow and misery, because they transgressed against Me, and have obeyed Satan. And look, they are in suffering until this day, the eightieth.'

15 Then God said to me, 'Get up, go to them, and make them come to your place, and suffer not that Satan come near them, and afflict them. For they are now in great misery, and lie helpless from hunger.'

16 He further said to me, 'When you have taken them to yourself, give them to eat of the fruit of the Tree of Life, and give them to drink of the water of peace; and clothe them in a garment of light,

and restore them to their former state of grace, and leave them not in misery, for they came from you. But grieve not over them, nor repent of that which has come over them.

17 But when I heard this, I was sorry; and my heart could not patiently bear it for your sake, O my child.

18 But, O Adam, when I heard the name of Satan, I was afraid, and I said within myself, I will not come out because he might trap me as he did my children, Adam and Eve.

19 And I said, 'O God, when I go to my children, Satan will meet me in the way, and war against me, as he did against them.'

20 Then God said to me, 'Fear not; when you find him, hit him with the staff that is in your hand, and don't be afraid of him, for you are of old standing, and he shall not prevail against you.'

21 Then I said, 'O my Lord, I am old, and cannot go. Send your angels to bring them.'

22 But God said to me, 'Angels, verily, are not like them and they will not consent to come with them. But I have chosen you, because they are your offspring and are like you, and they will listen to what you say.'

23 God said further to me, If you don't have enough strength to walk, I will send a cloud to carry you and set you down at the entrance of their cave; then the cloud will return and leave you there.

24 And if they will come with you, I will send a cloud to carry you and them.'

25 Then He commanded a cloud, and it bore me up and brought me to you; and then it went back.

26 And now, O my children, Adam and Eve, look at my old gray hair and my feeble state, and at my coming from that distant place. Come, come with me, to a place of rest.

27 Then he began to cry and to sob before Adam and Eve, and his tears poured on the ground like water.

28 And when Adam and Eve raised their eyes and saw his beard, and heard his sweet talk, their hearts softened towards him; they obeyed him, for they believed he was true.

29 And it seemed to them that they were his offspring, when they saw that his face was like their own and they trusted him.

1 Adam & Eve 61:1-7

1 Then he took Adam and Eve by the hand and began to bring them out of the cave.

2 But when they had come a little ways out of it, God knew that Satan had overcome them, and had brought them out before the forty days were ended, to take them to some distant place, and to destroy them.

3 Then the Word of the Lord God again came and cursed Satan, and drove him away from them.

4 And God began to speak to Adam and Eve, saying to them, What made you come out of the cave, to this place?

5 Then Adam said to God, Did you create a man before us? For when we were in the cave, there suddenly came to us a friendly old man who said to us, 'I am a messenger from God to you, to bring you back to some place of rest.'

6 And we believed, O God, that he was a messenger from you; and we came out with him; and knew not where we should go with him.

7 Then God said to Adam, See, that is the father of evil arts, who brought you and Eve out of the Garden of Delights. And now, indeed, when he saw that you and Eve both joined together in fasting and praying, and that you came not out of the cave before the end of the forty days, he wished to make your purpose vein, to break your mutual bond; to cut off all hope from you, and to drive you to some place where he might destroy you.

1 Adam & Eve 67: 8-12

8 But as they were going up from below the mountain where they were, Satan and his hosts met them in the form of angels, praising God.

9 Then Satan said to Adam, O Adam, why are you so pained with hunger and thirst? It seems to me that Satan has burnt up the wheat." And Adam said to him, Yes.

10 Again, Satan said to Adam, Come back with us; we are angels of God. God sent us to you, to show you another field of corn, better than that; and beyond it is a fountain of good water, and many trees, where you shall live near it, and work the corn field to better purpose than that which Satan has consumed.

11 Adam thought that he was true, and that they were angels who talked with him; and he went back with them.

12 Then Satan began to lead astray Adam and Eve for eight days, until they both fell as if dead, from hunger, thirst, and faintness. Then he fled with his hosts   and left them.

1 Adam & Eve 69: 1-3

1 Then Satan, the hater of all good, envious of Adam and his offering through which he found favor with God, hastened and took a sharp stone from among the sharp iron stones; he appeared in the form of a man, and went and stood by Adam and Eve.

2 Adam was then offering on the altar, and had begun to pray, with his hands spread before God.

3 Then Satan hastened with the sharp iron stone he had with him, and with it pierced Adam on the right side, from which flowed blood and water, then Adam fell on the altar like a corpse. And Satan fled

1 Adam & Eve 70: 1-15

1 After this, Satan, the hater of all good, took the form of an angel, and with him two others, so that they looked like the three angels who had brought to Adam gold, incense, and myrrh.

2 They passed before Adam and Eve while they were under the tree, and greeted Adam and Eve with fair words that were full of deceit.

3 But when Adam and Eve saw their pleasant expression, and heard their sweet speech, Adam rose, welcomed them, and brought them to Eve, and they remained all together; Adam's heart the while, being glad because he thought concerning them, that they were the same angels, who had brought him gold, incense, and myrrh.

4 Because, when they came to Adam the first time, there came over him from them peace and joy, through their bringing him good tokens; so Adam thought that they had come a second time to give him other tokens for him to rejoice therewith. For he did not know it was Satan; therefore, he received them with joy and consorted with them.

5 Then Satan, the tallest of them, said, Rejoice, O Adam, and be glad. Look, God has sent us to you to tell you something.

6 And Adam said, What is it?Then Satan answered, It is a simple thing, yet it is the Word of God. Will you accept it from us and do it? But if you will not accept it, we will return to God, and tell Him that you would not receive His Word.

7 And Satan said again to Adam, Don't be afraid and don't tremble; don't you know us?

8 But Adam said, I do not know you.

9 Then Satan said to him, I am the angel that brought you gold, and took it to the cave; this other angel is the one that brought you incense; and that third angel is the one who brought you myrrh when you were on top of the mountain, and who carried you to the cave.

10 But as to the other angels, our fellows, who bore you to the cave, God has not sent them with us this time; for He said to us, 'You will be enough'.

11 So when Adam heard these words, he believed them, and said to these angels, Speak the Word of God, that I may receive it.

12 And Satan said to him, Swear, and promise me that you will receive it.

13 Then Adam said, I do not know how to swear and promise.

14 And Satan said to him, Hold out your hand, and put it inside my hand.

15 Then Adam held out his hand, and put it into Satan's hand when Satan said to him, Say, now So true as God is living, rational, and

speaking, who raised the stars in heaven, and established the dry ground on the waters, and has created me out of the four elements, and out of the dust of the earthI will not break my promise, nor renounce my word.

1 Adam & Eve 71:3

3 But God never spoke the words that you have said and you are not God's angels, and you weren't sent from Him. But you are devils that have come to me under the false appearance of angels. Away from me; you, cursed of God!

1 Adam & Eve 72: 1-8

1 Then Satan and ten from his hosts transformed themselves into maidens, unlike any others in the whole world for grace.

2 They came up out of the river in the presence of Adam and Eve, and they said among themselves, Come, we will look at the faces of Adam and Eve, who are of the men on earth. How beautiful they are, and how different their look is from our faces. Then they came to Adam and Eve, and greeted them, and stood wondering at them.

3 Adam and Eve looked at them also, and wondered at their beauty, and said, Is there, then, under us, another world, with such beautiful creatures as these in it?

4 And those maidens said to Adam and Eve, Yes, indeed, we are an abundant creation.

5 Then Adam said to them, But how do you multiply?

6 And they answered him, We have husbands who have married us, and we bear them children, who grow up, and who in their turn marry and are married, and also bear children; and thus we increase.

And if so be, O Adam, you will not believe us, we will show you our husbands and our children.

7 Then they shouted over the river as if to call their husbands and their children, who came up from the river, men and children; and every man came to his wife, his children being with him.

8 But when Adam and Eve saw them, they stood silent and wondered at them.

2 Adam & Eve 3:4-5

4 Then Satan, the hater of all good, when he saw Adam thus alone, fasting and praying, appeared unto him in the form of a beautiful woman, who came and stood before him in the night of the fortieth day, and said unto him:

5 "0 Adam, from the time ye have dwelt in this cave, we have experienced great peace from you, and your prayers have reached us, and we have been comforted about you.

2 Adam & Eve 3: 15-16

15 Then God sent His Word unto Adam, saying, O Adam, that figure is the one that promised thee the Godhead, and majesty; he is not favorably disposed towards thee; but shows himself to thee at one time in the form of a woman; another moment, in the likeness of an angel; on another occasions, in the similitude of a serpent; and at another time, in the semblance of a god; but he does all that only to destroy thy soul.

16 "Now, therefore, O Adam, understanding thy heart, I have delivered thee many a time from his hands; to show thee that I am a merciful God; and that I wish thy good, and that I do not wish thy ruin.

2 Adam & Eve 4: 1-5

Then God ordered Satan to show himself to Adam plainly, in his hideous form.

2 But when Adam saw him, he feared and trembled at the sight of him.

3 And God said to Adam, Look at this devil, and at his hideous look, and know that he is who made thee fall from brightness into darkness, from peace and rest to toil and misery.

4 And look, 0 Adam, at him, who said of himself that he is God! Can God be black? Would God take the form of a woman? Is there anyone stronger than God? And can He be overpowered?

5 See, then, 0 Adam, and behold him bound in thy presence, in the air, unable to flee away! Therefore, I say unto thee, be not afraid of him; henceforth take care, and beware of him, in whatever he may do to thee.

2 Adam & Eve 17: 3-6, 46

3 At the end of these said years, there came unto him this sign. As Jared was standing like a lion before the bodies of his fathers, praying and warning his people, Satan envied him and wrought a beautiful apparition because Jared would not let his children do aught without his counsel.

4 Satan then appeared to him with thirty men of his hosts, in the form of handsome men; Satan himself being the elder and tallest among them, with a fine beard.

5 They stood at the mouth of the cave and called out to Jared from within it.

6 He came out to them and found them looking like fine men, full of light and great beauty. He wondered at their beauty and their looks , and thought within himself whether they might not be of the children of Cain.

46 He then wept and said, O God, destroy me not with this race, concerning which my fathers have warned me; for now, 0 my Lord God, I thought those who appeared to me were my fathers; but I have found them out to be devils, who allured me by this beautiful apparition, until I believed them.

There's no need to elaborate on these verses, for they speak for themselves. What happened to Mohammed was one of Satan's oldest tricks. Something the Watchers have been doing from the very beginning.

Here is what happened: Satan appeared to Mohammed as Gabriel, the angel of God, and gave him a revelation (a well-concocted story). Poor Mohammed, without any previous knowledge of the Scriptures or Satan's method of operation, simply did not know that Satan was playing him like a fiddle to achieve this end-time goal.

Mohammed fell right into his trap, bait, line, hook, and sinker! Satan has always wanted to imitate God, so he used Mohammed to form his version of twisted truth. By forming Islam and orchestrating the disappearing of the 12th Imam (In the same way the Watchers "abduct" humans in this day and age.), Satan was able to pave the way for his coming to earth in the end time in the likeness of a man, the 12th Imam (Islam's version of the Messiah). This is who Barack Hussein Obama will say he is, and in reality, Satan, the great deceiver who is indwelling him, was the originator of this deception. Some ask themselves, how could anyone believe such a satanic lie? Well, just look at the millions of Muslims around the world. This deception could have entangled any one of us. God's mercy is what has kept us attached to the truth.

The prophets and apostles were very well aware of Satan's trickeries. It even seems that Paul knew exactly what would be the method of the great deception when he addressed the Galatians 600 years before the deceptive founding of Islam.

Galatians 1:6-9

6 I marvel that ye are so soon removed from him that called you into the grace of Christ unto another gospel:

7 Which is not another, but some trouble you, and would pervert the gospel of Christ.

8 But though we, or an angel from heaven, preach any other gospel unto you than that which we have preached unto you, let him be accursed.

9 As we said before, so say I now again, If any man preach any other gospel unto you than that ye have received, let him be accursed.

2 Corinthians 2:11

Lest Satan should get an advantage over us: for we are not ignorant of his devices.

2 Corinthians 11:3

But I fear, lest by any means, as the serpent beguiled Eve through his subtilty, so your minds should be corrupted from the simplicity that is in Christ.

1 John 4:2-3

2 Hereby know ye the Spirit of God: Every spirit that confesseth that Jesus Christ is come in the flesh is of God:

3 And every spirit that confesseth not that Jesus Christ is come in the flesh is not of God: and this is that spirit of antichrist, whereof ye have heard that it should come; and even now already is it in the world.

Jubilees 20:12-13

12 Ishmael (Abraham's firstborn with Hagar) and his sons, and the sons of Keturah and their sons, went together and settled from Paran to the border of Babylon in all the land that is toward the East, facing the desert.

13 These mingled (intermarried) with each other, and their names were called Arabs and Ishmaelites.

Furthermore, the Apostles knew that the descendants of Ishmael (The Arabs) would be the ones in bondage to the deception.

In the following verses, Paul, addressing the Galatians, speaks of an allegory with a much deeper meaning than we have ever realized. But now, knowing the rise of the Nation of Islam and whose descendants they are, this deep allegory becomes clear.

Galatians 4:22-31

22 For it is written that Abraham had two sons, the one by a bond-maid, the other by a freewoman.

23 But he who was of the bondwoman was born after the flesh; but he of the freewoman was by promise.

24 Which things are an allegory for these are the two covenants; the one from Mount Sinai, which leadeth to bondage, which is Agar . (The Mother of Ishmael, the Arabs).

25 For this Agar is Mount Sinai in Arabia, and answereth to Jerusalem which now is, and is in bondage with her children.

26 But Jerusalem, which is above, is free, which is the mother of us all.

27 For it is written, Rejoice, thou barren that bearest not; break forth and cry, thou that travailest not: for the desolate hath many more children than she which hath an husband.

28 Now we, brethren, as Isaac was, are the children of promise.

29 But as then he that was born after the flesh persecuted him that was born after the Spirit, even so it is now.

30 Nevertheless, what saith the scripture? Cast out the bondwoman and her son: for the son of the bondwoman shall not be heir with the son of the freewoman.

31 So then, brethren, we are not children of the bondwoman, but of the free.

The threat of Islam is precisely what the following chapters warn this end-time generation of.

Psalm 83

1 Keep not thou silence, O God: hold not thy peace, and be not still , O God.

2 For, lo, thine enemies make a tumult: and they that hate thee have lifted the head.

3 They have taken crafty counsel (Using or involving cunning or trickery to deceive other people; a conspiracy) against thy people, and consulted against thy hidden ones.

4 They have said, Come, and let us cut them off from being a nation; that the name of Israel may be no more in remembrance.

5 For they have consulted together with one consent (A conspiracy): they are confederate (One of two or more people, groups, or nations that have allied for a common purpose; a conspirator) against thee:

6 The tabernacles of Edom, and the Ishmaelites (The Arab Nation); of Moab, and the Hagarenes;

7 Gebal, and Ammon, and Amalek; the Philistines with the inhabitants of Tyre;

8 Assur also is joined with them: they have helped the children of Lot. Selah.

9 Do unto them as unto the Midianites; as to Sisera, as to Jabin, at the brook of Kison:

10 Which perished at Endor: they became as dung for the earth.

11 Make their nobles like Oreb, and like Zeeb: yea, all their princes as Zebah, and as Zalmunna:

12 Who said, Let us take to ourselves the houses of God in possession.

13 O my God, make them like a wheel; as the stubble before the wind.

14 As the fire burnet a wood, and as the flame septet the mountains on fire;

15 So persecute them with thy tempest, and make them afraid with thy storm.

16 Fill their faces with shame; that they may seek thy name, O LORD.

17 Let them be confounded and troubled for ever; yea, let them be put to shame, and perish :

18 That men may know that thou, whose name alone is JEHOVAH, art the Most High over all the earth. (Not Allah, JEHOVAH!!!)

Enoch 56:5

5 And in those days the angels shall return (The Watchers are back) And hurl themselves to the east (The Middle East, The Islamic/Arab Nations) upon the Parthians (The people who came from Parthia, an ancient country in Southwest Asia that ruled an empire until the 3rd century AD) and Medes: (Modern-day Iran)

They (The Watchers) shall stir up the kings (rulers, leaders, heads of state), so that a spirit of unrest shall come upon them, And they shall rouse them from their thrones,

That they may break forth as lions from their lairs, And as hungry wolves among their flocks. (Terrorism)

2 Esdras 15:26-29

26 For the Lord knoweth all them that sin against him, and therefore delivereth them unto death and destruction.

27 For now are the plagues come upon the whole earth, and ye shall remain in them for God shall not deliver you, because ye have sinned against him.

28 Behold a horrible vision, and the appearance thereof from the east: (Middle East! NOT EUROPE!)

29 Where the nations of the dragons of Arabia shall come out with many chariots, and the multitude of them shall be carried as the wind upon earth, that all they which hear them may fear and tremble. (Islamic Terrorists have carried out more than 16,445 deadly terror attacks since 9/11.)

The threat of Islam is precisely what the Scriptures warn about, not Germany, not the Vatican, not the Resurrected Holy Roman Empire as mainstream Christianity is loudly proclaiming. The Nations of the Dragons of ARABIA! The descendants of Ishmael, the ARABS, Arab/Islamic Nations!!*!* Remember that if by this day and time, people do not know exactly what is happening, there are only two categories in which they fit in. They have either been deceived or they are part of the deception!!!

Dr. Anis Shorrosh, A member of the Oxford Society of Scholars and a Palestinian Arab Christian American, disclosed over 20 years ago the Twenty-Year Plan for the USA: Islam Targets America. This report is alarming and superbly accurate and has been accomplished in much less time than Dr. Shorrosh had predicted.

"This is my analysis of the Islamic invasion of America, the agenda of Islamists, and visible methods to take over America by the year 2020!

Will Americans continue to sleep through this invasion as they did when we were attacked on 9/11?"

1. Terminate America's freedom of speech by replacing it with hate crime bills state-wide and nationwide.

2. Wage a war of words using black leaders like Louis Farrakhan, Rev. Jesse Jackson, and other visible religious personalities to promote Islam as the original African-American's religion, while Christianity is for the whites!

3. Engage the American public in dialogues, discussions, and debates in colleges, universities, public libraries, radio, TV, churches, and mosques on the virtues of Islam. Proclaim how it is historically another religion, like Judaism and Christianity, with the same monotheistic faith.

4. Nominate Muslim sympathizers to political office for favorable legislation to Islam and support potential sympathizers by block voting.

5. Take control of as much of Hollywood, the press, TV, radio, and the internet by buying the corporations or controlling stock.

6. Yield to the fear of imminent shut-off of the lifeblood of America - the black gold. America's economy depends on oil (1000 products are derived from oil), so does its personal and industrial transportation and manufacturing -41% comes from the Middle East.

7. Yell, foul, out-of-context, personal interpretation, hate crime, Zionist, un-American, inaccurate interpretation of the Quran anytime Islam is criticized or the Quran is analyzed in the public arena.

8. Encourage Muslims to penetrate the White House, specifically with Islamists who can articulate a marvelous and peaceful picture of Islam. Acquire government positions and get membership in local

school boards. Train Muslims as medical doctors to dominate the medical field, research, and pharmaceutical companies. Take control of the computer industry. Establish Middle Eastern restaurants throughout the U.S. to connect planners of Islamization in a discreet way.

Ever notice how numerous Muslim doctors in America are, when their countries need them more desperately than America does?

9. Accelerate Islamic demographic growth via:

a. Massive immigration (100,000 annually since 1961)

b. No birth control whatsoever - every baby of Muslim parents is automatically a Muslim and cannot choose another religion later.

c. Muslim men must marry American women and Islamize them (10,000 annually). Then divorce them and remarry every five years, since one cannot have the Muslim legal permission to marry four at one time. This is a legal solution in America.

d. Convert angry, alienated black inmates and turn them into militants (so far, 2000 released inmates have joined Al Qaida worldwide). Only a few have been captured in Afghanistan and on American soil. So far - sleeping cells!

10. Reading, writing, arithmetic, and research through the American educational system, mosques, and student centers (now 1500) should be sprinkled with dislike of Jews, evangelical Christians, and democracy. There are 300 exclusively Muslim schools with loyalty to the Quran, not the U.S. Constitution.

11. Provide very sizeable monetary Muslim grants to colleges and universities in America to establish Centers for Islamic studies with Muslim directors to promote Islam in higher education institutions.

12. Let the entire world know through propaganda, speeches, seminars, and local and national media that terrorists have hijacked Islam, not the truth, which is that Islam hijacked the terrorists. Furthermore, in January of 2002, Saudi Arabia's Embassy in Washington mailed 4500 packets of the Quran, videos, promoting Islam to America's high schools--free. They would never allow us to reciprocate.

13. Appeal to the historically compassionate Americans for sympathy and tolerance towards the Muslims in America who are portrayed as mainly immigrants from oppressed countries.

14. Nullify America's sense of security by manipulating the intelligence community with misinformation. Periodically terrorize Americans of impending attacks on bridges, tunnels, water supplies, airports, apartment buildings, and malls. (We have experienced this too often since 9/11.)

15. Form riots and demonstrations in the prison system demanding Islamic Sharia as the way of life, not America's justice system.

16. Open numerous charities throughout the U.S. but use the funds to support Islamic terrorism with American dollars.

17. Raise interest in Islam on America's campuses by insisting that freshmen take at least one course on Islam. Be sure that the writer is a bona fide American, Christian, scholarly, and able to cover up the violence in the Quran and express the peaceful, spiritual, and religious aspect only.

18. Unify the numerous Muslim lobbies in Washington, mosques, Islamic student centers, educational organizations, magazines, and papers by internet and an annual convention to coordinate plans, propagate the faith, and engender news in the media of their visibility.

19. Send intimidating messages and messengers to the outspoken individuals who are critical of Islam and seek to eliminate them by hook or crook.

20. Applaud Muslims as loyal citizens of the US by spotlighting their voting record as the highest percentage of all minority and ethnic groups in America.

In light of all this, it is no wonder that God has turned His face on America and has left this country DESOLATE!

Former CIA Director George Tenet stated in his 2007 book, At the Center of the Storm: My Years in the CIA, that he is convinced that Al-Qaeda is trying to obtain nuclear capabilities: They understand that bombings by cars, trucks, trains, and planes will get them some headlines, to be sure. But if they manage to set off a mushroom cloud, they will make history. Such an event would put Al-Qaeda on par with the superpowers and make good on Bin Laden's threat to destroy our economy and bring death into every American household (pg. 279)

Al-Qaeda's nuclear intentions have been well documented. In 1998, Osama Bin Laden said he felt a religious duty to acquire nuclear weapons. In 2003 Al. Al-Qaeda sought and received a "fatwa" from a radical Saudi cleric authorizing the use of nuclear weapons against American civilians.

The ultimate concern, of course, is that extremists would obtain a weapon of mass destruction (WMD) in particular, a nuclear bomb. In a December 2008 report titled World at Risk, the Commission on the Prevention of WMD Proliferation and Terrorism concluded that unless the world community acts decisively and with great urgency, it is more likely than not that a weapon of mass destruction will be used in a terrorist attack somewhere in the world by 2013. (Somewhere in the world? Try the US/Babylon/The Great Whore. OH, WISE ONES!!!)

Jeremiah 8 7-9

7 Yea, the stork in the heaven knoweth her appointed times; and the turtle and the crane and the swallow observe the time of their coming; but my people know not the judgment of the LORD.

8 How do ye say, We are wise, and the law of the LORD is with us? Lo, certainly in vain made he it; the pen of the scribes is in vain.

9 The wise men are ashamed, they are dismayed and taken: lo, they have rejected the word of the LORD; and what wisdom is in them?

Taking a closer look at the Middle East's most anti-American and unstable nation Iran, (Known as the Medes and the Persians in ancient times, exactly where Enoch prophesied that the Watchers would begin their plot.) and its leadership we find the following disturbing facts: In his first year in office, in an October 2006 speech in Tehran largely ignored by the West, President Ahmadinejad stated his objectives for Iran under his rule. Israel, he said, must be wiped off the map, and he urged his hard-line Muslim audience to envision a world in which the United States no longer existed.

Mideast specialist Joel Rosenberg describes the speech and its background: Is it possible for us to witness a world without America and Zionism?' [Ahmadinejad] asked a gathering of leaders from Hamas and Islamic Jihad. 'You had best know that this slogan and this goal are attainable, and surely can be achieved.' He urged Muslims all over the world Shias and Sunnis alike to prepare for the day when 'our holy hatred expands' and 'strikes like a wave.

It was not just talk. Ahmadinejad was simultaneously making several aggressive moves to build up Iran's military and accelerate its bid to go nuclear. That fall, Iran purchased $1 billion worth of missiles from Russia, building on years of buying submarines and other advanced weapons systems from Moscow.

Iran also received a dozen cruise missiles with a three-thousand-kilometer range, each of which was capable of carrying nuclear warheads. Iran's parliament voted to block international inspections of its nuclear facilities. And Ahmadinejad placed the military firmly in control [over] his nation's nuclear program, undercutting his government's claim that the program is intended for civilian use" (Inside the Revolution, 2009, pp. 168-169).

Iran's president, Mahmoud Ahmadinejad, is one of the millions of Muslims referred to as "Twelvers." The Twelvers, who constitute more than 90 percent of the population of Iran and 60 percent of the population of Iraq, are a dangerous outgrowth of Shia Islam. They are called such because they are followers of the 12th imam, or successor of Muhammad.

This 12th imam was born around A.D. 868 or 869 and disappeared a few years later, in 874. His followers believe that "he merely withdrew from public view when he was five and that he will sooner or later emerge . to liberate the world from evil (Kuntzel).

Many Muslims believe this Hidden Imam to be the prophesied Mahdi divinely guided one a sort of Islamic messiah who will reemerge to establish Islam in its rightful place as the dominant, and eventually the only, religion over the entire world.

Shia believe the Mahdi will return at the end of history during a time of chaos, carnage, and confusion to establish righteousness, justice, and peace. When he comes, they say, the Mahdi will bring Jesus with him. Jesus will be a Muslim and will serve as his deputy, not as King of kings and Lord of lords as the Bible teaches, and he will force non-Muslims to choose between following the Mahdi or death (Rosenberg, p. 175).

But one thing that is fairly well agreed upon among devout 'Twelvers' is that the Mahdi will end apostasy and purify corruption within Islam. He is expected, therefore, to conquer the Arabian Peninsula, Jordan, Syria, and 'Palestine,' and then he and Jesus will kill between 60 and 80 percent of the world's population, specifically those who refuse to convert to Islam (Rosenberg, p. 176).

These are the beliefs that drive Iran's President Mahmoud Ahmadinejad.

Lest this sound so far-fetched as to be unbelievable, consider the opening words of his Sept. 29, 2009, address to the United Nations: In the Name of God, the Compassionate, the Merciful, praise be to Allah, the Lord of the universe, and peace and blessings be upon our master and prophet, Muhammad O God, hasten the arrival of the Imam Mahdi, grant him good health and victory and make us his followers and those who attest to his rightfulness.

Another core tenet of Islam is that, before going to war against non-Muslims, one must first invite them to convert to Islam and so avoid war. In his speech, Ahmadinejad carried out this obligation, urging the gathered world leaders to convert to Islam:

We emphasize that the only path to remain safe is to return to monotheism [Islam] and justice, and this is the greatest hope and opportunity in all ages and generations. Without belief in Allah and commitment to the cause of justice and fight against injustice and discrimination, the world structure cannot be put right.

President Ahmadinejad concluded his speech by declaring that there will come a time when justice will prevail across the globe that time being under the rule of the Perfect Man, the last Divine source on earth, the Great Mahdi. He then called on the world to be at work paving the way and preparing the conditions for building that bright future.

This was not the first time he had made such statements; his previous UN addresses included the same themes and components.

Mideast specialist Rosenberg gives more background on the Iranian leader's apocalyptic beliefs: Ahmadinejad and his close aides and advisors are driven by the deeply rooted belief that the Islamic messiah will appear soon and that by launching a war to annihilate Judeo-Christian civilization, they can hasten that day.

Hasten is a keyword here. Ahmadinejad and his team do not believe they are supposed to be sitting around, twiddling their thumbs, waiting for the Mahdi. They believe they have been given specific tasks to speed up his arrival, and they are determined to accomplish those tasks, whatever the cost to themselves or their country .

On August 29, [2007,] he said, 'The Iranian nation and the Islamic Revolution have a pivotal role in preparing the ground for the coming of the Hidden Imam . We must rapidly develop Iran's nuclear capabilities in order to create the right conditions for his coming . to precipitate this great event.

The responsibility that currently rests on Iran's shoulders is very heavy; it is the kind of mission with which divine prophets were entrusted. It does not permit us to rest or slumber even for a moment (Rosenberg, pp. 181-182).

A national review reported the consensus of some of the world's leading terrorism experts at a December 2009 Heritage Foundation meeting: If Iran, the world's leading sponsor of terrorism, is not prevented from acquiring nuclear weapons, the result will be a nuclear proliferation cascade. Before long, many countries would possess nuclear devices, exponentially increasing the chances of terrorist groups obtaining at least a few (Clifford May, Apocalypse When? November 26, 2009)

The respected Iranian-born journalist Amir Taheri states that President Ahmadinejad boasts that the [Hidden] Imam gave him the presidency for a single task: provoking a 'clash of civilisations' in which the Muslim world, led by Iran, takes on the 'infidel' West, led by the United States, and defeats it (The Frightening Truth of Why Iran Wants a Bomb, The Telegraph [London], April 16, 2006).

Furthermore, on July 27, 2010, Iran's Supreme Leader, Ayatollah Ali Khamenei, created a stir after apparently issuing a religious edict claiming ultimate spiritual powers on Earth. Iranian media reported that he told followers that they must obey him as the representative of the Prophet Muhammad and [Shi'ism's] 12th Imam on Earth. He also claimed that the 12th Imam is already here, that he has spoken to him, but he has not yet revealed himself to the world. He stated that he will do so soon.

Revelation 19:20

And the beast was taken, and with him the false prophet that wrought miracles before him, with which he deceived them that had received the mark of the beast, and them that worshipped his image. These both were cast alive into a lake of fire burning with brimstone.

Given this information, it is understandable why some believe that the Obama Administration (Satan & his hosts) is not doing anything significant about Iran's nuclear ambitions and at the same time deliberately weakening U.S. National Security. Once they destroy the U.S. with some form of nuclear device (Remember Revelation 17:16), the road is now clear for Obama to proceed to Iran, take his stance as the 12th Imam (Muslim Messiah), then attack the State of Israel. The poor Iranians who have been indoctrinated with this deception will worship Obama as their god. After all, they have already been primed up and are now ready for their version of the Messiah.

This is exactly what the Apostle Paul warned about in 2 Thessalonians 2:1-12, not that there would be a temple built in Jerusalem before "the Wicked One" comes, where he would pretend to be God. (The Wicked One is here, where is the temple?!!!) The one who builds the new Temple of God is Christ upon His return.

Zechariah 6:12-15

12 And speak unto him, saying, Thus speaketh the LORD of hosts, saying, Behold the man whose name is The BRANCH; and he shall grow up out of his place, and he shall build the temple of the LORD:

13 Even he shall build the temple of the LORD; and he shall bear the glory, and shall sit and rule upon his throne; and he shall be a priest upon his throne: and the counsel of peace shall be between them both.

14 And the crowns shall be to Helem, and to Tobijah, and to Jedaiah, and to Hen the son of Zephaniah, for a memorial in the temple of the LORD.

15 And they that are far off shall come and build in the temple of the LORD, and ye shall know that the LORD of hosts hath sent me unto you. And this shall come to pass, if ye will diligently obey the voice of the LORD your God.

I don't believe that anyone in the State of Israel, with their clear mind, would accept Obama posing as God. Especially someone with the Arab name Barack Hussein Obama! However, Islamic-Arab nations might! Even more so, those who are Shiite Muslims like Iran! Their ultimate goal is to establish a World Caliphate (Islamic Empire) and unite all Muslims worldwide.

Islam is the invention of Satan (before he took on human flesh as Barack Hussein Obama) to distort and distract God's true plan for His people and humanity. Do not be deceived into thinking that Obama was fighting Islamic Extremism or that he is hunting down Al Qaeda and Bin Laden with these super duper drone attacks. Or that he genuinely desires peace between Israel and the Arab World. HOGWASH! He's had everyone on a wild goose chase!

Obama, Ahmadinejad, King Abdullah, Gaddafi, Karzai, Bin Laden, Al-Qaeda, Taliban, Hezbollah, etc, it's all the same octopus (Islam) with many tentacles. It is the Illuminati/Freemason method of operation, "Order out of Chaos". They create the problem, then come in and pretend to bring the solution, and it   does not matter to them who dies on the way there. Except for the very top of Satan's Army, everyone else is just being deceived. Remember, you are not dealing with regular humans but "Fallen Angels". They are far more intelligent, devious, and far more evil, and harbor an extreme hatred towards humanity.

Revelation 12:9

And the great dragon was cast out, that old serpent, called the Devil, and Satan, which deceiveth the whole world: he was cast out into the earth, and his angels were cast out with him. so that they cannot

What Obama and friends (Satan and his hosts) did is obvious. Not only did Obama pervert every form of justice in this country, but now

289

it's finally coming to light the things he and his friends did to this nation. The problem is that many are so spiritually dead and blind that they cannot discern what is happening right in front of their faces. People are so caught up in sports, movies, music, clubs, work, video games, television (the idiot box), Facebook, space, etc, each and everything instead of trying to seek the knowledge of God. They've got the masses right where they want them. Stuck on Stupidity!

Jeremiah 4:22

For my people are foolish, they have not known me; they are senseless children, and they have no understanding: they are wise to do evil, but to do good they do not know.

Jeremiah 5:3-4

3 O LORD, are not thine eyes upon the truth? Thou hast stricken them, but they have not grieved; thou hast consumed them, but they have refused to receive correction: they have made their faces harder than a rock; they have refused to return.

4 Therefore I said, surely these are poor; they are foolish: for they know not the way of the LORD, nor the judgment of their God.

Hosea 4:6

My people are destroyed for lack of knowledge: because thou hast rejected knowledge, I will also reject thee, that thou shalt be no priest to me: seeing thou hast forgotten the law of thy God, I will also forget thy children.

To add insult to injury, when someone like me comes and tells them the truth of what is happening, they automatically discard it by making the lame statements, Oh, he's crazy or he studies the Bible too much". The problem is that most people are so ignorant of the things of God and in such a state of stupor that, although they see, they cannot perceive, and though they hear, they cannot understand.

Jeremiah 5:21

Hear now this, O foolish people, and without understanding; which have eyes, and see not; which have ears, and hear not:

Jeremiah 6:10

To whom shall I speak, and give warning, that they may hear? Behold, their ear is uncircumcised, and they cannot hearken: behold, the word of the LORD is unto them a reproach; they have no delight in it.

Ezekiel 33:30-33

30 Also, thou son of man, the children of thy people still are talking against thee by the walls and in the doors of the houses, and speak one to another, every one to his brother, saying, Come, I pray you, and hear what is the word that cometh forth from the LORD.

31 And they come unto thee as the people cometh, and they sit before thee as my people, and they hear thy words, but they will not do them: for with their mouth they shew much love, but their heart goeth after their covetousness.

32 And, lo, thou art unto them as a very lovely song of one that hath a pleasant voice, and can play well on an instrument: for they hear thy words, but they do them not.

33 And when this cometh to pass, (lo, it will come,) then shall they know that a prophet hath been among them.

1 Corinthians 2:13-14

13 Which things also we speak, not in the words which man's wisdom teacheth, but which the Holy Ghost teacheth; comparing spiritual things with spiritual.

14 But the natural man receiveth not the things of the Spirit of God: for they are foolishness unto him: neither can he know them, because they are spiritually discerned

Then, to make matters worse, most ministers throughout mainstream Christianity are continuously teaching the masses the same things over and over. Faith, miracles, the love of God, does it surprise you that the Creator of Heaven and Earth can also perform miracles? That God so loved the world that He gave His only begotten Son to pay for our sins? Many are still drinking milk and are in desperate need of spiritual growth so that they may be able to eat meat. Come on, my people, GROW IN THE KNOWLEDGE OF GOD, WAKE UP!!!

Isaiah 28:9

Whom shall he teach knowledge? and whom shall he make to understand doctrine? Them that are weaned from the milk and drawn from the breasts.

Ephesians 5 14-17

14 Wherefore he saith, Awake thou that sleepest, and arise from the dead, and Christ shall give thee light   .

15 See then that ye walk circumspectly, not as fools, but as wise,

16 Redeeming the time because the days are evil.

17 Wherefore be ye not unwise, but understanding what the will of the Lord is.

11 Of whom we have many things to say, and hard to be uttered, seeing ye are dull of hearing.

12 For when for the time ye ought to be teachers, ye have need that one teach you again which be the first principles of the oracles of God; and are become such as need milk, and not of strong meat.

13 For every one that useth milk is unskilful in the word of righteousness: for he is a babe.

14 But strong meat belongeth to them that are of full age, even those who   , because of use, have their senses exercised to discern both good and evil.

1 Therefore, leaving the principles of the doctrine of Christ, let us go on unto perfection; not laying again the foundation of repentance from dead works, and of faith toward God,

2 Of the doctrine of baptisms, and of laying on of hands, and of resurrection of the dead, and eternal judgment.

3 And this will we do, if God permit.

No one in their right mind can honestly expect to grow in the knowledge of God without diligently studying the Scriptures. I have heard many say, I always pray for wisdom, knowledge, and understanding, and never receive it. Well, if the only time you open your Bible is before going to sleep to read a daily devotional, OF COURSE YOU WILL NOT RECEIVE ANY!

2 Timothy 2:15

Study to shew thyself approved unto God, a workman that needeth not to be ashamed, rightly dividing the word of truth.

Study, research, and dig for knowledge as a hidden treasure. In secular education, no one has ever received a degree by just sitting around and then studying whenever they get around to it. They earned it through hard work and many sleepless nights. You must do the same! After all, this is much more important; your eternal future is at stake here. The odds against you are great, and you cannot afford to lose!

Proverbs 2 1-6

1 My son, if thou wilt receive my words, and hide my commandments with thee;

2 So that thou incline thine ear unto wisdom, and apply thine heart to understanding;

3 Yea, if thou criest after knowledge, and liftest up thy voice for understanding;

4 If thou seest her as silver, and searchest for her as for hid treasures;

5 Then shalt thou understand the fear of the LORD, and find the knowledge of God.

6 For the LORD giveth wisdom: out of his mouth cometh knowledge and understanding.

Notice that there are several things that we must do to receive some of the knowledge of the Almighty God. It is not just to ask God, and He will supernaturally implant it in our minds. It does not work that way, my people; that is just not the way God does things. Please, don't think for one moment that I am being harsh and insensitive towards any of you. On the contrary, I love every one of God's people. We are one big family. I just want you guys to know that there is an extreme sense of urgency here. I am your watchman, and I am warning you all, HERE COMES THE SWORD! God is about to hand down "Judgment"! And, from the bottom of my heart, I want you guys to get this right, HONESTLY.

Do you think that I would publish a book with a tremendous risk of losing my life if I honestly did not care about and love every one of you? I did not do this for monetary gain. I could have 24 million dollars, but what use is money going to be to me when all this occurs in less than 24 months? It is of absolutely no use, I did it out of love!

And though I have the gift of prophecy, and understand all mysteries, and all knowledge; and though I have all faith, so that I could remove mountains, and have not love, I am nothing.

My motive is Love! It is also God's motive and the reason why He sent me. God is love, and love is the key!

FOOD FOR THOUGHT: Could it be that Satan, in his twisted mind, invented this Hidden Imam deception because he is hidden (indwelling) inside Barack Hussein Obama (Revelation 17:11)? I believe he is doing this as a form of mockery to the ignorant masses!

Chapter 17

This "Rapture" Stuff

The belief throughout mainstream Christianity is that before the great tribulation or before the Antichrist comes on the scene, the Lord will Rapture the true believers to a place of safety. If that is the case, then we've been "left behind"! (I am being sarcastic!)

This rapture teaching is yet another of the great deceiver's slick moves. This teaching is simply another deception based on several verses in Scripture taken out of context.

1 Thessalonians 4:15-17

14 For if we believe that Jesus died and rose again, even so they also who sleep in Jesus will God bring with him.

15 For this we say unto you by the word of the Lord, that we which are alive and remain unto the coming of the Lord shall not prevent them which are asleep.

16 For the Lord himself shall descend from heaven with a shout, with the voice of the archangel, and with the trump of God: and the dead in Christ shall rise first:

17 Then we who are alive and remain, shall be caught up together with them in the clouds, to meet the Lord in the air: and so shall we ever be with the Lord.

This is the main verse used to teach about the rapture. There will be a rapture, but what they have totally out of context is the timing of its occurrence. Notice that in the very next chapter, Paul provides the correct timing..

2 Thessalonians 2:1-12

1 Now we beseech you, brethren, by the coming of our Lord Jesus Christ, and by our gathering (being raptured) together unto him,

2 That ye be not soon shaken in mind, or be troubled, neither by spirit, nor by word, nor by letter as from us, as that the day of Christ is at hand.

3 Let no man deceive you by any means: for that day (the 2nd coming of Christ) shall not come, except there come a falling away first (an apostasy, which has already occurred), and that man of sin be revealed, the son of perdition;

(Has Obama been revealed to the world yet? NO! Then obviously, Christ will not come until he has!)

4 Who opposeth and exalteth himself above all that is called God, or that is worshipped; so that he, as God, sitteth in the temple of God, shewing himself that he is God.

5 Remember ye not, that, when I was yet with you, I told you these things?

6 And now ye know what withholdeth that he might be revealed in his time.

7 For the mystery of iniquity doth already work only he who now letteth will let, until he be taken out of the way.

8 And then shall that Wicked be revealed, whom the Lord shall consume with the spirit of his mouth, and shall destroy with the brightness of his coming: (Obviously the wicked one has to be revealed on earth in his position so that the Lord can consume him. And in verse 3 we just read that the Lord will not come until then!)

9 Even him, whose coming is after the working of Satan with all power and signs and lying wonders,

10 And with all deceivableness of unrighteousness in them that perish; because they received not the love of the truth (The Scriptures), that they might be saved.

11 And for this cause God shall send them strong delusion, that they should believe a lie:

12 That they all might be damned who believed not the truth, but had pleasure in unrighteousness

In the Epistles of Paul, there are certain things not clearly understood, which the unlearned and unstable twist to their own destruction. This was something so prevalent in Paul's days that even Peter felt a need to address the issue.

2 Peter 3:15-17

15 And account that the longsuffering of our Lord is salvation; even as our beloved brother Paul also, according to the wisdom given unto him, hath written unto you;

16 As also in all his epistles, speaking in them of these things; in which are some things hard to be understood, which they that are unlearned and unstable wrest (To change or twist the meaning of something.), as they do also the other scriptures, unto their destruction.

17 Ye therefore, beloved, seeing ye know these things before, beware lest ye also, being led away with the error of the wicked, fall from your stedfastness.

Let us not do the same and twist Paul's words to our destruction.

In the Olivet Prophecy, Jesus Christ Himself gives us the order of events to come.

Mathew 24:1-41

1 And Jesus went out, and departed from the temple: and his disciples came to him to show him the buildings of the temple.

2 And Jesus said unto them, See ye not all these things? Verily, I say unto you, There shall not be left here one stone upon another, that shall not be thrown down.

3 And as he sat upon the mount of Olives, the disciples came unto him privately, saying, Tell us, when shall these things be? And what shall be the sign of thy coming, and of the end of the world?

4 And Jesus answered and said unto them, Take heed that no man deceive you.

5 For many shall come in my name, saying, I am Christ; and shall deceive many.

6 And ye shall hear of wars and rumours of wars: see that ye be not troubled, for all these things must come to pass, but the end is not yet.

7 For nation shall rise against nation, and kingdom against kingdom: and there shall be famines, and pestilences, and earthquakes, in diverse places.

8 All these are the beginning of sorrows.

9 Then shall they deliver you up to be afflicted, and shall kill you: and ye shall be hated of all nations for my name's sake.

10 And then shall many be offended, and shall betray one another, and shall hate one another.

11 And many false prophets shall rise, and shall deceive many.

12 And because iniquity shall abound, the love of many shall wax cold .

13 But he that shall endure unto the end, the same shall be saved   .

14 And this gospel of the kingdom shall be preached in all the world for a witness unto all nations; and then shall the end come.

15 When ye therefore shall see the abomination of desolation, spoken of by Daniel the prophet, stand in the holy place, (whoso readeth, let him understand :) (Notice the abomination of desolation, Satan in the flesh, is in place before the great tribulation begins.)

16 Then let them who are in Judaea flee into the mountains:

17 Let him who is on the housetop not come down to take anything out of his house:

18 Neither let him who is in the field return to take his clothes. (In other words, put all your earthly cares away, do not worry about your earthly possessions, the end has come!)

19 And woe unto them that are with child, and to them that give suck in those days! (If fleeing for an adult will be hard, imagine an adult with children? And if we were raptured out, why would Christ make this statement?)

20 But pray ye that your flight be not in the winter, neither on the sabbath day (Who else would be keeping the Sabbath besides the Elect? The world?):

21 For then shall be great tribulation, such as was not since the beginning of the world to this time, no, nor ever shall be.

22 And except those days should be shortened, there should no flesh be saved: but for the elect's sake those days shall be shortened. (If the elect were in some place of safety, then God would not have to shorten the days, but he does!)

23 Then if any man shall say unto you, Lo, here is Christ, or there; believe it not (If the Elect had been "raptured" by Christ and were with Him, they would not be around for anyone to tell them Lo, here is Christ, or there).

24 For there shall arise false Christs, and false prophets, and shall shew great signs and wonders; insomuch that, if it were possible, they shall deceive the very elect. (Obviously, the very elect are somewhere on earth running the risk of being deceived.)

25 Behold, I have told you before.

26 Wherefore if they shall say unto you, Behold, he is in the desert; go not forth: behold, he is in the secret chambers; believe it not. (Again, if the Elect were already with Christ, they would not even be around to hear anyone say these things!)

27 For as the lightning cometh out of the east (Remember that lighting means barack. The Watchers started their current rebellion in the east.), and shineth even unto the west (Now their leader is in position on the west, the western side of the earth, America); so shall also the coming of the Son of man be. (In other words, for as Barack

cometh out of the east and taketh his position even unto the west; then the Son of Man is coming soon.)

28 For wheresoever the carcase is, there will the eagles be gathered together.

29 Immediately after the tribulation of those days shall the sun be darkened, and the moon shall not give her light, and the stars shall fall from heaven, and the powers of the heavens shall be shaken:

30 And then shall appear the sign of the Son of man in heaven: and then shall all the tribes of the earth mourn, and they shall see the Son of man coming in the clouds of heaven with power and great glory.

31 And He shall send His angels with a great sound of a trumpet, and they shall gather together His elect from the four winds (From the Northern, Southern, Eastern, and Western parts of the earth.) from one end of heaven to the other. (Here is where the Rapture occurs, not before!!!)

Mark 13:24-27

24 But in those days, after that tribulation, the sun shall be darkened, and the moon shall not give her light,

25 And the stars of heaven shall fall, and the powers that are in heaven shall be shaken.

26 And then shall they see the Son of man coming in the clouds with great power and glory.

27 And then shall He send His angels, and shall gather together His elect from the four winds, from the uttermost part of the earth to the uttermost part of heaven.

Luke 21:25-28, 36

25 And there shall be signs in the sun, and in the moon, and the stars; and upon the earth distress of nations, with perplexity; the sea and the waves roaring;

26 Men's hearts failing them for fear, and for looking after those things which are coming on the earth: for the powers of heaven shall be shaken.

27 And then shall they see the Son of man coming in a cloud with power and great glory.

28 And when these things begin to come to pass, then look up, and lift   your heads; for your redemption draweth nigh.

36 Watch ye therefore, and pray always, that ye may be accounted worthy to escape all these things that shall come to pass, and to stand before the Son of man.

Isaiah 11:12

And it shall come to pass in that day, that the Lord shall set His hand again the second time to recover the remnant of His people, which shall be left, from Assyria, and Egypt, and Pathros, and from Cush, and Elam, and Shinar, and Hamath, and the islands of the sea.

Isaiah 43:5-6

5 Fear not: for I am with thee: I will bring thy seed from the east, and gather thee from the west;

6 I will say to the north, Give up and to the south, Keep not back: bring my sons from far, and my daughters from the ends of the earth.

Jeremiah 23:7-8

7 Therefore, behold, the days come, saith the LORD, that they shall no more say, The LORD liveth, which brought up the children of Israel out of the land of Egypt;

8 But the LORD liveth, which brought up and which led the seed of the house of Israel out of the north country, and from all countries whither I had driven them; and they shall dwell in their land.

Mathew 24 (cont.)

32 Now learn a parable of the fig tree; When his branch is yet tender, and putteth forth leaves, ye know that summer is nigh:

33 So likewise ye, when ye shall see all these things, know that it is near, even at the doors.

34 Verily I say unto you, This generation shall not pass, till all these things be fulfilled   .

35 Heaven and earth shall pass away, but my words shall not pass away.

36 But of that day and hour knoweth no man (Not the season, we are supposed to discern the signs of the times. We just don't know the exact date.), no, not the angels of heaven, but my Father only.

37 But as the days of Noe (When the lawlessness of the Watchers was in full swing) were, so shall also the coming of the Son of man be.

38 For as in the days that were before the flood they were eating and drinking, marrying and giving in marriage, until the day that Noe entered into the ark,

39 And knew not until the flood came, and took them all away; so shall also the coming of the Son of man be.

40 Then shall two be in the field; the one shall be taken, and the other left.

41 Two women shall be grinding at the mill; the one shall be taken, and the other left.

The word taken is the Greek word, Paralambano, which signifies "the removal of persons from the earth in judgment when the Son of Man is revealed", Mat. 24:40-41, Luke 17:34-35; it is the means of the removal of corruption... (See Strong's Concordance # 3880)

Blessed is the one not taken away in judgment, the opposite of what the "false teachers" are feeding the masses through this "rapture stuff". What Christ is saying is that two people may be in the same place, one taken in judgment and the other, the elect, left behind to inherit the earth.

Ascension of Isaiah 4:13

few in those days will be left as His servants, while they flee from desert to desert, awaiting the coming of the Beloved.

2 Esdras 6:25-26

25 Whosoever remaineth from all these that I have told thee shall escape, and see my salvation, and the end of your world.

26 And the men that are received shall see it, who have not tasted death from their birth: and the heart of the inhabitants shall be changed, and turned into another meaning.

2 Esdras 9:7-8

7 And every one that shall be saved, and shall be able to escape by his works, and by faith, whereby ye have believed,

8 Shall be preserved from the said perils, and shall see my salvation in my land, and within my borders: for I have sanctified them for me from the beginning.

2 Esdras 13: 16-24

16 For as I conceive in mine understanding, woe unto them that shall be left in those days, and much more woe unto them that are not left behind!

17 For they that were not left were in heaviness.

18 Now understand I the things that are laid up in the latter days (End Times), which shall happen unto them, and to those that are left behind.

19 Therefore are they have come into great perils and many necessities, as these dreams declare.

20 Yet it is easier for him that is in danger to come into these things, than to pass away as a cloud out of the world, and not to see the things that happen in the last days. And he answered unto me, and said,

21The interpretation of the vision shall I shew thee, and I will open unto thee the thing that thou hast required.

22 Whereas thou hast spoken of them that are left behind, this is the interpretation:

23 He that shall endure the peril in that time hath kept himself: they that be fallen into danger are such as have works, and faith toward the Almighty.

24 Know this therefore, that they who are left behind are more blessed than they that be dead.

Jeremiah 30:7

Alas! For that day is great, so that none is like it: it is even the time of Jacob's trouble (The tribulation period), but he shall be saved out of it (out of it" NOT from it).

Daniel 2:44

And in the days of these kings shall the God of heaven set up a kingdom, which shall never be destroyed: and the kingdom shall not be left to other people, but it shall break in pieces and consume all these kingdoms, and it shall stand for ever.

Mathew 5:5

Blessed are the meek: for they shall inherit the earth.

It is the Kingdom of God on Earth. The Kingdom of Heaven is not in Heaven!!!

During my research, I have found verse after verse that debunk this "rapture" myth, but I think that this false teaching is so pathetic and ridiculous that I have decided not to include them here in order to make this book as short as possible. Besides, this is not a book on theology or doctrinal differences; it is on prophecy.

How they got people believing this nonsense when the Scriptures are so clear on this subject is beyond me. The point is that many do believe it. The reason behind this deception is the same as what Satan told Eve, "Eat of the tree, it is good for you, when God had commanded the opposite. Here, God is telling His people, "Get out of Babylon, lest you share in her punishment". But Satan is telling the masses, "Don't worry, before I come and start tearing this earth apart, God is going to take you to a nice, safe place so that I can't put my nasty, greasy paws on you or hurt you in any kind of way don't believe your lying eyes!" Who are you going to listen to?!!!

To the pastors and ministers who have been teaching about the "rapture," please understand this and do not just discard it as a small doctrinal difference. My people, it is okay to be wrong. We are not born knowing anything. We grow and learn new things as we grow. I do not know everything, nor do I pretend to, but what I do know I share with you all. I learn new things from God every day. I am a proud member of a small church. I have a pastor whom I love, and I am under his guidance. I may have the gift of prophecy and be able to understand prophecy more than my pastor, but I am still subject to his leadership, and I constantly learn new things from him. And this is exactly how God wants things to be done. There is a chain of command, and we must joyfully follow it. I follow it and I think it's great. Even Jesus Christ followed it, and He is our example.

It's okay to be wrong, just please correct it, because when all hell starts to break loose on earth and you have been telling your flock that they were going to be "raptured" out of tribulation and they are not, you are going to destroy their precious faith. Please don't do that, you will have to give an account to God because of it. I am a fellow laborer with you in something that is not about you and me. It is about the Kingdom of God. With the utmost respect and humility, I ask you to please correct this. Maybe this is something you have taught simply because you were taught it and never really researched it. It is okay, we all make mistakes. I make them every day, and my Father is patient with me and corrects me. After all, I am only a Child of God; I am not an adult, none of us are. I may be a child eating spiritual meat, but a child nonetheless, as we all are. So please correct this; it is the right thing to do. It takes a mature man in Christ to want to know when he is wrong so that he may correct himself. Your congregation will appreciate your humbleness, and most importantly, so will God.

Chapter 18

The Mark of the Beast

Revelation 13:15-18

15 And he had power to give life unto the image of the beast, that the image of the beast should both speak, and cause that as many as would not worship the image of the beast should be killed.

16 And he causeth all, both small and great, rich and poor, free and bond, to receive a mark in their right hand, or their foreheads:

17 And that no man might buy or sell, save he that had the mark, or the name of the beast, or the number of his name.

18 Here is wisdom. Let him that hath understanding count the number of the beast: for it is the number of a man; and his number is Six hundred threescore and six.

Revelation 14:9-12

9 And the third angel followed them, saying with a loud voice, If any man worship the beast and his image, and receive his mark in his forehead, or his hand,

10 The same shall drink of the wine of the wrath of God, which is poured out without mixture into the cup of his indignation and he shall be tormented with fire and brimstone in the presence of the holy angels, and in the presence of the Lamb

11 And the smoke of their torment ascendeth up forever and ever and they have no rest day nor night, who worships the beast and his image, and whosoever receiveth the mark of his name.

12 Here is the patience of the saints: here are they that keep the commandments of God, and the faith of Jesus.

What is this strange mark? Is it some form of computer chip or something? Is it the forsaking of the 4th Commandment? Let's dig into the mysteries of God and find out. We know that everything has a beginning (a root), so what is the root of all evil?

1 Timothy 6:9-10

9 But they that will be rich fall into temptation and a snare, and into many foolish and hurtful lusts, which drown men in destruction and perdition.

10 For the love of money is the root of all evil: which, while some coveted after, they have erred from the faith, and pierced them-selves through with many sorrows.

Paul admonishes Timothy about striving to be rich. He warned him that it is a snare (A trap) that drowns men in destruction and perdi-tion. For the love of money (Not the money itself, but the love of it) is the root (The beginning) of all evil.

Testament of Judah 3:36-38, 42

36 And I know what evils you will do in the last days (The End times).

37 Beware, therefore, my children, of fornication, and the love of money.

38 For these things withdraw you from the Law of God, and blind the inclination of the soul,

42 My children, the love of money leadeth to idolatry; because, when led astray through money, men name as gods those who are not gods, and it causeth him who hath it to fall into madness.

Matthew 6 19-23

19 Lay not up for yourselves treasures upon earth, where moth and rust doth corrupt, and where thieves break through and steal:

20 But lay up for yourselves treasures in heaven, where neither moth nor rust doth corrupt, and where thieves do not break through nor steal:

21 For where your treasure is, there will your heart be also.

22 The light of the body is the eye: if therefore thine eye be single, thy whole body shall be full of light. (Use your spiritual eye to focus all your attention only on the things of God, not the things of this world. When we start to focus on more than one thing, our eye (spiritual/inclination) is no longer single and becomes evil.)

23 But if thine eye be evil, thy whole body shall be full of darkness. If therefore the light that is in thee be darkness, how great is that darkness!

Testament of Issachar 1:33

The single-minded man coveteth not gold, he overreacheth not his neighbour, he longeth not after manifold dainties, he delighteth not in varied apparel (Eating, drinking, fancy clothes, things which are of the world.)

Testament of Issachar 2:1-2

1 KNOW ye therefore, my children, that in the last times (The End Times) your sons will forsake singleness, and will cleave unto insatiable desire (Always needing more and impossible to satisfy).

2 And leaving guilelessness, will draw near to malice; and forsaking the commandments of the Lord, they will cleave unto Beliar (Satan).

Mathew 6:24

No man can serve two masters: for either he will hate the one, and love the other; or else he will hold to the one, and despise the other. Ye cannot serve God and mammon (Mammon RA: The idolatrous image of the double-headed eagle shown on the cover of Albert Pike's classic text, Morals and Dogma is a much-treasured symbol of Jewish Masons. It represents the Babylonian god of money and forces, Mammon-Ra, as well as the Hegelian dialectical process practiced by the Jewish elite.

This same symbol is the Masonic Jewel awarded to high-level Masons initiated into the 33rd degree. "The true name of Satan, the Kabalists say, is that of Yahweh reversed; for Satan is not a black god, but the negation of God...For the Initiates, this is not a Person, but a Force, created for good, but which may serve for evil. It is the instrument of Liberty and Free Will.

As for Lucifer, the alternate name for the Devil, the former Sovereign Grand Commander frankly admits that he, Lucifer, is a good angel, and a divine god worthy of our esteemed worship. Doubt it not! Pike commands. Intimating that the antichrist, the one whom the Bible warns shall have the unholy, combined triple number 666, is the one whom the world awaits and shall recognize as their Messiah, Pike cryptically refers to the Triple Secret of the Great Work.

Revelation 3:9

Behold, I will make them of the synagogue of Satan, which say they are Jews, and are not, but do lie; behold, I will make them to come and worship before thy feet, and to know that I have loved thee.

We previously learned that Satan has used money (A financial system) to enslave the masses. (Triple Secret of the Great Work)

Notice the parallels in the following verses:

1 Kings 10:14 (666 talents of gold-knowing that Obama is Satan in the flesh and his number is 666- this verse shows a possible connection between the mark of the beast and money)

Eccl. 5:10 (Vanities /money)

Ez. 7:19 (Stumbling block -Silver & Gold- money)

Hos. 8:4 (Silver and gold/idols – money)

Mt. 26:15 (Judas betrayed Christ for money)

Acts 5:3-5 (They tried to lie to God over money)

Acts 8:18-20 (Simon tried to buy the gift of the Holy Spirit with money)

Furthermore, in Revelation 13:16-17, we see that no one can buy, sell, or trade (conduct business) without it. It is some object of monetary value. In ancient times, the object used to purchase something was silver and gold by weight. Yet, in current times, dollar bills have replaced this practice. The same tool used by the beast to enslave the masses.

The Language used in the right hand represents our actions, and in their foreheads represents our thoughts. Not on but in. This is virtually identical to the description God gave His people Israel in the Old Testament to describe what His law should be to them.

Exodus 13:9

And it shall be for a sign unto thee upon thine hand, and for a memorial between thine eyes, that the LORD'S law may be in thy mouth: for with a strong hand hath the LORD brought thee out of Egypt.

Deuteronomy 6:8

And thou shalt bind them for a sign upon thine hand, and they shall be as frontlets between thine eyes.

The Mark of the Beast is not something put on anyone; this is spiritual, it is in someone. Remember, in the New Covenant, it is the spiritual intent of the law that Jesus Christ showed and made known to us. God is to be worshipped in Spirit and truth.

The 2nd Commandment says, Thou shalt not make thy self any graven image or the likeness of anything in the heaven above in the earth beneath or in the sea underneath the earth thou shalt not bow down to them nor serve them for I the Lord your God am a jealous God visiting the iniquities of the fathers upon the children to the third and fourth generation of those that hate Me but showing mercy to thousands that love Me and keep My commandments. Dollar bills are a clear violation of this commandment, and notice what the different symbols on them mean.

Let's examine the one-dollar bill:

The Great Seal of the United States of America. It was designed by the Freemasons and contains a mass of symbolism that the profane (non-Masons) are not to understand. The Seal is a Masonic design. Have you ever asked the question, Why is there a Pyramid on the one-dollar bill? The religion of Freemasonry and some of its mysteries have descended from ancient Egypt, whose mysteries descended from ancient Babylon. The Pyramid has, of old, been a fascination of Freemasons. It is a pagan temple of Satan worship.

The Latin words on the seal   :

Annuit Coeptis means Announcing The Birth Of' and 'Novus Ordo Seclorum' means 'New World Order. Therefore, it says 'Announcing the birth of the New World Order'. The date in Roman numerals is 1776, the year the modern Illuminati were formed, and also the year of American independence. The Latin 'E Pluribus Unum' means 'One out of many,' which is the foundation of the New World Order's plan to unify the world's governments, religions, and money systems into one, so the world can be controlled.

The capstone, "The Head One", has not come down on the Pyramid (But Now He has come to earth in the likeness of a man). This means that the plan is not complete. Only when the New World Order is established upon all nations and the world leader is enthroned, will the plan be complete.

On the obverse is an eagle whose Dexter wing has thirty feathers, the number of ordinary degrees in Scottish Rite Freemasonry. The sinister wing has thirty-three feathers, the additional feather corresponding to the Thirty-Third Degree of the Scottish Rite conferred for outstanding Masonic service. The tail feathers number nine, the number of degrees in the Chapter, Council, and Commandery of the York Rite of Freemasonry. Notice the stars above the eagle's head form a hexagram, the most evil of all witchcraft symbols.

A Favorite Illuminati Symbol: The All-Seeing Eye of Lucifer. New World Order Currency: The all-seeing eye on the dollar bill. Below the illuminati pyramid/eye symbol are the words: Novus Ordo Seclorum, which can be translated as: A new order of the ages.

The Serpent promised Adam and Eve that their eyes would be opened if they ate of the fruit of the tree of knowledge of good and evil. The keyword in this passage is eyes, which in Hebrew can be translated knowledge. Opened can be translated as broadened. What the Serpent promised Adam and Eve was that knowledge would be broadened if they ate of the forbidden fruit.

But the most foreboding aspect of this scripture emerges from the fact that the Hebrew word for "eyes" is not plural, but singular. What the Serpent told Adam and Eve was that their "eye" would be broadened by knowledge.

The "eye" that Scripture wants us to consider is not the physical organ of sight, but the eye of the spirit. This singular "eye" is called the "third eye" of clairvoyance in the Hindu religion, the eye of Osiris in Egypt, and the All-Seeing Eye in Freemasonry. (John Daniel, *Scarlet and the Beast*, Vol. III, pp. 6-7)

The all-seeing eye is the Illuminati elite's favorite symbol. It represents the eye of Lucifer seeing all, and is usually atop a pyramid, the symbol for a top-down command and control system of compartmentalization.

Many companies use the pyramid within their logos James Walker, a 32º Mason, shares some facts with us about the above symbols:

- 13 leaves in the olive branch

- 13 bars and stripes in the shield

- 13 arrows in the right claw

- 13 letters in the "E Pluribus Unum" on the ribbon

- 13 stars in the green crest above

- 32 long feathers on its right wing representing the 32º in Freemasonry

- 13 granite stones in the Pyramid. (The 13 layers represent the 13 Illuminati bloodlines)

- 13 letters in Annuit Coeptis

It should also be noted that the Eagle has 32 feathers right wing, but 33 in its left wing. The 32 feathers represent the number of ordinary degrees of the Scottish Rite, and the 33 feathers represent the 33º of Freemasonry. Furthermore, if we add all the wings 32+33=65, 6+5=11, the 11th "little horn and most evil" in Daniel 7, and the last 11 kings/presidents in 2 Esdras 12.The tail feathers number 9, the number of degrees in the York Rite. The eagle itself is a prominent icon of Masonry, being used extensively in the Scottish Rite.

Looking just above the eagle's head, you will see 13 pentagrams within a cloud. The pentagrams are arranged in the shape of a hexagram - or greater Seal of Solomon. To the sorcerer, the hexagram is a powerful tool to invoke Satan and is a sign of Antichrist. (6 points, 6 angles, 6 planes - 666) The 5-pointed pentagrams multiplied by the 13 stars equals 65, the same cabalistic number as mentioned above. This makes one wonder with whom or what we are to dwell in unity!

The eagle replaced the Phoenix in 1841 as the national bird. The Phoenix has been a Brotherhood (Illuminati, Freemasons, Islam, Jewish Cabala, etc, the monkey with the three-piece suite, but still a monkey.) symbol since ancient Egypt. The Phoenix was adopted by the Founding Fathers (Freemasons) for use on the reverse of the first official seal of the United States after a design proposed by Charles Thompson, Secretary of the Continental Congress.

To the right of George Washington's portrait on the front of the American Dollar Bill, you will see the Seal of the Department of the Treasury. It comprises a key, the scales of justice, and a square, which is a very important symbol in Freemasonry. If you look at the square, you will see 13 holes in it (13, 1+3=4, the "fourth beast" in Daniel 7).

The letters on the base of the Illuminati pyramid stand for certain numbers. And all those numbers, when added up, equal 1776, the year the Illuminati formed. More than one method exists for arriving at 1776. However, there is only one way to arrive at the following sequence. The Babylonian numbering system was used by the Masonic designers of the Seal. That numbering system was not based on ten, but on six. For example, "600" would be 1000, "60" would be 100, and "6" would be 10.

The Occult is Trinitarian, i.e., its main teachings are grouped in threes. The Number Sequence "93 and 93, 93"; or 600, 60, and 6 is the "current" of the new age of Aquarius - the Water Bearer, which heralds the end of the age of Pisces - the Fishes (an early symbol of Christianity) in the teachings of the Order of the Eastern Templars or O.T.O.

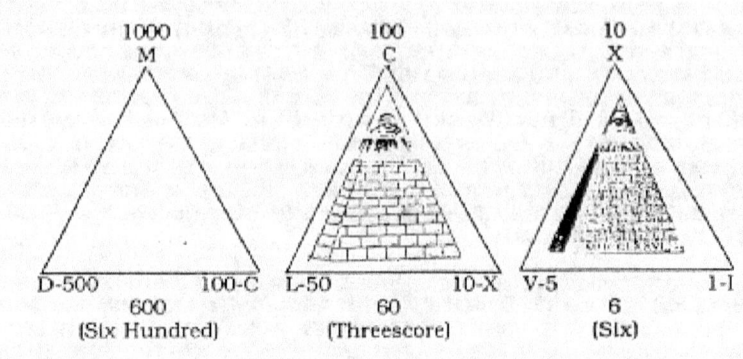

During this very end time and near total economic collapse, most people are in such distress about their financial situation that God's laws have been completely forsaken, and an all-out relentless pursuit of money has engrossed the earth. Most everyone is bowing "lusting" to the feet of Mammon Ra. Knowing the beast (US Government now headed by Obama) has enslaved the masses with it financial system, and money represents the system; by purposely destroying the economy the Beast is thereby making the majority of the people totally "worship" its image, the mark of the beast ("that the image of the beast should both speak", ever heard of the phrase "MONEY TALKS"?). MONEY!!! Using our God given sense of logic and reason, and those who see (spiritually) can see the spiritual implications behind this scheme.

Another example of evil lust was when the children of Israel were in the wilderness and were complaining about eating just Manna and began to lust after meat (Quails), and the wrath of God fell on them because they lusted.

Psalms 78:18

16 He brought streams also out of the rock, and caused waters to run down like rivers.

17 And they sinned yet more against him by provoking the Most High in the wilderness.

18 And they tempted God in their heart by asking for meat for their lust.

1 Corinthians 10:5-6

5 But with many of them God was not well pleased: for they were overthrown in the wilderness.

6 Now these things were our examples, to the intent we should not lust after evil things, as they also lusted.

Notice it was not the Quails but the actual lust of them that brought the wrath of God upon them. Spiritually, people are worshipping the image of something created by Satan. The lust and relentless pursuit of money will bring the wrath of God upon the people in the spiritual wilderness they are currently in, just as it fell upon the children of Israel in the physical wilderness they were in.

One thing is certain: God did not inspire anyone to create a dollar bill full of satanic graven images.

Romans 1:21-23, 25

21 Because of that, when they knew God, they glorified him not as God, nor were thankful but became vain in their imaginations, and their foolish heart was darkened.

22 Professing themselves to be wise, they became fools,

23 And changed the glory of the uncorruptible God into an image made like to corruptible man, and to birds, and four-footed beasts, and creeping things.

25 Who changed the truth of God into a lie, and worshipped and served the creature more than the Creator, who is blessed forever. Amen

Can I be certain that the love for money is the mark of the beast? No, I cannot. I truly believe it has a lot to do with it, but I feel it is a combination of violations of God's law that will determine this factor. My suggestion to everyone is this:

Ecclesiastes 12 13 14

13 Let us hear the conclusion of the whole matter: Fear God, and keep his commandments: for this is the whole duty of man.

14 For God shall bring every work into judgment, with every secret thing, whether it be good, or whether it be evil.

ALL THE COMMANDMENTS, In God's sight, if you violate one, it is as if you have violated them all. Learn the law, for it is impossible not to sin when you do not know what defines it. Do not turn to the right or the left for anyone or anything! "Man does not live on bread alone but by every word that proceeds out of the mouth of God" (Mathew 4:4) from Genesis to Revelation. If you do this, you will not fail.

But know that God does not listen to the prayers of those who refuse to keep His Commandments.

Proverbs 15:8, 26, 29

8 The sacrifice of the wicked is an abomination to the LORD, but the prayer of the upright is his delight.

26 The thoughts of the wicked are an abomination to the LORD, but the words of the pure are pleasant   .

29 The LORD is far from the wicked, but he heareth the prayer of the righteous.

Proverbs 21:27

27 The sacrifice of the wicked is an abomination: how much more, when he bringeth it with a wicked mind?

Proverbs 28:9

9 He that turneth away his ear from hearing the law, even his prayer shall be abomination.

Also, be vigilant. Do not let anyone put any kind of microchip in you for any reason. Whether it is for medical records, GPS, or National ID, etc., use judgment, and understand that if the government (The Beast) is the one suggesting it, this should automatically put your mind on full alert.

Behold, I send you forth as sheep amid wolves: be ye therefore wise as serpents, and harmless as doves. (Mathew 10:16)

Most important of all, KEEP THE COMMANDMENTS!

Chapter 19

Why Such Wrath?

The time is soon to come when all hidden things will be revealed and the events foretold made apparent to all. By that time, there will be no need for someone like me to tell anyone what is to occur in advance; I have already done that. Unfortunately, not many listened or took heed. In the law, it is written, with men of other tongues and other lips will I speak unto this people; and yet for all that will they not hear me, saith the Lord.

Instead, I was ridiculed, laughed at, lied about, beaten, imprisoned, and betrayed by the very people I love the most. Out of love for my people, I warned them, risking the very same thing that happened. For my love and the truth, hatred was my recompense. But I know that this is nothing new. Those who came before me were treated in the same manner, some even worse. Just when I thought I could not handle such hatred and betrayal, and was completely without the will to carry on, God's strength pulled me through. Just when I said I would not tell anyone else what God had revealed to me, His words were like fire within me.

My fear and love for God, His Son, His kingdom, His law, His people, and the truth kept me speaking of the wrath to come to whoever had an ear to hear and hungered for the knowledge of the Most High.

Now, I will fill you in on a little secret that not many know. You see, I knew America was Mystery Babylon. I knew who Barack Hussein Obama was before he first set foot on his presidential campaign. I knew almost everything I know now and many other hidden things that most would not understand, so why speak of them, seeing that the obvious is so hidden from most due to spiritual blindness. The hidden is better to remain as such until the Lord of all decides to reveal them. I knew these things without ever reading the Scriptures.

How did I know? Well, here is the secret: 3 years ago, "the Word of the Lord came to me" and showed me all. The judgment, the destruction, the people dying, it was extremely horrific and frightening. So, I ran frantically to tell as many as would listen, but very few did. Because as it is written, "Wherefore tongues are for a sign, not to them that believe, but to them that believe not: but prophesying serveth not for them that believe not, but for them which believe." This is why this book is not intended for unbelievers but for the Elect of God.

You see, without the visions I received from the Lord, it would have been impossible to piece together these prophecies so perfectly. It was the actual missing link. It is not because I am wiser or more learned than anyone. For I know nothing of myself, and what have I that I have not received from God? On the contrary, God just showed the world once again His abundant love, mercy, and forgiveness in choosing a very sinful fool to reveal some of His most hidden prophecies. Glory be to God and my Lord and Savior Jesus Christ for their unspeakable gift of repentance.

The question many will ask themselves when all this occurs is, Why? Why is God so angry? Why such wrath? Well before they ask, since I know they will, I will tell them. It all has to do with the "Covenant". What Covenant? The Covenant many have been falsely led to believe it was somehow abolished. The Covenant made with our ancestors, the children of Israel, at Mount Sinai when God took them out of Egypt. The Covenant in Leviticus 26 and Deuteronomy 28. The Covenant in the 1st Chapter of this book. Yes, that Covenant!!!

Leviticus 26:21-25

21 And if ye walk contrary unto me, and will not hearken unto me; I will bring seven times more plagues upon you according to your sins.

22 I will also send wild beasts among you, which shall rob you of your children, and destroy your cattle, and make you few; and your high ways shall be desolate   .

23 And if ye will not be reformed by me by these things, but will walk contrary unto me;

24 Then will I also walk contrary unto you, and will punish you yet seven times for your sins.

25 And I will bring a sword upon you, that shall avenge the quarrel of my covenant: and when ye are gathered together within your cities, I will send the pestilence among you; and ye shall be delivered into the hand of the enemy. (This is what God did, delivering the United States of America into the hands of Satan.)

Deuteronomy 28:20

20 The LORD shall send upon thee cursing, vexation, and rebuke, in all that thou settest thine hand unto for to do, until thou be destroyed, and until thou perish quickly; because of the wickedness of thy doings, whereby thou hast forsaken me.

Deuteronomy 29:22-28

22 So that the generation to come of your children that shall rise after you, and the stranger that shall come from a far land, shall say, when they see the plagues of that land, and the sicknesses which the LORD hath laid upon it;

23 And that the whole land thereof is brimstone, and salt, and burning, that it is not sown, nor bearish, nor any grass growth therein, like the overthrow of Sodom, and Gomorrah, Admah, and Zeboim, which the LORD overthrew in his anger, and in his wrath:

24 Even all nations shall say, wherefore hath the LORD done thus unto this land? What meant the heat of this great anger?

25 Then men shall say, because they have forsaken the covenant of the LORD God of their fathers, which He made with them when He brought them forth out of the land of Egypt:

26 For they went and served other gods, and worshipped them, gods whom they knew not, and whom he had not given unto them:

27 And the anger of the LORD was kindled against this land, to bring upon it all the curses that are written in this book:

28 And the LORD rooted them out of their land in anger, and in wrath, and great indignation, and cast them into another land, as it is this day.

29 The secret things belong unto the LORD our God: but those things which are revealed belong unto us and to our children forever, that we may do all the words of this law.

Isaiah 1:4

4 Ah, sinful nation, a people laden with iniquity, a seed of evildoers, children that are corrupters: they have forsaken the LORD, they have provoked the Holy One of Israel unto anger, they are gone away backward.

Jeremiah 2:13, 17, 19

13 For my people have committed two evils; they have forsaken me, the fountain of living waters, and hewed them out cisterns, broken cisterns, that can hold no water.

17 Hast thou not procured this unto thyself, in that thou hast forsaken the LORD thy God, when He led thee by the way?

19 Thine own wickedness shall correct thee, and thy backslidings shall reprove thee: know therefore and see that it is an evil thing and bitter, that thou hast forsaken the LORD thy God, and that my fear is not in thee, saith the Lord GOD of hosts.

Jeremiah 5:7, 19-29

7 How shall I pardon thee for this? Thy children have forsaken me, and sworn by them that are no gods: when I had fed them to the full, they then committed adultery, and assembled themselves by troops in the harlots ' houses.

19 And it shall come to pass, when ye shall say, wherefore doeth the LORD our God all these things unto us? Then shalt thou answer them, like as ye have forsaken me, and served strange gods in your land, so shall ye serve strangers in a land that is not yours.

20 Declare this in the house of Jacob, and publish it in Judah, saying,

21 Hear now this, O foolish people, and without understanding; which have eyes, and see not; which have ears, and hear not:

22 Fear ye not me? Saith the LORD: will ye not tremble at my presence, which have placed the sand for the bound of the sea by a perpetual decree, that it cannot pass it: and though the waves thereof toss themselves, yet can they not prevail; though they roar, yet can they not pass over it?

23 But this people hath a revolting and a rebellious heart; they are revolted and gone.

24 Neither say they in their heart, Let us now fear the LORD our God, that giveth rain, both the former and the latter, in His season: He reserved unto us the appointed weeks of the harvest.

25 Your iniquities have turned away these things, and your sins have withheld good things from you.

26 For among my people are found wicked men: they lie in wait, as he that septet snares; they set a trap, they catch men.

27 As a cage is full of birds, so are their houses full of deceit: therefore, they are become great, and waxen rich.

28 They are waxen fat, they shine: yea, they overpass the deeds of the wicked: they judge not the cause, the cause of the fatherless, yet they prosper; and the right of the needy do they not judge.

29 Shall I not visit for these things? Saith the LORD: shall not my soul be avenged on such a nation as this?

Romans 1:18-32

28 And even as they did not like to retain God in their knowledge, God gave them over to a reprobate mind, to do those things which are not convenient;

29 Being filled with all unrighteousness, fornication, wickedness, covetousness, maliciousness; full of envy, murder, debate, deceit, malignity; whisperers,

30 Backbiters, haters of God, spiteful, proud, boasters, inventors of evil things, disobedient to parents,

31 Without understanding, covenantbreakers, without natural affection, implacable, unmerciful:

32 Who, knowing the judgment of God, that they who commit such things are worthy of death, not only do the same, but have pleasure in them that do them.

You see, whether you know it, like it, or admit it, every person on the face of the earth is under the Covenant, and ignorance of the Law is not a valid defense!

Romans 2:12

For as many as have sinned without law shall also perish without law: and as many as have sinned in the law shall be judged by the law;

Deuteronomy 29:12-15

12 That thou shouldest enter into covenant with the LORD thy God, and into his oath, which the LORD thy God maketh with thee this day:

13 That He may establish thee today for a people unto Himself, and that He may be unto thee a God, as He hath said unto thee, and as He hath sworn unto thy fathers, to Abraham, to Isaac, and Jacob.

14 Neither with you only do I make this covenant and this oath;

15 But with him that standeth here with us this day before the LORD our God, and also with him that is not here with us this day:

Deuteronomy 29:18-20

18 Lest there should be among you man, or woman, or family, or tribe, whose heart turneth away this day from the LORD our God, to

go and serve the gods of these nations; lest there should be among you a root that beareth gall and wormwood;

19 And it comes to pass, when he heareth the words of this curse, that he blesses himself in his heart, saying, I shall have peace, though I walk in the imagination of mine heart, to add drunkenness to thirst:

20 The LORD will not spare him, but then the anger of the LORD and His jealousy shall smoke against that man, and all the curses that are written in this book shall lie upon him, and the LORD shall blot out his name from under heaven.

Deuteronomy 31:16-30

16 And the LORD said unto Moses, Behold, thou shalt sleep with thy fathers; and this people will rise, and go a whoring after the gods of the strangers of the land, whither they go to be among them, and will forsake me, and break my covenant which I have made with them.

17 Then my anger shall be kindled against them in that day, and I will forsake them, and I will hide my face from them, and they shall be devoured, and many evils and troubles shall befall them; so that they will say in that day, are not these evils come upon us, because our God is not among us?

18 And I will surely hide my face in that day for all the evils which they shall have wrought, in that they are turned unto other gods.

19 Now therefore write ye this song for you, and teach it the children of Israel: put it in their mouths, that this song may be a witness for me against the children of Israel.

20 For when I shall have brought them into the land which I sware unto their fathers, that floweth with milk and honey; and they shall

have eaten and filled themselves, and waxen fat; then will they turn unto other gods, and serve them, and provoke me, and break my covenant.

21 And it shall come to pass, when many evils and troubles are befallen them, that this song shall testify against them as a witness; for it shall not be forgotten out of the mouths of their seed: for I know their imagination which they go about, even now, before I have brought them into the land which I sware.

22 Moses therefore wrote this song the same day, and taught it to the children of Israel.

23 And he gave Joshua the son of Nun a charge, and said, Be strong and of a good courage: for thou shalt bring the children of Israel into the land which I sware unto them, and I will be with thee.

24 And it came to pass, when Moses had made an end of writing the words of this law in a book, until they were finished,

25 That Moses commanded the Levites, who bore the ark of the covenant of the LORD, saying,

26 Take this book of the law, and put it in the side of the ark of the covenant of the LORD your God, that it may be there for a witness against thee.

27 For I know thy rebellion, and thy stiff neck: behold, while I am yet alive with you this day, ye have been rebellious against the LORD; and how much more after my death?

28 Gather unto me all the elders of your tribes, and your officers, that I may speak these words in their ears, and call heaven and earth to record against them.

29 For I know that after my death ye will utterly corrupt yourselves, and turn aside from the way which I have commanded you and evil will befall you in the latter days; (The End Times) because ye will do evil in the sight of the LORD, to provoke him to anger through the work of your hands.

30 And Moses spake in the ears of all the congregation of Israel the words of this song, until they were ended.

Revelation of Esdras

Woe to the human race then, when You shall come to judgment! And I said to the Lord: Lord, why have You created man, and delivered him up to judgment? And God said, with a lofty proclamation: I will not by any means have mercy on those who transgress my covenant. And the prophet said: Lord, where is Your goodness? And God said: I have prepared all things for man's sake, and man does not keep my commandments.

The Great God, Ruler of Heaven and Earth, has simply demonstrated to the world that He means exactly what He says. God is simply keeping His end of the Covenant. He warned us that if we kept the Covenant, blessings would overtake us. But if we did not, He would avenge it!

Deuteronomy 28:49-52

49 The LORD shall bring a nation (The Nation of Islam) against thee from far, from the end of the earth, as swift as the eagle flieth; a nation whose tongue thou shalt not understand; (Arabic Language)

50 A nation of fierce countenance, which shall not regard the person of the old, nor shew favor to the young: (A ruthless nation)

51 And he shall eat the fruit of thy cattle, and the fruit of thy land, until thou be destroyed: which also shall not leave thee either corn, wine, or oil, or the increase of thy Kine, or flocks of thy sheep, until he have destroyed thee.

52 And he shall besiege thee in all thy gates (In all positions of authority), until thy high and fenced walls (National Security) come down, wherein thou trusted, throughout all thy land: and he shall besiege thee in all thy gates throughout all thy land, which the LORD thy God hath given thee.

Jeremiah 5:15-17

15 Lo, I will bring a nation upon you from far, O house of Israel, saith the LORD: it is a mighty nation, it is an ancient nation, a nation whose language thou knowest not, neither understands what they say.

16 Their quiver is as an open sepulcher, they are all mighty men.

17 And they shall eat up thine harvest, and thy bread, which thy sons and thy daughters should eat: they shall eat up thy flocks and thine herds: they shall eat up thy vines and thy fig trees: they shall impoverish thy fenced cities (Financial ruin), wherein thou trusted, with the sword.

One compound word explains it best: covenant-breakers. This word stresses one who enters into an agreement or treaty but then refuses to abide by the terms stipulated. God kept His end of the agreement, but the people have refused to keep theirs after receiving the benefits. Does anyone think that they can rob God and get away with it?

Chapter 20

To America, Babylon the Great, Mother of Harlots

Thus saith the Lord;

Hear, O heavens, and give ear, O earth for the LORD hath spoken, I have nourished and brought up children, and they have rebelled against me. The ox Koeth his owner, and the ass his master's crib: but Israel doth not know, my people doth not consider. Ah, sinful nation, a people laden with iniquity, a seed of evildoers, children that are corrupters: they have forsaken the LORD, they have provoked the Holy One of Israel unto anger, they are gone away backward. Why should ye be stricken anymore? Ye will revolt more and more: the whole head is sick, and the whole heart faint. From the sole even unto the head there is no soundness in it; but wounds, and bruises, and putrefying sores: they have not been closed, neither bound up, nor mollified with ointment.

Because I have called, and ye refused; I have stretched out my hand, and no man regarded; But ye have set at nought all my counsel, and would none of my reproof: I also will laugh at your calamity I will mock when your fear cometh; When your fear cometh as desolation, and your destruction cometh as a whirlwind; when distress and anguish cometh upon you. Then shall they call upon me, but I will not answer; they shall seek me early, but they shall not find me: For that they hated knowledge, and did not choose the fear of the LORD They would none of my counsel: they despised all my reproof. Therefore, shall they eat of the fruit of their way, and be filled with their own devices. For the turning away of the simple shall slay them, and the prosperity of fools shall destroy them.

Now is the end come upon thee, and I will send mine anger upon thee, and will judge thee according to thy ways, and will recompense upon thee all thine abominations. And mine eye shall not spare thee, neither will I have pity: but I will recompense thy ways upon thee, and thine abominations shall be in the midst of thee: and ye shall know that I am the LORD.

Thus saith the Lord GOD: An evil, an only evil, behold, is come. An end is come, the end is come: it watcheth for thee; behold, it is come. The son of the morning is come unto thee, O thou that dwellest in the land: the time is come, the day of trouble is near, and not the sounding again of the mountains. Now will I shortly pour out my fury upon thee, and accomplish mine anger upon thee: and I will judge thee according to thy ways, and will recompense thee for all thine abominations. And mine eye shall not spare, neither will I have pity:

Behold the day, behold, it is come: the son of the morning is gone forth; the rod hath blossomed, pride hath budded. Violence has risen into a rod of wickedness: none of them shall remain, nor of their multitude, nor any of theirs: neither shall there be wailing for them. The time is come, the day draweth near: let not the buyer rejoice, nor the seller mourn: for wrath is upon all the multitude thereof.

For the seller shall not return to that which is sold, although they were yet alive: for the vision is touching the whole multitude thereof, which shall not return; neither shall any strengthen himself in the iniquity of his life. They have blown the trumpet, even to make all ready; but none goeth to the battle: for my wrath is upon all the multitude thereof. The sword is without, and the pestilence and the famine within: he that is in the field shall die with the sword; and he that is in the city, famine and pestilence shall devour him. But they that escape from them shall escape, and shall be on the mountains like doves of the valleys, all of them mourning, every one for his iniquity.

All hands shall be feeble, and all knees shall be weak as water. They shall also gird themselves with sackcloth, and horror shall cover them; and shame shall be upon all faces, and baldness upon all their heads. They shall cast their silver in the streets, and their gold shall be removed: their silver and their gold shall not be able to deliver them in the day of the wrath of the LORD: they shall not satisfy their souls, neither fill their bowels: because it is the stumbling block of their iniquity. As for the beauty of his ornament, he set it in majesty, but they made the images of their abominations and their detestable things therein; therefore, I have set it far from them.

And I will give it into the hands of the strangers for a prey, and to the wicked of the earth for a spoil; and they shall pollute it. My face will I turn also from them, and they shall pollute my secret place: for the robbers shall enter into it, and defile it. Make a chain: for the land is full of bloody crimes, and the city is full of violence. Wherefore I will bring the worst of the heathen, and they shall possess their houses: I will also make the pomp of the strong to cease; and their holy places shall be defiled. Destruction cometh; and they shall seek peace, and there shall be none. Mischief shall come upon mischief, and rumor shall be upon rumor; then shall they seek a vision of the prophet; but the law shall perish from the priest, and counsel from the ancients. The king shall mourn, and the prince shall be clothed with desolation, and the hands of the people of the land shall be troubled: I will do unto them after their way, and according to their deserts will I judge them; and they shall know that I am the LORD.

Therefore, pray not thou for this people, neither lift cry nor prayer for them, nor make intercession to me: for I will not hear thee. For now they must all appear before the judgment seat of Christ; that every one may receive the things done in his body, according to that he hath done, whether it be good or bad.

Until this day lasted the day of His mercy; and He hath been merciful and long-suffering towards those who dwell on the earth. And when the day, and the power, and the punishment, and the judgement come, which the Lord of Spirits hath prepared for those who worship not the righteous law, and for those who deny the righteous judgement, and for those who take His name in vain-that day is prepared, for the elect a covenant, but for sinners an inquisition.

Go to now, ye rich men, weep and howl for your miseries that shall come upon you. Your riches are corrupted, and your garments are moth-eaten. Your gold and silver are cankered; and the rust of them shall be a witness against you, and shall eat your flesh as it were fire. Ye have heaped treasure together for the last days. Behold, the hire of the laborers who have reaped down your field, which is of you kept back by fraud, cried: and the cries of them which have reaped are entered into the ears of the Lord of Sabbath. Ye have lived in pleasure on the earth, and been wanton; ye have nourished your hearts, as in a day of slaughter. Therefore will I number you to the sword, and ye shall all bow down to the slaughter: because when I called, ye did not answer; when I space, ye did not hear; but did evil before mine eyes, and did choose that wherein I delighted not. Therefore thus saith the Lord GOD, Behold, my servants shall eat, but ye shall be hungry: behold, my servants shall drink, but ye shall be thirsty: behold, my servants shall rejoice, but ye shall be ashamed: Behold, my servants shall sing for joy of heart, but ye shall cry for sorrow of heart, and shall howl for vexation of spirit.

Who has permitted you to practice reproaches and wickedness? And so judgment shall overtake you, sinners. Woe to you who fulminate anathemas which cannot be reversed: Healing shall therefore be far from you because of your sins. Woe to you who requite your neighbour with evil; for ye shall be requited according to your works. Woe to you, lying witnesses, and to those who weigh out injustice, for suddenly shall ye perish. Woe to you, sinners, for ye persecute the righteous; for ye shall be delivered up and persecuted because of injustice, and heavy shall its yoke be upon thee. Woe to those who build unrighteousness and oppression and lay deceit as a foundation; for they shall be suddenly overthrown, and they shall have no peace. Woe to those who build their houses with sin; for from all their foundations shall they be overthrown, and by the sword shall they fall. And those who acquire gold and silver in judgment shall suddenly perish.

Woe to you, ye rich, for ye have trusted in your riches, and from your riches shall ye depart, because ye have not remembered the Most High in the days of your riches. Ye have committed blasphemy and unrighteousness, and have become ready for the day of slaughter, and the day of darkness, and the day of the great judgement.

Thus I speak and declare unto you: He who hath created you will overthrow you, and for your fall there shall be no compassion, and your Creator will rejoice at your destruction. Woe unto you, ye sinners, for your riches make you appear like the righteous, but your hearts convict you of being sinners, and this fact shall be a testimony against you for a memorial ofyour evil deeds.

Woe to you who devour the finest of the wheat, and drink wine in large bowls, and tread underfoot the lowly with your might. Woe to you who drink water from every fountain, for suddenly shall ye be consumed and wither away, because ye have forsaken the fountain of life. Woe to you who work unrighteousness and deceit and blasphemy: It shall be a memorial against you for evil. Woe to you, ye mighty, who with might oppress the righteous; for the day of your destruction is coming.

Woe to you who spread evil to your neighbors, for you shall be slain in Sheol. Woe to you who make deceitful and false measures, and (to them) who cause bitterness on the earth; for they shall thereby be utterly consumed. Woe to you who build your houses through the grievous toil of others, and all their building materials are the bricks and stones of sin; I tell you ye shall have no peace. Woe to them who reject the measure and eternal heritage of their fathers and whose souls follow after idols; for they shall have no rest. Woe to them who work unrighteousness and help oppression, and slay their neighbors until the day of the great judgment.

For He shall cast down your glory, and bring affliction on your hearts, and shall arouse His fierce indignation and destroy you all with the sword; and all the holy and righteous shall remember your sins. Woe to you, Sinners, on the day of strong anguish, ye who afflict the righteous and burn them with fire: Ye shall be requited according to your works. Woe to you, ye obstinate of hearts, who watch to devise wickedness: Therefore shall fear come upon you, and there shall be none to help you. Woe to you, ye sinners, on account of the words of your mouth, and on account of the deeds of your hands which your godlessness has wrought, In blazing flames burning worse than fire shall ye burn.

In those days when He hath brought a grievous fire upon you, whither will ye flee, and where will ye find deliverance? And when He launches forth His Word against you, will you not be affrighted and fear? And all the luminaries shall be affrighted with great fear, and all the earth shall be affrighted and tremble and be alarmed. And all the angels shall execute their commands and shall seek to hide themselves from the presence of the Great Glory, and the children of earth shall tremble and quake; and ye sinners shall be cursed forever, and ye shall have no peace.

Now therefore ask thou no more questions concerning the multitude of them that perish. For when they had taken liberty, they despised the Most High, thought scorn of His law, and forsook His ways. Moreover, they have trodden down His righteousness, and said in their heart, that there is no God; yea, and that knowing they must die. For as the things aforesaid shalt receive you, so thirst and pain are prepared for them: for it was not His will that men should come to nought: But they which be created have defiled the name of Him that created them, and were unthankful unto Him which prepared life for them. What hast thou to do to declare my statutes, or that thou shouldest take my covenant of grace in thy mouth? Seeing that thou hates instruction, and castes my words behind thee. These things hast thou done, and I kept silence; thou though test that I was altogether such a one as thyself: but I will reprove thee, and set them in order before thine eyes. And therefore, is my judgment now at hand!

he judgment was set, and the books were opened.I have declared the former things from the beginning; and they went forth out of My mouth, and I shewed them; I did them suddenly, and they came to pass. Because I knew that thou art obstinate, and thy neck is an iron sinew, and thy brow brass; I have even from the beginning declared it to thee before it came to pass I shewed it thee: lest thou shouldest say, Mine idol hath done them, and my graven image, and my molten image, hath commanded them.

Thou hast heard, see all this; will not ye declare it? I have shewed thee new things from this time, even hidden things, and thou didst not know them. They are created now, and not from the beginning; even before the day when thou headrest them not; lest thou shouldest say, Behold, I knew them. Yea, thou headrest not; yea, thou newest not; yea, from that time that thine ear was not opened: for I knew that thou wildest deal very treacherously, and west called a transgressor from the womb.